ARMY HISTORICAL SERIES

COMBAT ACTIONS IN KOREA

Russell A. Gugeler

CENTER OF MILITARY HISTORY
UNITED STATES ARMY
WASHINGTON, D.C., 1987

Library of Congress Catalog Card Number: 70-603408

First Printed 1954—CMH Pub 30-2

For sale by the Superintendent of Documents, U.S. Government Printing Office
Washington, D.C. 20402

Foreword

★ This book was originally published in 1954, revised in 1970, and in demand and print since then. The accounts of small-unit actions were written primarily for junior officers, noncommissioned officers, and privates of the United States Army who had not yet been in battle. The object was to acquaint them with the realities of their own fields.

Since the Korean War, some of the tools and procedures of battle have changed, but the basic conditions of combat have not. Indeed, the surprises, confusion, and problems faced on one battlefield generally resemble the difficulties met on another. Accounts of battle experience at other times in other places, then, continue to have instructive value. It is with this fact in mind that this book is being reprinted.

One of the accounts contained in the original version was omitted after a review of the source material on which it was based revealed several irreconcilable errors. All of the other episodes appearing in the 1970 revised edition continue to appear in their original form. Those who absorb the lessons they offer can substantially increase their competence as leaders and members of small units in battle, and all students of military history should find profit in these intimate and objective stories of combat action.

The Center of Military History is pleased to continue this popular work.

Washington, D.C.   DOUGLAS KINNARD
20 July 1984   *Brigadier General, USA (Ret.)*
                                                 Chief of Military History

Preface

★ This book is a collection of accounts describing the combat action of small Army units—squads and platoons, companies and batteries. These are the units that engage in combat, suffer the casualties, and make up the fighting strength of the battalions, regiments, divisions, corps, and finally, of the field army. Combat is a very personal business to members of such a small unit. Concerned with the fearful and consuming tasks of fighting and living, these men cannot think of war in terms of the Big Picture as it is represented on the situation maps at corps or army headquarters. Members of a squad or platoon know only what they can see and hear of combat. They know and understand the earth for which they fight, the advantage of holding the high ground, the protection of the trench or hole. These men can distinguish the sounds of enemy weapons from those of their own; they know the satisfying sound of friendly artillery shells passing overhead and of friendly planes diving at an objective. They know the excitement of combat, the feeling of exhilaration and of despair, the feeling of massed power, and of overwhelming loneliness.

The author has tried to describe combat as individuals have experienced it, or at least as it has appeared from the company command post. In so doing, much detail has been included that does not find its way into more barren official records. The details and the little incidents of combat were furnished by surviving members of the squads and companies during painstaking interviews and discussions soon after the fighting was over. Conversely, many facts have been omitted from the narrative presented here. The accounts tell only part of the complete story, intentionally ignoring related actions of cause and effect in order to keep one or two small units in sharper focus. The story of action on Heartbreak Ridge, for example, describes fighting that lasted only one or two hours, whereas the entire battle for that hill went on for several weeks. Sometimes there are obvious gaps because important information was lost with the men who died in the battle. Sometimes the accounts are incomplete because the author failed to learn or to recount everything of importance that happened.

The stories that follow have been selected as representative of the important battles of the Korean conflict. In chronological sequence, they follow the fighting beginning on the second day of the participation of United States troops until the war settled into a static defense of fortified lines.

Because most of the peninsula is covered with an intricate mass of hills and ridges, many of the battles in Korea took place on hilltops. The typical Korean ridge rises from rice paddies and a stream at its base and slants upward at an angle of forty-five or more degrees. It takes an hour of steady climbing to reach the top and, once they have reached the path-wide crest, the sweating infantrymen see only another ridge ahead, and others beyond it, stretching in row after row to the purple haze at the horizon. In the wintertime the hills are windblown and harsh but when summer rains come to Korea and the morning mist drifts along the ridgelines there is a fresh beauty to the land. The hills become verdant and between them the rice paddies, in delicate shades of green, are so neat they look as if someone had combed them by hand and set them out in the sun. Other than the beauty of the landscape, American soldiers find little that is desirable in Korea. It has always been a poor land, and the shifting combat has reduced many of the villages to heaps of red ashes, many of the people to destitution. In the combat zone only the hills seem unchanged, and even a few of them are beaten up and bare from the fighting. This is the setting for the stories that follow.

The preparation of this book has not been a one-man project. Major General Orlando Ward, U.S. Army (now retired), is responsible for the book, having planned it and furnished much of the enthusiasm and inspiration necessary to get the writing done. It is a personal pleasure for the author to share the credit for the book with nine officers with whom he worked and often shared tents in Korea. These officers, members of historical detachments, were engaged in collecting and preserving accurate historical records of the Korean conflict. From the large number of accounts that they prepared, the author has included eleven that were either partially or almost wholly prepared by them. To the following officers the author is indebted for this valuable assistance and for the pleasure of sharing the experiences of Korea: Major Edward C. Williamson, Captain John Mewha, Captain Martin Blumenson, Major B. C. Mossman, Major Pierce Briscoe, Major William J. Fox, Lieutenant Bevin R. Alexander, Lieutenant Edgar Denton, and Major Robert H. Fechtman.

The author reserves a special acknowledgment of indebtedness and an expression of appreciation to Lt. Col. Roy E. Appleman. During both World War II and the Korean War, the author benefited from Colonel Appleman's familiarity with military history and from his sturdy good judgment.

Except for one, the discussions following most of the action accounts were compiled by Lt. Colonel Carl D. McFerren of the Office of the Chief of Military History, and based upon comments from the Army schools at Fort Benning, Fort Sill, and Fort Knox. At the request of the Chief of Military History, Lieutenant Nicholas A. Canzona, U.S. Marine Corps, wrote the discussion following "Attack Along a Ridgeline." The discussions do not necessarily reflect the official view of the Department of the Army, but are included to stimulate thought and promote discussion. No attempt has been made to mention everything that is either good or bad about the conduct of the battles described and, in many cases, the obvious has been intentionally avoided. Neither has there been any attempt to place blame, since no one can claim that, in the same circumstances, he could have done better.

Miss Mary Ann Bacon has been generous in giving skillful editorial guidance to the author. Mr. Alfred M. Beck accomplished the numerous tasks required to convert the original publication into the present edition. Mrs. Vivian Brooks prepared all maps illustrating the text, and Mr. Robert Johnstone prepared the two pen-and-ink sketches. To them the author is deeply grateful.

Finally, the author is anxious to thank several hundred men and officers of the United States Army who have been both patient and generous in furnishing the information upon which the accounts are based. Without their cooperation this book could not have been written and eventually much of the information presented here would have been lost, just as the dust and smoke disappear from the battlefield when the fighting is over.

RUSSELL A. GUGELER
Stuttgart, Germany
30 September 1969

Contents

		Page
FOREWORD		iii
PREFACE		v
1	WITHDRAWAL ACTION	3
2	ATTACK ALONG A RIDGELINE	20
3	DEFENSE OF A BATTERY POSITION	31
4	TANK ACTION AT CHONGJU	39
5	ARTILLERY AT KUNU–RI	45
6	CHOSIN RESERVOIR	54
7	TWIN TUNNELS PATROL AMBUSH	80
8	CHIPYONG–NI	100
9	TASK FORCE CROMBEZ	126
10	TANK SUPPORT	137
11	A RIFLE COMPANY AS A COVERING FORCE	144
12	ARTILLERY IN PERIMETER DEFENSE	154
13	HILL 800 (BUNKER HILL)	166
14	TASK FORCE GERHARDT	183
15	MILLION DOLLAR HILL	193
16	BLOODY RIDGE	202
17	HEARTBREAK RIDGE	215
18	OUTPOST EERIE	222
19	COMBAT PATROL	236
LEGEND TO SYMBOLS ON MAPS		246
INDEX		247

Combat Actions in Korea

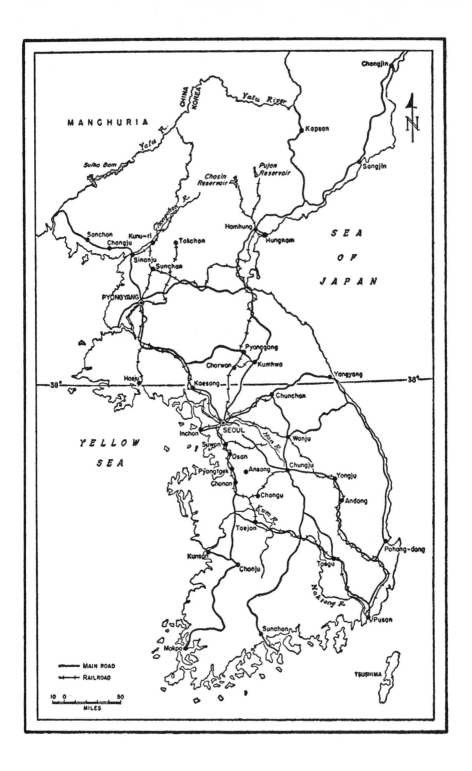

I

Withdrawal Action

★ Korean summers are wet. It was raining and unseasonably cold during the dark early morning hours of 5 July 1950 when the 1st Battalion, 34th Infantry, reached Pyongtaek. Approximately forty miles south of Seoul, the village was near the west coast of Korea on the main road and railroad between the capital city and Taejon, Taegu, and Pusan to the south. Pyongtaek was a shabby huddle of colorless huts lining narrow, dirt streets.

The infantrymen stood quietly in the steady rain, waiting for daylight. They grumbled about the weather but, in the sudden shift from garrison duties in Japan, few appeared to be concerned about the possibility of combat in Korea. None expected to stay there long. High-ranking officers and riflemen alike shared the belief that a few American soldiers would restore order within a few weeks.[1]*

"As soon as those North Koreans see an American uniform over here," soldiers boasted to one another, "they'll run like hell." American soldiers later lost this cocky attitude when the North Koreans overran their first defensive positions. Early overconfidence changed suddenly to surprise, then to dismay, and finally to the grim realization that, of the two armies, the North Korean force was superior in size, equipment, training, and fighting ability.

As part of the 24th Infantry Division, the 1st Battalion, 34th Infantry, was one of several unprepared American battalions rushed from Japan to help halt the North Korean invasion of the southern end of the Korean

* Notes are at the end of chapters.

peninsula. The change from garrison to combat duties had come abruptly on the morning of 1 July 1950 when the division commander (Maj.Gen. William F. Dean) called the commander of the 34th Infantry and alerted the entire regiment for immediate movement to Korea. At the time the regiment consisted of only two under-strength battalions. Twenty-four hours later they sailed from Sasebo, Kyushu, arriving in Pusan that evening. After spending two days checking equipment, organizing supplies, and arranging for transportation north, the regiment, crowded onto five South Korean-operated trains, had started north on the afternoon of 4 July.[2]

The 34th Infantry had not been the first unit of the United States Army to reach Korea. Part of the 1st Battalion, 21st Infantry (24th Division), had been airlifted from Japan on the morning of 1 July. After landing at Pusan it had boarded trains immediately, and rushed northward. The battalion commander (Lt.Col. Charles B. Smith) had the mission of setting up roadblocks to halt the North Korean southward thrust. Part of this force had gone to Pyongtaek and part to Ansong, a village ten miles east of Pyongtaek.[3] Without making contact with North Koreans, the two task forces from Colonel Smith's battalion had reached their assigned areas during the morning of 3 July. A field artillery battery arrived at Pyongtaek the next day, and that evening, 4 July, Smith's entire force had moved twelve miles north of Pyongtaek where it set up another blocking position just north of Osan.[4]

About the same time that Smith's battalion had started for Osan, the two battalions of the 34th Infantry, heading north, had passed through Taejon. One battalion was to reestablish the blocking position at Ansong; the 1st Battalion was going to Pyongtaek with a similar mission. A new commander—an experienced combat officer—had joined the 1st Battalion as the trains moved through Taejon. He told his company commanders that North Korean soldiers were reported to be farther north but that they were poorly trained, that only half of them had weapons, and that there would be no difficulty in stopping them. Junior officers had assured their men that after a brief police action all would be back in Sasebo. Officers of the 34th Infantry knew that the 21st was ahead of the 34th in a screening position. Overconfidence was the prevailing note.

This was the background and the setting for the rainy morning when the 1st Battalion—and especially Company A, with which this account is mainly concerned—waited in the muddy streets of Pyongtaek. When daylight came, the companies marched north to the hills upon which they were to set up their blocking positions.

A small river flowed along the north side of Pyongtaek. Two miles north of the bridge that carried the main highway across the river there were two grass-covered hills separated by a strip of rice paddies three quarters of a mile wide. The railroad and narrow dirt road, both on eight- to ten-foot-high embankments, ran through the neatly patterned fields. The battalion commander stationed Company B on the east side of the road, Company A on the west, leaving Company C in reserve positions in the rear. Once on the hill, the men dropped their packs and began digging into the coarse red earth to prepare defensive positions for an enemy attack few

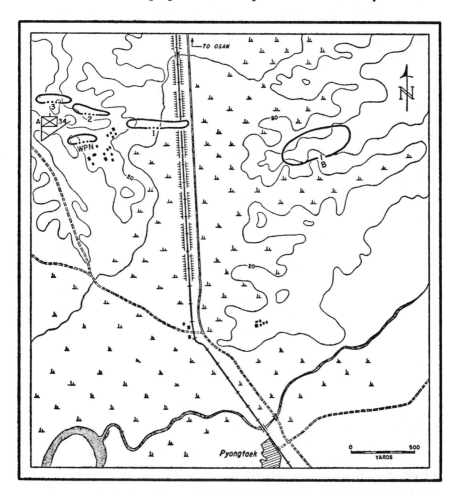

of them expected. In Company A's sector the positions consisted of two-man foxholes dug across the north side of the hill, across the rice paddies to the railroad embankment, and beyond that to the road. Company A (Capt. Leroy Osburn) consisted of about 140 men and officers at the time.[5] With two men in each position, the holes were so far apart that the men had to shout to one another. Each man was equipped with either an M1 rifle or a carbine for which he carried between eighty and one hundred rounds of ammunition. The Weapons Platoon had three 60mm mortars. There were also three light machine guns—one in each of the rifle platoons—and four boxes of ammunition for each machine gun. Each platoon had one BAR and two hundred rounds of ammunition for it. There were no grenades nor was there any ammunition for the recoilless rifles.[6]

To the north of Osan, meanwhile, Colonel Smith's 1st Battalion, 21st Infantry, and an attached battery of artillery completed the occupation of the high ground north of the village by daylight on 5 July. Smith had orders to hold in place to gain time, even though his forces might become surrounded.[7] That same morning, at 0745, enemy tanks approached from the north. The Americans opened fire with artillery and then with bazookas, but the tanks rammed through the infantry positions and on south past the artillery, after losing only 4 of 33 tanks. Enemy infantrymen followed later, engaged Colonel Smith's force and, after a four-hour battle, almost surrounded it. About 1400, Colonel Smith ordered his men to leave the position and withdraw toward Ansong. Smith's force carried out as many wounded as possible, but abandoned its equipment and dead. The survivors, traveling on foot in small groups or on the few artillery trucks, headed southwest toward Ansong.[8] This was the result of the first engagement between North Korean and American soldiers.

Brig.Gen. George B. Barth (commander of 24th Division Artillery and General Dean's representative in the forward area) was at Osan with the battery of artillery when the first "Fire mission!" was relayed to the battery position. When it became apparent that neither the infantry nor the artillery could stop the tanks, General Barth had gone back to Pyongtaek to alert the 1st Battalion, 34th Infantry, which was still digging in.

The 1st Battalion's command post was in one of the dirty buildings on the road north of Pyongtaek. It was apparent to General Barth, by the time he arrived there, that enemy tanks would break through the Osan position. He therefore warned the 1st Battalion commander and instructed him to dispatch a patrol northward to make contact with the enemy column. Barth's instructions to the 1st Battalion, 34th Infantry, differed from those he had given to Colonel Smith at Osan. Since General Barth now believed the Pyongtaek force could hold out only a short time if encircled, as apparently was happening to the battalion at Osan, he ordered the battalion at Pyongtaek to hold only until the enemy threatened to envelop the position, and then to delay in successive rearward positions to gain time.[9]

A rifle platoon from the 34th Infantry went north to make contact with the enemy tanks. About halfway between Pyongtaek and Osan the platoon met several enemy tanks and fired upon them without effect. The tanks made no effort to advance. The opposing forces settled down to observing each other.[10]

While these events were taking place only a few miles away, men of Company A at Pyongtaek finished digging their defensive positions or sat quietly in the cold rain. In spite of the fact that a column of enemy tanks had overrun the Osan position and was then not more than six miles from

Pyongtaek, the infantrymen did not know about it. They continued to exchange rumors and speculations. One of the platoon leaders called his men together later that afternoon to put an end to the growing anxiety over the possibility of combat. "You've been told repeatedly," he explained, "that this is a police action, and that is exactly what it is going to be." He assured them that the rumors of a large enemy force in the area were false, and that they would be back in Sasebo within a few weeks. He directed them to put out only the normal guard for the night. Later that evening, however, Captain Osburn told some of the men that four Americans who had driven north of Osan toward Suwon had failed to return, and that he had heard an estimate that 12,000 North Koreans were in the area to the north. He considered an attack possible but not probable.

It rained steadily all night. Beyond the fact that tanks had penetrated the Osan position, no more information about the fight there came through until nearly midnight, when five survivors from Osan arrived at the 1st Battalion command post with a detailed account of that action. The 1st Battalion commander passed word of the Osan defeat along to his company commanders, warning them to be on the lookout for stragglers from the 21st Infantry. Apparently no one passed the information on down to the platoons. The battalion commander then sent a patrol from Company C to blow up a small bridge about 600 yards north of his two forward companies. It was about 0300 when this was done. Startled by the explosions, infantrymen of Company A showed some concern until they learned the cause. Then they settled back to wait for daylight, or to sleep if possible. At 0430 they began to stir again. SFC Roy E. Collins, a platoon sergeant, walked along the row of foxholes in the center of the company position. One of a group of combat-experienced men recently transferred from another division, he had joined Company A only the day before. He advised his men to get up and break out their C rations and eat while they had a chance. The evening before, Collins had stationed a two-man listening post in the rice paddies about 75 yards north of the company. He called down and told them to come back to the company perimeter. It was only a few minutes after daylight.

The battalion commander walked down the road between Companies A and B, stopping to talk with a group of 17 men manning a roadblock on Company A's side of the road. Lt. Herman L. Driskell was in charge of the group, which consisted of an eight-man machine-gun squad from his 1st Platoon, and three 2.36-inch bazooka teams from the Weapons Platoon.[11]

After telling Driskell to get his men down in their holes because he planned to register the 4.2-inch mortars, the battalion commander walked west across the soggy rice paddies toward Company A's command post on top of the hill. Lieutenant Driskell's men did not, however, get into their holes—the holes were full of water. A Weapons Platoon sergeant, SFC Zack C. Williams, and PFC James O. Hite, were sitting near one hole. "I sure would hate to have to get in that hole," Hite said. In a few minutes they heard mortar shells overhead, but the shell bursts were lost in the morning fog and rain. In the cold rain, hunched under their ponchos, the men sat beside their holes eating their breakfast ration.

Up on the hill, Sergeant Collins was eating a can of beans. He had eaten about half of it when he heard the sound of engines running. Through the fog he saw the faint outline of several tanks that had stopped just beyond the bridge that the detail from Company C destroyed two hours earlier. North Korean soldiers from the lead tank got out and walked up to inspect the bridge site. At the same time, through binoculars, Collins could see two columns of infantrymen moving beyond the tanks, around both ends of the bridge, and out across the rice paddies. He yelled back to his platoon leader (Lt. Robert R. Ridley), "Sir, we got company." Lieutenant Ridley, having been warned that part of the 21st Infantry might be withdrawing down this road, said it was probably part of that unit. "Well," said Collins, "these people have tanks and I know the 21st hasn't any." The battalion commander arrived at Captain Osburn's command post just in time to see the column of enemy infantrymen appear. Deciding it was made up of men from the 21st Infantry, the two commanders watched it for several minutes before realizing it was too large to be friendly troops. They could see a battalion-size group already, and others were still coming in a column of fours.[12] At once, the battalion commander called for mortar fire. When the first round landed, the enemy spread out across the rice paddies on both sides of the road but continued to advance. By this time Collins could count thirteen tanks from the blown bridge north to the point where the column disappeared in the early morning fog.

Within a few minutes the men from the enemy's lead tank returned to their vehicle, got in, closed the turret, and then swung the tube until it pointed directly toward Company A.

"Get down!" Sergeant Collins yelled to his men. "Here it comes!"

The first shell exploded just above the row of foxholes, spattering dirt over the center platoon. The men slid into their holes. Collins and two other combat veterans of World War II began shouting to their men to commence firing. Response was slow although the Americans could see the North Korean infantrymen advancing steadily, spreading out across the flat ground in front of the hill. In the same hole with Sergeant Collins were two riflemen. He poked them. "Come on," he said. "You've got an M1. Get firing."

After watching the enemy attack for a few minutes, the battalion commander told Captain Osburn to withdraw Company A, and then left the hill, walking back toward his command post, which he planned to move south.

Out in front of the company hill, the two men at the listening post, after gathering up their wet equipment, had been just ready to leave when the first enemy shell landed. They jumped back into their hole. After a short time one of them jumped out and ran back under fire. The other, who stayed there, was not seen again.

The entire 1st Platoon was also in the flat rice paddies. Lieutenant Driskell's seventeen men from the 1st and the Weapons Platoons who were between the railroad and road could hear some of the activity but they could not see the enemy because of the high embankments on both sides. Private Hite was still sitting by his water-filled hole when the first enemy shell exploded up on the hill. He thought a 4.2-inch mortar shell had fallen short. Within a minute or two another round landed near Osburn's command post on top of the hill. Private Hite watched as the smoke drifted away.

"Must be another short round," he remarked to Sergeant Williams.

"It's not short," said Williams, a combat-experienced soldier. "It's an enemy shell."

Hite slid into his foxhole, making a dull splash like a frog diving into a pond. Williams followed. The two men sat there, up to their necks in cold, stagnant water.

It was fully fifteen minutes before the two Company A platoons up on the hill had built up an appreciable volume of fire, and then less than half of the men were firing their weapons. The squad and platoon leaders did most of the firing. Many of the riflemen appeared stunned and unwilling to believe that enemy soldiers were firing at them.

About fifty rounds fell in the battalion area within the fifteen minutes following the first shell-burst in Company A's sector. Meanwhile, enemy troops were appearing in numbers that looked overwhelmingly large to the American soldiers. "It looked like the entire city of New York moving against two little under-strength companies," said one of the men. Another large group of North Korean soldiers gathered around the tanks now lined up bumper to bumper on the road. It was the best target Sergeant Collins had ever seen. He fretted because he had no ammunition for the recoilless rifle. Neither could he get mortar fire because the second enemy tank's shell had exploded near the 4.2-inch mortar observer who, although not wounded, had suffered severely from shock. In the confusion no one else attempted to direct the mortars. Within thirty minutes after the action began, the leading North Korean foot soldiers had moved so close that Company A men could see them load and reload their rifles.

About the same time, Company B, under the same attack, began moving off of its hill on the opposite side of the road. Within another minute or two Captain Osburn called down to tell his men to prepare to withdraw, "but we'll have to cover Baker Company first."

Company A, however, had no effective fire power and spent no time covering the movement of the other company. Most of the Weapons Platoon, located on the south side of the hill, left immediately, walking down to a cluster of about fifteen straw-topped houses at the south edge of the hill. The two rifle platoons on the hill began to move out soon after Captain Osburn gave the alert order. The movement was orderly at the beginning although few of the men carried their field packs with them and others walked away leaving ammunition and even their weapons. However, just as the last two squads of this group reached a small ridge on the east side of the main hill, an enemy machine gun suddenly fired into the group. The men took off in panic. Captain Osburn and several of his platoon leaders were near the cluster of houses behind the hill re-forming the company for the march back to Pyongtaek. But when the panicked men raced past, fear spread quickly and others also began running. The officers called to them but few of the men stopped. Gathering as many members of his company as he could, Osburn sent them back toward the village with one of his officers.

By this time the Weapons Platoon and most of the 2d and 3d Platoons had succeeded in vacating their positions. As they left, members of these units had called down telling the 1st Platoon to withdraw from its position blocking the road. Strung across the flat paddies, the 1st Platoon was more exposed to enemy fire. Four of its men started running back and one, hit by rifle fire, fell. After seeing that, most of the others were apparently too frightened to leave their holes.

As it happened, Lieutenant Driskell's seventeen men who were between the railroad and road embankments were unable to see the rest of their company. Since they had not heard the shouted order they were unaware that an order to withdraw had been given. They had, however, watched the fire fight between the North Koreans and Company B, and had seen Company B leave. Lieutenant Driskell and Sergeant Williams decided they would hold their ground until they received orders. Twenty or thirty minutes passed. As soon as the bulk of the two companies had withdrawn, the enemy fire stopped, and all became quiet again. Driskell and his seventeen men were still in place when the North Koreans climbed the hill to take over the positions vacated by Company B. This roused their anxiety.

"What do you think we should do now?" Driskell asked.

"Well, sir," said Sergeant Williams, "I don't know what you're going to do, but I'd like to get the hell out of here."

Driskell then sent a runner to see if the rest of the company was still in position. When the runner returned to say he could see no one on the hill, the men started back using the railroad embankment for protection. Nine members of this group were from Lieutenant Driskell's 1st Platoon; the other eight were with Sergeant Williams from the Weapons Platoon. A few of Lieutenant Driskell's men had already left but about twenty, afraid to move across the flat paddies, had stayed behind. At the time, however, Driskell did not know what had happened to the rest of his platoon so, after he had walked back to the vicinity of the group of houses behind the hill, he stopped at one of the rice-paddy trails to decide which way to go to locate his missing men. Just then someone walked past and told him that some of his men, including several who were wounded, were near the base of the hill. With one other man, Driskell went off to look for them.

By the time the panicked riflemen of Company A had run the mile or two back to Pyongtaek they had overcome much of their initial fear. They gathered along the muddy main street of the village and stood there in the rain, waiting. When Captain Osburn arrived he immediately began assembling and reorganizing his company for the march south. Meanwhile, two Company C men were waiting to dynamite the bridge at the north edge of the village. One of the officers found a jeep and trailer that had been abandoned on a side street. He and several of his men succeeded in starting it and, although it did not run well and had apparently been abandoned for that reason, they decided it would do for hauling the company's heavy equipment that was left. By 0930 they piled all extra equipment, plus the machine guns, mortars, bazookas, BARs, and extra ammunition in the trailer. About the same time, several men noticed what appeared to be two wounded men trying to make their way along the road into Pyongtaek. It was still raining so hard that it was difficult to distinguish details. Pvt. Thomas A. Cammarano and another man volunteered to take the jeep and go after them. They pulled a BAR from the weapons in the trailer, inserted a magazine of ammunition, and drove the jeep north across the bridge, not realizing that the road was so narrow it would have been difficult to turn the vehicle around even if the trailer had not been attached.

During the period when the company was assembling and waiting in Pyongtaek, Sergeant Collins, the platoon sergeant who had joined the company the day before, decided to find out why his platoon had failed to fire effectively against the enemy. Of 31 members of his platoon, 12 complained that their rifles would not fire. Collins checked them and found the rifles were either broken, dirty, or had been assembled incorrectly. He sorted out the defective weapons and dropped them in a nearby well.

Two other incidents now occurred that had an unfavorable effect on morale. The second shell fired by the North Koreans that morning had landed near Captain Osburn's command post where the observer for his 4.2-inch mortars was standing. The observer reached Pyongtaek while the men were waiting for Cammarano and his companion to return with the jeep. Suffering severely from shock, the mortar observer could not talk coherently and walked as if he were drunk. His eyes showed white, and he stared wildly, moaning, "Rain, rain, rain," over and over again. About the same time, a member of the 1st Platoon joined the group and claimed that he had been with Lieutenant Driskell after he walked toward the cluster of houses searching for wounded men of his platoon. Lieutenant Driskell with four men had been suddenly surrounded by a group of North Korean soldiers. They tried to surrender, according to this man, but one of the

North Korean soldiers walked up to the lieutenant, shot him, and then killed the other three men. The narrator had escaped.

Of the approximately 140 men who had been in position at daybreak that morning, only a few more than 100 were now assembled in Pyongtaek. In addition to the 4 men just reported killed, there were about 30 others who were missing. The first sergeant with 8 men had followed a separate route after leaving the hill that morning and did not rejoin the company until several days later. One man failed to return after having walked down to a stream just after daylight to refill several canteens. There were also the others who had been either afraid or unable to leave their foxholes to move back with the rest of the company. This group included the man from the listening post and about twenty members of the 1st Platoon who had stayed in their holes in the rice paddies.[13]

Ten or fifteen minutes went by after Cammarano and his companion drove off in the jeep. Through the heavy rain and fog neither the jeep nor the wounded men were visible now. Suddenly there was the sound of rifle fire in the village and Captain Osburn, assuming that the two men (together with the vehicle and all company crew-served weapons) were also lost, gave the word to move out. Forming the remainder of his company into two single-file columns, one on each side of the street, he started south. The men had scarcely reached the south edge of the village when they heard the explosion as the Company C men destroyed the bridge. One fourth of the company and most of its equipment and supplies were missing as the men set off on their forced march.

A few scattered artillery shells followed the columns. None came close, but they kept the men moving fast. "This was one time," said one of the sergeants later, "when we didn't have to kick the men to get them to move. They kept going at a steady slow run." Captain Osburn did not try to follow the high ground but, when he could, he kept off the road and walked across rice paddies. There were several wounded men but the 4.2-inch mortar observer was the only one in the group unable to walk by himself. The others took turns supporting and helping him. His eyes still showed white and he kept moaning "rain" and the men near him wished he would shut up.

Occasionally the men made wise cracks about the police action: "I wonder when they're going to give me my police badge," or "Damned if these cops here don't use some big guns." But mostly they were quiet and just kept moving.

The rain continued hard until about noon. Then it began to get hot— a moist, sultry heat. The clouds hung low on the mountains. Nevertheless, Captain Osburn kept up a steady pace. Before leaving Pyongtaek he had warned that the column would not stop and any men who fell out would be left behind. The men were thirsty but few of them had canteens. They drank from the ditches along the roads, or from the rice paddies.

By noon the column had outrun the enemy fire, and Osburn halted it for a ten-minute rest. Thereafter he set a slower pace, usually following the road, and took a ten-minute break each hour. The column had no communication with any other part of the 24th Division, since the company radios had been abandoned that morning. Nor did anyone know of a plan except to go south. There was no longer any serious talk of a police action—by this time the soldiers expected to go straight to Pusan and back to Japan. The Company A men frequently saw pieces of equipment along the road, and from this they assumed the rest of the battalion was on the same road ahead of them. Later they began to overtake stragglers from other companies. By the middle of the day the men were hungry.

By mid-afternoon wet shoes caused serious foot trouble. Some of the men took off their shoes and carried them for a while, or threw them away. It was easier walking barefoot in the mud. Other equipment was strewn along the road—discarded ponchos, steel helmets, ammunition belts, and even rifles that men of the battalion had dropped. As the afternoon wore on the two columns of Company A men lengthened, the distance between the men increasing. They kept trading places in the line and took turns helping the mortar observer. At breaks, Captain Osburn reminded them to stay on or near the road and, if they were scattered by a sudden attack, to keep moving individually.

Late that afternoon, during a ten-minute rest period, an American plane flew low over the men who were lying along the road near a few straw-roofed houses. The pilot suddenly dipped into the column and opened fire with his caliber .50 machine guns. Only one man was hit—a South Korean soldier. The bullet struck him in the cheeks, tearing away his lower jaw and part of his face. This incident further demoralized the men. When a South Korean truck came by, they put the wounded Korean on it.

Early that evening Captain Osburn, at the head of his company, reached the town of Chonan and there found other elements of the 1st Battalion which had arrived earlier. It was a shabby-looking outfit. Many men were asleep on the floor of an old sawmill and others were scattered throughout the town in buildings or along the streets, sitting or sleeping. Captain Osburn immediately set out to locate officers of the other units to learn what he could of the situation. The remainder of Company A was strung out for a mile and a half or two miles to the north. As the men reached the town they lay down to rest. There was no organization—they were just a group of tired, disheartened men. The last men in the column did not straggle in until two hours later. By then Captain Osburn had borrowed three trucks from the South Korean Army with which he moved his company to defensive positions a few miles south of Chonan. General Barth had selected these positions after leaving the 1st Battalion's command post at Pyongtaek early that morning. He had gone to Chonan to brief the regimental commander of the 34th Infantry and then south to select terrain from which the 24th Division could stage a series of delaying actions. He returned to Chonan late in the afternoon to learn that the 1st Battalion had withdrawn the entire distance to Chonan, instead of defending the first available position south of Pyongtaek from which it could physically block the enemy tank column. Believing that the North Koreans were in pursuit, he directed the 1st Battalion to occupy the next defensive position, which happened to be about two miles south of Chonan.[14]

It was dark by the time Company A began to dig in at this position. The company, of course, had no intrenching tools but a few of the men scraped out shallow holes. Most of them just lay down and went to sleep. The next morning (7 July) Captain Osburn got the men up and ordered them to go on digging foxholes. Groups of men went off to nearby villages looking for spades or shovels. They also got a small supply of food from the Koreans, many of whom were abandoning their homes and fleeing south. When they had finished digging their positions, Osburn's men sat barefoot in the rain, nursing their feet. Hopefully, they discussed a new rumor: they were going to a railway station south of their present location, then by train to Pusan, and from there to Japan. There was some argument about the location of the railway station, but most of the men were agreed that they were returning to Japan. The rumor pleased everyone. Nothing of importance happened to Company A during the day, although the other battalion of the 34th Infantry, after having moved from Ansong to Chonan on the previous evening, was engaged in heavy fighting just north of Chonan.

Full rations were available on the morning of 8 July, thus relieving one kind of discomfort. The fighting for Chonan continued and, by midmorning, the remaining American forces began to withdraw and abandon the town.[15] In Company A's area, the day was quiet until early afternoon, when enemy artillery rounds suddenly exploded in the battalion's area. Within a few minutes after the first shell landed, Captain Osburn gave the order to pull out. The entire battalion moved, part of it on three trucks still in its possession, but Company A marched, Captain Osburn in the lead and again setting a fast pace. This time he kept his company together. About the middle of the night the company stopped and took up positions on a hill adjoining the road, staying there until the first signs of daylight when Osburn roused his men and resumed the march. After several hours the three trucks returned and began shuttling the remainder of the battalion to new positions just north of the Kum River and the town of Konju. There the entire battalion formed a perimeter in defensive positions—the best they had constructed since coming to Korea.

By the time the trenches and holes were dug in, it was mid-afternoon of 9 July. Company A got an issue of rations and, for the first time, one of ammunition. The Weapons Platoon received one 60mm mortar. This preparation for combat weakened the rumor about returning to Japan. Instead,

Captain Osburn and his officers told the men of another infantry division then en route from Japan. The sky was clear, the sun hot and, for the first time in several days, the men had dry clothing. The battalion remained in the area without incident until 12 July. That morning it registered the 81mm and the 4.2-inch mortars and issued more ammunition to the men. It

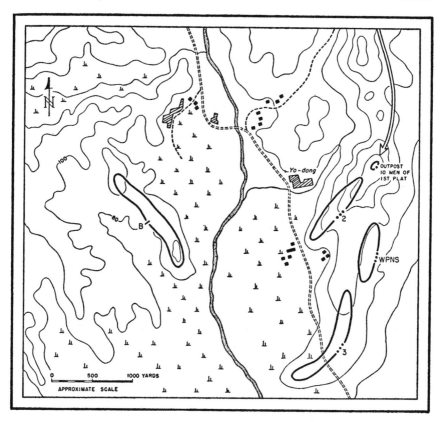

had the first friendly mortar fire and the first abundant supply of ammunition since early morning of 6 July. That afternoon, at 1700, an enemy shell landed in the area. Others followed and within a few minutes North Korean soldiers appeared in large numbers. Instead of hitting frontally, the leading enemy soldiers circled wide and attacked the 1st Platoon, which was outposting a high point of the hill, on the right flank. After suffering heavy losses on the morning of 6 July, only ten men remained in that platoon. Five of these were killed at the very outset of the fighting on the 12th when the North Koreans overran their positions and shot them in their holes. The five remaining men from the 1st Platoon escaped and joined one of the others.

The sudden collapse of the outpost placed the enemy directly to the right and above the 2d Platoon. SFC Elvin E. Knight, platoon guide, turning to determine the source and cause of the firing, noticed a flag up where the 1st Platoon had been.

"What the hell's that flag doing up here?" he asked. Suddenly he yelled, "That's a North Korean flag!"

About twenty enemy soldiers appeared on the high knob. They began firing down upon the 2d Platoon and several of them started sliding down the steep hill toward the men, shouting and firing as they came. The flank attack completely surprised the men of the 2d Platoon, whose positions, selected for firing toward the front, were unsuitable for firing at the high ground on the right. Almost immediately someone began shouting, "Let's get the hell out of here!" and the men started back individually or in small groups. They did, however, take their weapons and several of the wounded. The rest of the company—those in the 3d and Weapons Platoons—held their ground and rapidly increased their rate of fire as soon as they saw what had happened to the other two platoons. Most of the 2d Platoon moved back several hundred yards, where the other two platoons were located, and resumed fighting. Until dark there was a heavy volume of fire and after that occasional exchanges with small arms until about 0230 on 13 July when, under orders, Company A abandoned its hill and moved very quietly back, following a river south for a short distance until it was beyond range of North Koreans' rifles.

After daylight Osburn and his men crossed the long bridge over the Kum River. For another day Company A and the rest of the battalion stayed there while North Koreans assembled on the north bank of the river. Then, on 14 July, one group of North Koreans crossed the Kum River and successfully attacked a battery of artillery in that vicinity. The entire battalion moved out by truck on the 15th and fell back to the city of Taejon, closing there late in the afternoon. Other units of the 24th Division, already assembled, were preparing to defend the town. The 1st Battalion took up defensive positions on the northeast side of Taejon, on high ground between the main part of the town and the airstrip used by the division liaison planes.[16] American forces destroyed the bridge over the Kum River before withdrawing to Taejon, but the North Koreans succeeded in crossing and followed in close pursuit.

After the next heavy enemy attack Company A, and the remainder of the entire 24th Division, fell back again, this time to the Pusan perimeter. The attack began soon after daybreak on the morning of 20 July. In Company A's area, Sergeant Williams and three other members of the Weapons Platoon were among the first to discover it. They were manning bazookas with the mission of blocking the main road leading from the north into Taejon. As daylight increased on the morning of 20 July Williams noticed movement on hills about three hundred yards to the right. He watched as three skirmish lines of North Koreans came over the hilltop. Other enemy soldiers appeared on hills to the left of the road. After watching for several minutes, he raced back about five hundred yards to a Korean house in which the battalion's command post was located. The other three men followed.

There was a high, mud wall around the command post. Williams ran through the gate and into the house, where he hurriedly described the enemy force, claiming that North Koreans were "just boiling over the hill!"

"Well, Sergeant," answered the battalion commander, "you're a little excited, aren't you?"

"Yes, sir, I am," said Williams. "And if you'd seen what I just saw, you'd be excited too."

Just as the two men went through the gate to look, several flares appeared to the north. Suddenly the enemy began firing tank guns, artillery, mortars, and machine guns in a pattern that covered the entire city, including the immediate area of the 1st Battalion's headquarters.

"I guess we'd better get out of here," said the commander, and turned back into the building.

It was only a few minutes after dawn. Soon the entire battalion was moving south again. Captain Osburn kept Company A together as a unit—at the beginning at least—but many men from the battalion were on their own, units were mixed together, and organization was lost in the confusion. Some men threw away their shoes again and walked barefoot. Most of them had trouble finding food, and for all of them it was a disheartening repetition of their first contact with the North Korean Army. They did not go back to Japan. They had seen only the beginning of fighting on the Korean peninsula. But when they again came to a halt beyond the Naktong River, and turned to make another defensive stand against the North Koreans, they had ended the first phase of the Korean conflict. Other United Nations troops had arrived in Korea. The period of withdrawal was over. Members of Company A and the rest of the 34th Infantry had lost their overconfidence and had gained battle experience. They soon settled down to a grim defense of the Pusan perimeter.

★ DISCUSSION

Before 25 June 1950 Korea was of little import to the American soldiers in Japan and to the citizens of our nation. Defense of the United Nations' principles was given lip service but few among us thought of action. Korea was not in the public mind.

The North Korean Army marched. Our leaders met. And Company A, with its peacetime thoughts, unprepared both psychologically and militarily, found itself faced with the stark reality of war. With this deal, victory could not be in the cards for Company A nor for any other company so prepared and so committed. We should take advantage of their mistakes —all too evident. We invite attention to them with great humility, for who among us must not say, "There, but for the grace of God, go I"?

What were some of the specific causes that contributed to the debacle experienced by Company A? Faulty orientation, poor intelligence, and a lack of communications are evident. The exact level at which orientation and intelligence ceased to be adequate cannot be determined by this narrative. However, Company A was not prepared to fight intelligently when it was called upon to do so. The individual actions and reactions—the failure to differentiate between enemy tank fire coming from the front and supposed short rounds from supporting mortars—indicate a lack of imaginative and realistic combat training. The inability of the troops to remedy minor weapons malfunctions is further indication of inadequate training.

Examples of faulty leadership are frequent in the narrative. Where was the combat outpost, or adequate local security, of the 1st Battalion? Evidently, there was none.

Why was a platoon permitted to occupy a nearby position from which it could not support the fires of an adjacent platoon?

Why was a patrol permitted to rest within three hundred yards of the enemy without establishing security positions?

It was to take many months of combat and the physical hardening of several campaigns before the military potential of both officers and men was realized and they achieved the high military proficiency of which they were capable.

★ NOTES

1. 21st Infantry: war diary, 29 June 1950. See also Marguerite Higgins, *War in Korea*, 33, 47–48, 59; and Lt.Col. Roy E. Appleman's combat history of the Korean War, a manuscript in preparation for the Office of the Chief of Military History's Korean series. The details of this action, unless otherwise cited, are based upon a series of interviews with MSgt. Roy E. Collins and with MSgt. Zack C. Williams, both of whom were platoon sergeants at the time of the action. These men presented the action at the platoon level. For a general account of activities in Korea during this time, especially in reference to the 34th Infantry, see the article by Brig.Gen. George B. Barth, "The First Days in Korea," *Combat Forces Journal* (March 1951).

2. 24th Division, unit war diaries: 34th Infantry Regiment, 28 June to 4 July 1950; 24th Division: G3 journal, Vol. 3A, 4 July 1950.

3. 24th Division, unit war diaries: 21st Infantry Regiment, 29 June to 4 July 1950; 24th Division: G3 journal, message ROB 052, 031710 July. The dates and times given here do not always agree with the official records, which are often incorrect, having been prepared from memory at some later date. See Appleman, *op. cit.*, chapter 3.

4. 24th Division, unit war diaries: 21st Infantry Regiment, 4 July 1950, and 52d FA Battalion, 4 July 1950. Also Appleman, *loc. cit.*

5. The company's morning report lists 138 men and 5 officers for 5 July. These reports, however, appear to have been made up at some later date, and they do not accurately record all the changes and events as they occurred.

6. Letters, Major Leroy Osburn to OCMH, 21 January and 5 March 1952. Osburn states the mission of his company at that time. It appears from General Barth's article (cited in note 1) that General Barth changed the mission from one of defense to one of delaying action before contact was made with the enemy force.

7. Barth, *op. cit.*

8. For a more complete account of this action, see Appleman, *loc. cit.* See also 24th Division: G3 journal, report of interrogation of CO, 1st Battalion, 21st Infantry, 7 July 1950; and 24th Division, unit war diaries: 21st Infantry Regiment, 5 July 1950. The number of tanks varies in these reports, but the best evidence indicates there were 33 in the first column, of which only 4 were knocked out.

9. Barth, *op. cit.*

10. SFC Alfred Beauchamp, Company A, 34th Infantry, in an interview by the author, 7 August 1951.

11. Letter, Osburn to OCMH, 5 March 1952.

12. *Ibid.*, 21 January 1952.

13. Company A's morning reports for this period list twenty-seven men missing in action. The report was made up on 8 July, apparently after the first sergeant and the several men with him rejoined the company. These reports do not include at least one man (Pvt. Joseph P. Krahel) who was missing in action after the engagement on the morning of 6 July 1950.

14. Barth, *op. cit.*

15. For a more complete account of the fighting in Chonan by the 3d Battalion, 34th Infantry, see Appleman, *loc. cit.*

16. 24th Division: G3 journal, 15 to 18 July 1950.

The god of war hates those who hesitate.

EURIPIDES: HERACLIDÆ (*circa* 425 B.C.)

2

Attack Along a Ridgeline

★ The first break in the Naktong defense line at the central sector of the Pusan perimeter occurred during the early morning of 6 August 1950 when an estimated one thousand enemy troops crossed the Naktong River and penetrated the zone of the 34th Infantry (24th Infantry Division). The regimental commander immediately committed his reserve and counterattacked, but the North Koreans clung to their bridgehead on the east side of the river. During the night the enemy moved sufficient forces across the Naktong to replace their losses and increase their strength.[1] When the division commander (Maj.Gen. John H. Church) learned that the enemy had crossed the last good natural barrier in southern Korea, he committed his reserve, the 19th Infantry (24th Infantry Division), in an effort to drive the enemy back across the river. During the next few days General Church attacked with all the troops he could muster from his own under-strength division and from units attached to it by Eighth Army. The North Koreans, however, continued to build up their forces east of the Naktong.[2]

By 8 August North Koreans, totaling a reinforced regiment, had waded the river and pulled raftloads of heavy equipment including trucks, across with them. Two days later they appeared to have two regiments in strong positions east of the Naktong.[3] Consolidating all troops in the southern part of his division zone under the command of Col. John G. Hill (whose 9th Infantry Regiment, 2d Infantry Division, was attached to the 24th Division to help restore the Naktong line), General Church ordered a counterattack on 11 August.[4] Task Force Hill's attack ran squarely into strong enemy attacks, and the entire operation lost its direction and impetus in the resulting confusion. With communications lacking much of the time and enemy forces scattered throughout a large area, one regimental commander summed up the chaos by saying, "There are dozens of enemy and American forces all over the area, and they are all surrounding each other." [5] During this period of grim combat, a desperate effort was made to prevent collapse of the Naktong line, while North Koreans fought back with equal determination. Task Force Hill, now comprising three infantry regiments, launched a full-scale attack again on 14 August. It failed once more.

General Church ordered the attack to continue at 0630, 15 August. It would commence on the left (south) flank of the task force zone where the 1st Battalion, 34th Infantry, was to lead off in a column of companies. The battalion commander chose Company A to lead the attack.[6]

Eighth Army planned maximum artillery support and gave Task Force Hill priority on tactical airplanes. Early that morning, however, it began to rain, and thick clouds along the ridgelines interfered with effective operation of the planes.

Soon after first light on the morning of 15 August, the commander of Company A summoned the leader of the 1st Platoon (Lt. Melvin D. Schiller), to whom he briefly outlined the plan of attack. Lieutenant Schiller, whose platoon was to lead the company column, had time only to take his squad leaders to high ground where he could point out to them the objective and the general route to be followed. The 1st Battalion's objective was a ridgeline a mile and a half long and approximately four hundred feet higher than the stream and the rice paddies at the ridge's base. There were several separate peaks along the crest of the ridgeline.[7]

Followed by the rest of Company A, Lieutenant Schiller's platoon proceeded to the southeast end of the ridge, took up its attack formation, waited a few minutes until the end of a fifteen-minute artillery preparation, and then started up the ridge in a general northwest direction. Members of the platoon, knowing that the North Koreans had repulsed a similar attack that Company B had made two days before, expected trouble. For about a quarter of the distance, however, the platoon moved up the ridgeline without interference. Then two enemy machine guns, firing from the left, forced the platoon to the ground. When this happened, the company commander called Lt. Edward L. Shea and told him to take his 2d Platoon through the stalled unit and continue the advance. Lieutenant Shea and one of his squad leaders (SFC Roy E. Collins) exchanged dubious glances. Their platoon consisted of 9 inexperienced men and 24 replacements who had joined the company three days before.

Motioning his men to follow, Lieutenant Shea started up the ridge.

"Let's take a look at it," he said, as he strode off erectly. As he neared the 1st Platoon's position, enemy fire forced him to the ground. He crawled up beside Lieutenant Schiller who was lying on his stomach behind a native grave mound which was about four feet high, four feet in diameter, and covered with neatly trimmed grass. Lieutenant Schiller was trying to locate the two enemy machine guns that were holding up the advance. He and Lieutenant Shea suspected that the guns were located on the short hill on the left flank, since the string of enemy bullets seemed to cross just above the grave. Just as the two platoon leaders reached this conclusion, a bullet struck Schiller's helmet. It cut his head, followed the curve of his helmet,

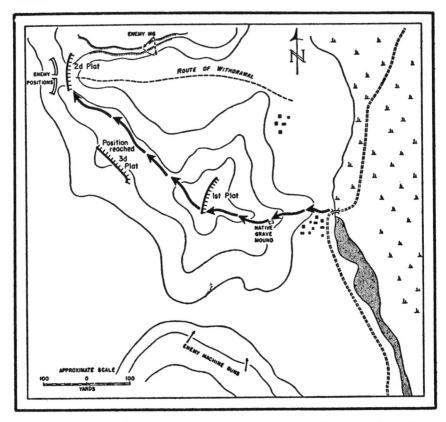

passed through his shoulder, and emerged to lodge in Shea's leg just above the knee. The two officers, both casualties, immediately directed their platoons to open fire against the enemy guns. Friendly fire caused the enemy guns to suspend fire, and the attack moved forward along the ridge top with the company commander (Lt. Albert F. Alfonso) directing the platoons.

The two platoons worked well together, one group moving forward while the other fired at the enemy positions. Moving steadily, Company A soon reached the first high peak at the southwestern end of the ridgeline. It was about 0830 when the company stopped to plan for the continuation of the attack. There were freshly dug holes, but no enemy in the area.

Beyond this point the narrow crest of the ridge dipped slightly before rising again at the next peak. Formed by a spur ridge, the next high point appeared to be a rocky cliff, about four hundred yards away, which lay athwart the long ridgeline and the direction of attack. Just in front of the point where the cliff joined the main ridgeline, there was a depression, or saddle. During the few minutes that the company spent preparing to continue the attack, several of the men observed enemy soldiers moving near the saddle. On the previous day, members of Company A had seen an enemy machine gun firing from the top of the rocky cliff.

Lieutenant Alfonso pointed out the saddle in front of the rocky cliff and told MSgt. Willie C. Gibson (now leading the 2d Platoon) to secure it. Alfonso then lined up the 1st Platoon behind an embankment on the high ground and assigned to it the mission of firing at any enemy interference, and especially to silence the enemy machine gun, if it fired. Under the protection of the 1st Platoon's base of fire, the 2d Platoon would dash along the 500-yard-long ridge. Once the 2d was in the saddle, the 3d Platoon would follow and reinforce it.

Sergeant Gibson lined up his four squads in the order they were to leave. He planned to follow the 2d Squad. He detailed Sergeant Collins at the end of the line to make certain that every man in the platoon moved out. Cpl. Leo M. Brennen (a squad leader and veteran of the Pacific War who had joined the company three days before) straightened and partially pulled the pin on a grenade he carried.

"I'll be the first man to go," Brennen said. "The rest of you guys follow me."

Brennen jumped over the embankment and started running toward the objective. Sergeant Collins checked his watch. It was 0845. Three other men followed Brennen at fifteen-yard intervals, all of them running just below the crest of the ridge since enemy guns fired from the opposite, or southwest, side of the ridge. Just after the fourth man left, the North Koreans fired several short bursts from the machine gun on the rock cliff, hitting two men from the 1st Platoon, one in the eye and the other in the neck. Both were killed at once.

"After that," one of the surviving men said, "it was just like jumping into ice water."

But the rest of the platoon followed, each man about ten or fifteen steps behind the man in front. No one was wounded until the next to the last man —Cpl. Joseph H. Simoneau—rose to go. A burst from the North Korean gun struck him in the leg and shoulder. He yelled, "I'm hit!" and fell back toward Sergeant Collins. Collins pulled him back, called the medics, and then, after notifying the leader of the 3d Platoon that he was the last man from the 2d, jumped over the protective hump of dirt and ran.

This had taken no longer than five minutes. Sergeant Collins had gone only a few steps when Corporal Brennen, the lead man, reached the end of the ridge. After running the entire distance, Brennen looked over the low, pinched ridge separating him from the enemy-occupied ground and saw three North Koreans sitting around their machine gun as if they were relaxing. The gun was about twenty yards in front of him. Brennen had one grenade ready to throw and he tossed it. As he did this, he noticed movement to his left and turned to see another enemy light machine gun and its crew nearer than the first. He fired one clip from his rifle at them at the same time the machine gun fired at him. Corporal Brennen hit both enemy soldiers manning the gun, and believed he killed them, but not until they had shot him through the leg. He slid down the hill a short distance to a protected area. A brief period of noisy, confused, and furious fighting followed.

As the members of the 2d Platoon reached the saddle, they formed a firing line along their side of the little ridge. Lying close to the ground, they peered over the ridge frequently to observe and fire at the enemy, who was often only a few yards away. Three or four men who became casualties within a few minutes slid down the slope to join Corporal Brennen. There, Sergeant Gibson and a medic were now caring for the wounded.

Sergeant Collins, whom Lieutenant Shea had appointed second in command, reached the combat area a few minutes after the first burst of activity and took over the direction of the 2d Platoon. Like Corporal Brennen, Sergeant Collins carried a grenade with the cotter pin straightened and the ring over his index finger so that he could flip out the pin quickly. A few seconds after he reached the saddle there was a burst of fire from an enemy burp gun on the left flank. Collins ran back toward the bank on the left end of the firing line and looked over the ridge just as a North Korean raised to fire into the American line. Collins dropped his grenade on the enemy side of the hill and jumped to one side as a burst from the burp gun dug into the ground near him. His grenade-burst threw the burp gun into the air, and as Collins raised up to look over the ridgeline again another North Korean picked up the gun and tried to reload it. Sergeant Collins shot him with his rifle. At this moment SFC Regis J. Foley of the 3d Platoon came up to Collins.

According to the plan, the 3d Platoon was to follow immediately after the 2d Platoon. Sergeant Foley, the first man behind Sergeant Collins, reached the saddle, but the next man mistakenly turned into another narrow area about two thirds of the way across. Consequently, the entire 3d Platoon was lost to the action since it came under such heavy enemy fire that it could move neither forward nor to the rear.

"Foley," said Sergeant Collins, "you watch this end and don't let them get up here."

Collins then started back along the line of riflemen where several gaps had occurred as men became casualties. Some men were already yelling that they were out of ammunition, even though each rifleman had carried two bardoleers and a full belt of M1 clips—a total of 176 rounds. Sergeant Collins knew they would need help to win the battle they had started. Unaware that the 3d Platoon had gone to the wrong area and was now pinned down by heavy enemy fire, and believing that it would soon join him, Collins sent a runner to the company commander asking for more help and for more ammunition. He especially wanted grenades, which were easy to toss over the ridgeline. While he waited for word from the company commander, he went along the line, taking ammunition from those who were wounded or dead and distributing it to the men who were effective. By this time most of the men in the platoons were calling for help, wanting either ammunition or medics. In addition to the close-in fighting that continued, the enemy machine gun up on the rocky cliff had turned and was firing at the exposed rear of the 2d Platoon. Fire from this gun varied according to the amount of fire that the 1st Platoon's base of fire delivered against it. When the covering fire was heavy, the enemy gun was quiet; but it resumed firing as soon, and as often, as the 1st Platoon quit.

It took Sergeant Collins's runner eight minutes to make his round trip. He returned with a note from Lieutenant Alfonso which read, "Pull out."

At the far right of the line, Cpl. Joseph J. Sady yelled for a grenade. "They're pulling up a machine gun here," he shouted.

Collins threw Lieutenant Alfonso's note down and took a grenade to Corporal Sady who tossed it over on the enemy gunners.

"That took care of them," he said.

An enemy rifleman, firing from a distance of ten steps, hit Corporal Sady in the head and killed him. The next man in the line killed the North Korean.

Sergeant Collins worked back along the line. At the left end Sergeant Foley, who had been stationed there to hold that flank, came sliding down the ridge bareheaded and bleeding. He had been hit by a split bullet that had apparently ricocheted from a rock and had cut into his head. Collins bandaged him and told him to go back and ask the company commander for more help. But as soon as he was gone, Sergeant Collins realized that because his ammunition was so low, and because less than half of his original strength remained, he had no alternative but to break contact and withdraw. He called down to tell Sergeant Gibson to start getting the wounded men out. Six men were wounded, two of them seriously, and Gibson started to evacuate them by moving them down a gully between the two hills to a road at the bottom.

Near the center of the saddle a Negro rifleman, PFC Edward O. Cleaborn, concentrated on keeping an enemy machine gun out of action. Standing up on the ridgeline and shooting down into the enemy side of the hill, he kept killing North Koreans who tried to man the gun. He was excited and kept firing rapidly, calling for ammunition and yelling, "Come on up, you sons of bitches, and fight!"

Sergeant Collins told him to get down on the ground, but Cleaborn said, "Sergeant, I just can't see them when I get down."

About this time an enemy soldier jumped over the little ridge and landed on top of Sergeant Collins who was stripping ammunition from one of his men who had just been killed. The North Korean grabbed Sergeant Collins by the waist and held on tightly. Seeing this, Cleaborn jumped down and started after the North Korean who kept hiding behind Sergeant Collins. Collins eventually persuaded Cleaborn that the enemy soldier wanted to surrender, and Cleaborn went back to the firing line. Collins pushed his prisoner down to the ditch where Gibson was evacuating the wounded. Sergeant Gibson loaded the prisoner with the largest wounded man who had to be carried out, and started him down the gully toward the road.

By the time Sergeant Foley returned with a renewal of the company commander's instructions to withdraw, the evacuation of all wounded men was under way. As men left the firing line, they helped the wounded. Only six men remained in firing positions and several of these were so low on ammunition they had fixed their bayonets. Sergeant Collins told the six to fire a heavy blast at the enemy's position, and then move out quickly. All but Cleaborn fired a clip of ammunition and then started to leave. He reloaded his rifle and said he wanted to fire one more clip. As he jumped back on the ridge to fire again, he was killed by a bullet through his head. Sergeant Collins and the remaining five men ran back along the ridgeline, the route of their advance.

It was 0932 when the men reached the little spur from which the 1st Platoon had been firing, just forty-seven minutes after the attack had begun. Of the original 36 men in the 2d Platoon that morning, only 10 were unharmed. Nine wounded men walked or were carried down the ditch to the road, three dying before reaching the road. The other members of the platoon were dead.[8]

The 1st Battalion's attack had been stopped. Other elements of Task Force Hill encountered similarly stubborn resistance, and during the afternoon the commander of the force recommended to General Church that the attack be discontinued and that the force dig in to defend the ground it occupied.[9]

★ DISCUSSION

While the American soldier is typified by courage, he is, at the same time, universally marked as an impulsive, intelligent individualist. Thus it is that strong leadership and guidance are necessary to weld a group of American soldiers into a singular unit of specific purpose. Without this directing strength at command level, each in the group will nobly carry on in his own merry way; and though the individual conduct of each might be highly commendable, the unit's mission can end in complete failure.

This fact is the underlying cause for the failure of Company A, 34th Infantry, in its attack on 15 August 1950.

If the aggressiveness and heroism of Brennen, Collins, Cleaborn, Sady, and others had been organized into a single, vigorous effort against the enemy, the objective would have been secured. Instead, each of these able fighters carried on his own private war, while the acting leader of the 2d Platoon was caring for wounded, and the company commander was entrenched with a base of fire five hundred yards away.

Correct and successful command at the platoon and company levels is not conducive to long life, because the commander must constantly expose himself in order to lead and maintain control. The commanding officer of Company A was conspicuously absent in action and decision from the time that he failed to join the 1st Platoon when it was first hit by long-range fire, until the very end of the engagement when the survivors of the 2d Platoon withdrew from the bloody threshold of victory.

It was unfortunate that the leading platoons lost their brave but reckless lieutenants when the battle had hardly begun. Had the leader of the 1st Platoon considered the enemy's point of view for only a moment, he would have realized that a conspicuous grave mound would be top priority for a machine gunner firing from a distance of several hundred yards. Taking extreme ranges into consideration, it is highly possible that the North Korean gunner did not even see the lieutenant, but was merely firing at a likely target. The 2d Platoon leader committed a grave error and set a poor example by joining the other officer within the narrow confines of the tempting target. What more bitter lesson against bunching up could be learned than to have two unit commanders become casualties as a result of *one* bullet? This disaster was an appropriate climax to the scene which just previously found the 2d Platoon leader walking erect along the crest of a hill that was under fire.

A study of the terrain would indicate that the company commander could have moved his entire unit into position on the high ground of the larger hill. Had he taken advantage of the natural cover afforded by the ridgeline, his company might have accomplished this movement without sustaining a casualty. Then, with the company organized in the area which was used for the base of fire, the commander could have devised any number of plans involving maneuver, supporting arms, and assault for seizing the remainder of his objective.

But he first set a bad precedent when he allowed the 1st Platoon to halt as it came under long-range machine-gun fire. Instead of directing that unit to continue the attack, he impulsively pushed the 2d Platoon into the lead. It is noteworthy here that another platoon became lost and immobilized later, during the crucial stage of the battle.

The company commander should have been the key figure in the final phase of the attack; he should have been the spirit of a two-platoon assault which never materialized. Instead, remaining five hundred yards behind with the base of fire, he was so unable to control the two leading platoons that one of them even became lost and completely ineffective.

Judging from the fact that the 2d Platoon fought a large number of enemy at a distance of only a few yards, it is evident that the Americans were practically in the heart of the North Korean position when they came to a halt. Then, for several minutes, bravery and sacrifice—which could have won the day—went for naught; and a great number of casualties was sustained without a decision being forced.

Had the company commander followed the 2d Platoon, he could have spurred it into an assault. With men like Cleaborn and Collins setting the pace, the North Korean soldiers probably would have reeled back and retreated or surrendered. Moreover, it is probable that the 3d Platoon would not have strayed into temporary oblivion had it been following on the heels of a watchful company commander. Even after this unit had wandered into the draw, it certainly could have been retrieved under sufficient prodding. Could it have fared any worse than to lie exposed and immobile under the barrels of two enemy automatic weapons? Hardly!

Although the enemy force could have been eliminated by a combination of aggressive leadership and small-arms fire, the apparent lack of artillery support during this attack is enough to shake the foundations of The Artillery School at Fort Sill. In the introduction to the battle account, there is mention of the fact that Eighth Army planned "full artillery support." Where was it? Why was it not employed when a relatively small group of enemy on a prominent terrain feature held up a battalion attack? If the enemy's guns were periodically silenced by sporadic bursts from Company A's base of fire, surely white phosphorus and high-explosive shells would have wrought havoc with such cautious defenders.

Once again the big gap between tactical theory and practice is glaringly exposed by the bland statement: "*After* an artillery preparation, the attack moved off about 0700." Company A then had to proceed a mere one and one half miles, while unmolested enemy gunners lolled pleasantly in their holes and fingered their triggers expectantly.

When once the area occupied by the enemy was known, not only artillery, but also mortars and recoilless rifles could have rained a devastating barrage of steel and fire into the hostile position. The layout of the terrain and the location of the enemy's defenses were ideal for maximum fire support throughout all but the assault phase of the attack. Shielded with covering fire, Company A could have retained excellent control to a point from which the final, victorious assault could have been launched.

Another deadly, disquieting annoyance for the North Koreans might have been in the form of flanking and frontal machine-gun and rocket-launcher fire delivered from the center and northwest portions of the larger hill. Such weapons would have been able to give added protection to the 2d and 3d Platoons until they were in position to assault.

Why small-unit commanders overlook the life-saving potential of supporting arms, and why higher commanders tolerate that oversight, are questions which cry futilely for logical answers.

In general, nothing but the highest praise is sufficient for the individual conduct of the soldiers of Company A throughout this action. Although their lieutenants were wounded early, leaving them nothing in the way of leadership except long-range encouragement from their company commander, they closed with the enemy, clung tenaciously to a position of bitter attrition, and inflicted many casualties on a foe who was flushed with victory and confidence. When ordered to withdraw, they did so in an orderly fashion, ensuring that wounded comrades among them were first removed to safety. Even in this last, most distasteful of all military maneuvers, they acquitted themselves with honor, despite the fact that they had no really effective covering fire.

It was indeed fortunate for the men of the 2d Platoon that the flame of natural leadership in Sergeant Collins burned brightly during this engagement. Had it not been for his initiative and exemplary action, the plight of the platoon might have ended as complete catastrophe.

Noble as his sentiments might have been, the NCO acting as 2d Platoon leader picked a poor time to work as a medic. While his command was being decimated, he should have played a role far more active than that of comforter to the afflicted.

That Cleaborn and others were probably carried away by temporary fanaticism—to the point of paying for it with their lives—is certainly not to the discredit of these men. Had an experienced commander been present to maintain control and demand discipline, it is very possible that these soldiers might still be alive. Or, at least, they would have had a victory in return for their supreme sacrifice.

★ NOTES

1. 24th Infantry Division: war diary, 6 and 7 August 1950.

2. *Ibid.*, 6–8 August 1950.

3. *Ibid.*, 7–10 August 1950.

4. *Ibid.*, 10 August 1950.

5. *Ibid.*, 8–11 August 1950; 24th Infantry Division: periodic operations report No. 36, 112400 August 1950.

6. Unless otherwise noted, all information about the combat action was obtained from Capt. Edward L. Shea (the platoon commander at the time of the action)

and First Sgt. Roy E. Collins (the platoon sergeant on 15 August 1950), in interviews by the author.

7. Statement by Lieutenant Schiller in first draft of this account, OCMH files.

8. Morning reports of Company A, 34th Infantry, 14–20 August 1950. The report for 15 August lists 35 casualties for Company A, including 17 missing in action, 13 wounded in action, and 5 killed in action. At least one man known to have been killed on 15 August is listed on the morning report for 14 August.

9. 24th Infantry Division: war diary, 15 August 1950.

3
Defense of a Battery Position

★ North Korean Communist forces appeared to be near complete victory at the end of August and during the first part of September of 1950. Along the southern coast of Korea enemy troops were within thirty miles of Pusan, the only port and supply base left to the United Nations army. American troops holding this Pusan perimeter at the time consisted of four divisions and a brigade occupying a line in the general area of the Naktong River from Waegwan south to Masan—a straight-line distance of seventy miles. The irregular front line was twice that long. South Korean soldiers manned the northern section of the perimeter from Waegwan to Pohang-dong on the east coast.

At the beginning of September the North Koreans began a powerful drive against the southern end of the perimeter defended by the U.S. 2d and 25th Infantry Divisions. These attacks achieved limited success and carried the combat into the rear areas behind the American front lines. One penetration fell against the 35th Infantry, a regiment of the 25th Division, soon after midnight on the morning of 3 September. The enemy pushed Company B from its position, surrounded Company G and the 1st Battalion command post, and then attacked several batteries of artillery. Among the artillery units, the heaviest fighting took place within the gun position of Battery A, 64th Field Artillery Battalion, which was in direct support of the 35th Infantry. The headquarters of each of these units was located in Haman at that time.

On the night of 2–3 September Battery A was in position two and a half miles north of Haman near a main road and single-track railroad running east and west between Masan and Chinju. The narrow road from Haman joined the Masan–Chinju road at the small village of Saga, the buildings of which were strung along the main road.[1] Because of North Korean infiltrators, artillery units were alert to the necessity of defending their own positions and the battery commander (Capt. Leroy Anderson) kept his area as compact as possible. Three or four hundred yards south of the road there was a low ridge shaped like a half circle and forming a shallow bowl. Here Captain Anderson positioned five of his six howitzers. Since the area was too small to accommodate all of the pieces, he placed the other howitzer on the north side of a railroad track that paralleled the Masan road and divided the battery area. The fire direction center, on the south side of the tracks, was operating in a tent erected in a four-foot-deep dugout within shouting distance of the guns. The wire section had its switchboard north of the tracks in a dugout fifteen to twenty yards south of the cluster of houses, a few of which were used by men of the wire section as living quarters. In addition to the low ridge, there was only one other terrain feature of importance—a gully, about four feet deep, next to the railroad tracks.

Around the battery position Captain Anderson set up ten defensive posts including four .50-caliber machine guns, three .30-caliber machine guns, one observation and listening post, and two M16 halftracks each mounting four .50-caliber machine guns. Four of the posts were on the. ridge around the gun position and were connected by telephone wire. The others were within shouting distance.

Until 0245 on 3 September the battery fired its usual missions in support of the 35th Infantry. The night was dark, and there was a heavy fog in the area—a condition common along the southern coast of Korea during the summer. The battery first sergeant (MSgt. William Parker) was the first to suspect trouble. He was standing near the switchboard dugout when he noticed several men moving along the main road.

He called to them, "Who's there?" and then, when they continued walking, he yelled "Halt!"

Three North Koreans were pulling a machine gun (the type mounted on small, cast-iron wheels) down the road. They moved down the road a few more steps and then dropped into a ditch, turned their gun toward the battery position, and opened fire. Almost immediately there was enemy fire from several other directions, a large part of it coming from the ridge-line that partially surrounded the main part of the battery. At the south end of the battery position the North Koreans had three machine guns in action against the gun sections and, soon after the first shots were fired, they had pulled another machine gun into place along the road in Saga. From the beginning, the action was divided between the two parts of the battery, divided by the railroad tracks.

Sgt. Herbert L. Rawls, Jr., the wire team chief, saw the North Koreans

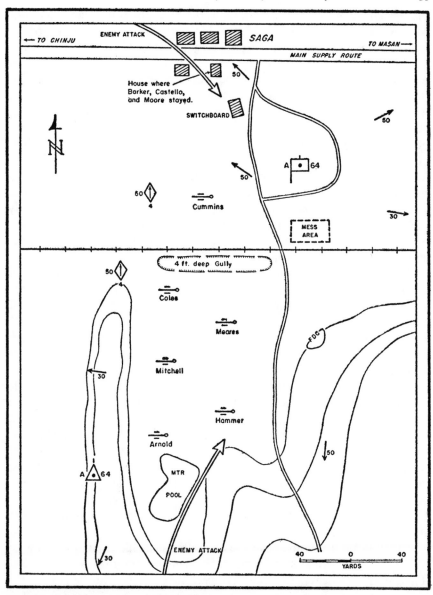

at the time Sergeant Parker challenged them. Realizing that there would be trouble, he ran first to one of the native houses by the road to awaken several men from his section who were sleeping there, then to the switchboard dugout to warn those men. Near the edge of the switchboard hole Sgt. Joseph R. Pursley was kneeling on the ground splicing a wire. Just as Rawls got there a North Korean appeared and killed both men with a burp gun. He then threw a grenade into the switchboard dugout. The explosion killed two of the three men in the hole; the third man, Cpl. John M. Pitcher, was not seriously injured. He continued to operate the switchboard throughout the night with the two bodies beside him in the hole.

All this had occurred within a few minutes. At the same time two other events were taking place in the same area. At the first sign of action, Cpl. Bobbie H. McQuitty ran to his ¾-ton truck upon which was mounted a machine gun. He had parked his truck near the road and now, by the time he reached it, the North Koreans had rolled one of their machine guns (one of the two they had in Saga) up just in front of it. With the two machine guns pointed toward each other at a distance of not more than thirty yards, McQuitty's gun failed to fire. He jumped from the truck and ran across the rice paddies toward the front lines of the infantrymen where he had seen a tank the previous afternoon. He now hoped to get help from it. By this time, neither the other two machine guns on that side of the railroad, nor the quad .50s, could fire against the North Koreans in that area without endangering men of the wire section.

Meanwhile, the communications men whom Sergeant Rawls had awakened just before he was killed tried to get away from the building in which they had been sleeping, hoping to rejoin the main section of the battery. In one room of the building were three men, PFC Harold W. Barker, PFC Thomas A. Castello, and PFC Santford B. Moore. Barker left first, running. He had gone only a few steps when he saw one of the North Korean machine guns directly ahead. He turned quickly and dashed back to the house, but as he reached the doorway a bullet struck his knee. Castello and Moore pulled him back into the building and decided to remain in the house. They put Barker on the floor, and then stood in a corner of the room as close to the wall as possible. Unfortunately, several days before this Barker and Castello had picked up two small pups, which now shared the same room. The pups chewed on some paper and made considerable noise. In an adjoining room there had been another man who also tried to escape, but as he stepped from the building he encountered fifteen or twenty Communist soldiers standing in a group just outside the door. One of them shot him in the mouth and killed him.

Within a few minutes after the North Koreans appeared, five members of the communications section were dead and another man was wounded. Thereafter the enemy fired the two machine guns toward the area of the howitzers but made no attempt to move against the guns or even to search the area for other Americans.

Immediately after the first shot was fired against the men near the switchboard, three machine guns at the south end of the battery position opened fire against the howitzer sections. Two of these were in place on the low ridgeline at the left front of the guns and a third fired from the left rear. In addition, there was fire from a half dozen or more enemy riflemen. Of the six guns, the three nearest the ridge were under the heaviest fire. There was an immediate interruption of the fire missions while the crews took cover in their gun pits, which were deep enough to afford some protection. There was a period of several minutes, then, before the artillery-men realized what was happening and determined the extent of and direction of the enemy fire.

Meanwhile, on the left, an enemy soldier threw several grenades at the pit occupied by MSgt. Frederick J. Hammer's section. One of the grenades exploded inside the pit, killing one man and wounding several others; another exploded in an ammunition pit and set fire to over a hundred 105mm shells stored there. The men manning the machine-gun posts along the ridge opened fire when the action began but soon realized the enemy had already penetrated to the battery position. They pulled back, going north toward the other halftrack mounting the quad .50s. This weapon fired just a few rounds before its power traversing mechanism failed and, when it could not be operated by hand, the gun crew backed the vehicle a short distance to the gully by the railroad tracks.

It was just about this time that the battalion headquarters called Battery A to ask the reason for interrupting the fire mission. The battery executive officer (Lieut. Kincheon H. Bailey, Jr.) answered the telephone at the fire direction tent. Bailey had heard the machine guns firing but was not concerned about it since at that time the front-line infantrymen were not far away and the artillerymen could often hear the noise of automatic weapons and small arms. In turn, he called the gun crews to ask them. Sergeant Hammer and four other gun sections reported their situation but the sixth section, commanded by PFC Ernest R. Arnold, was under such intense machine-gun fire that no one wanted to reach for the telephone on the edge of the gun pit. Bailey reported back to the battalion and went out to investigate for himself.

During the several minutes required to relay this information to battalion headquarters the situation in the battery position developed fast. Sergeant Hammer, seeing his ammunition burning, ordered the men in his section to make a dash for the gully by the railroad tracks. Within the next few minutes the men manning two other guns managed to escape and get back to this gully. Meanwhile, one of the platoon sergeants (MSgt. Germanus P. Kotzur) had raced over to the howitzer north of the railroad tracks and ordered the gun section to lay direct fire against the hill from which the enemy soldiers had apparently come.

It was about the time the first of these shells landed that Lieutenant Bailey left the fire direction tent to find out what was happening. The powder in Hammer's ammunition pit was burning brightly by this time, illuminating one end of the battery position. As Bailey walked toward that area he saw North Koreans walking around the gun and concluded the crew was dead or gone. He ran back to the nearest howitzer and told the chief of section (Cpl. Cecil W. Meares) to start firing against the ridge.

Two howitzers fired a total of eighteen rounds, which burst a hundred and fifty to two hundred yards away. Bailey also urged the gun crew to start firing their side arms against the North Koreans who now occupied the next gun pit—the one Sergeant Hammer's crew had abandoned. For five or ten minutes Corporal Meares's men fired at the enemy soldiers and threw grenades toward the gun pit. Then Bailey and Kotzur decided it would be best to get the crews back to the protection of the gully. They stopped the artillery fire and began calling for the other crews to move back. To give these men some protection, Sgt. Henry E. Baker ran to a nearby 2½-ton truck which carried a ring-mounted caliber .50 machine gun and began firing this toward the North Koreans. PFC Richard G. Haussler went with Baker to feed the ammunition belts through the gun. These two men, although up high where they could be seen from the entire area as long as the ammunition was burning brightly, fired five boxes of ammunition (1,250 rounds) through the gun in about ten minutes. The battery commander (Captain Anderson) set out on an inspection of the battery position to make certain none of his men remained in foxholes or in the gun pits.

It was about 0315 when all of the cannoneers reached the gully by the railroad tracks—half an hour after the action began. As it happened, the Catholic chaplain of the 25th Division (Capt. John T. Schag) had visited the battery earlier in the day and had decided to spend the night there. When the fighting began Father Schag took charge of a group of men who had been sleeping near him and guided them to the gully then used as the battery defensive position. Once in the gully, he gathered the wounded men together and then helped the medics care for them. Captain Anderson and Sergeant Kotzur organized the men for the defense of the gully. Everyone was now in this gully except for three men in the fire direction tent; Corporal Pitcher, who was still operating the battery switchboard; and Barker, Castello, and Moore, who were still waiting quietly in the house in Saga.

Enemy activity decreased after the men of the battery consolidated their position in the gully although there was a brisk exchange of rifle fire. The battalion commander (Lt.Col. Arthur H. Hogan) called several times to find out what was happening and offered help from one of the other batteries in the battalion. One man at the fire direction tent (Sgt. Carl Francis) yelled to Lieutenant Bailey to ask if he wanted some 155mm fire placed in the area, and Bailey said they'd like to have some on the hill in front of the guns. Colonel Hogan was familiar with the hill and, having good original data, got the first shells squarely on the hill.

Bailey yelled back to the fire direction center, "Right 50; drop 100; fire for effect."

The men around him groaned when they heard this command, so Bailey changed it to "drop 50; fire for effect."

Colonel Hogan asked for two rounds from the battery of medium artillery and the rounds fell just in front of the guns. Soon after this a tank came down the Masan road from the north and began firing into the enemy positions. It was the tank for which Corporal McQuitty had gone after his machine gun jammed at the beginning of the action. This helped to reduce the enemy activity although there was scattered rifle fire until the first signs of light that morning. The enemy soldiers then disappeared, and the gun sections returned to their howitzers to assess the damage. The North Koreans had killed 7 men and wounded 12 others of Battery A, destroyed four trucks, and let the air out of the tires on one of the howitzers. On three of the howitzer tubes they had written in chalk the numbers of their company, platoon, and squad. Otherwise, the guns were not damaged. There were 21 dead North Korean soldiers in the battery position when the action was all over. Captain Anderson regrouped his battery on the north side of the tracks and resumed the firing of normal supporting missions.

★   DISCUSSION

Every soldier must be mentally trained for the shock of battle and prepared for instant defense of his own and his unit's position. In fluid situations, it must be expected that the front will not be stabilized and that hostile action will develop well to the rear. Under these conditions, artillery position areas must be selected that not only will permit accomplishing the primary mission of fire support but will also facilitate local defense against enemy action that might interrupt the fire support.

This example demonstrates how an attack of limited strength against an inadequately prepared battery position can be effective in neutralizing a battery. To avoid such interruptions in fire support, batteries must obtain an all-around, completely integrated defense. This is accomplished by assigning primary and contingent sectors of responsibility to each gun section, by preparing the firing positions of the individual pieces to insure complete cannon fire coverage of the position's perimeter, and by developing fire plans to cover all possible avenues of approach. Into this plan is integrated the fire of the battery's automatic weapons and rocket launchers. Each individual of the battery must be assigned and be ready to occupy a specific defense position. Specific personnel must be designated in advance as a reserve force.

An alarm system must be established and all battery personnel actually rehearsed in the actions they will take when the alarm is given. Day and night security must be completed by installing sufficient observation and listening posts, coupled with adequate communications and patrols that visit and maintain contact with adjacent units.

This action contains incidents of individual bravery and courage, of demonstrated devotion to duty, of the use of initiative, and of leadership in an emergency. But how was it possible for the enemy to walk down the road and into the battery position? The obvious answer is that the defensive organization was unsatisfactory. Weapons had not been checked to insure that they would fire. An alarm or alert system, if used, did not work. How much better to stop the enemy outside a battery position than to let him neutralize the battery, kill and wound soldiers, and destroy matériel. A well-organized and alert defense would have enabled Battery A to repel this attack with a minimum of effort.

★ NOTE

1. Information used to prepare this account is based upon a personal interview with Capt. Kincheon H. Bailey and six members of Battery A, 64th FA Battalion. This interview was conducted by the author on 3 September 1951 near Kumhwa, Korea. Captain Bailey also furnished additional information in four letters to the author. These were dated 13 October 1951, 4 February, 22 February and 1 March 1952.

*Effective pursuit requires the highest degree of
leadership and initiative.*

FM 7–40: INFANTRY REGIMENT
(JANUARY 1950)

4

Tank Action at Chongju

★ Following the capture of Pyongyang, the enemy's capital
city, in October 1950, the left-flank unit of Eighth Army hurried north
to fulfill the long-range mission of reaching the Yalu River and the end of
the war. This force was built around the British 27 Commonwealth
Brigade which, at the time, consisted of a battalion from the Royal Australian Regiment, a battalion from the Argyle and Sutherland Regiment,
and a battalion from the Middlesex Regiment. Since these infantry battalions were without supporting arms or services of their own, Eighth
Army attached to the brigade U.S. artillery units, engineers, and the 89th
Medium Tank Battalion. This combined force, commanded by Brig. B. A.
Coad of the British Army, was under the operational control of the 1st
Cavalry Division, but worked as a separate task force at a considerable
distance from, and without physical contact with, that division or other
friendly units.[1]

Starting early on the morning of 22 October 1950, the task force
resumed its advance from Pyongyang north. Usually the infantrymen
rode on the tanks or in trucks near the end of the column that stretched
for two and a half to three miles. A platoon of tanks led. Nothing unusual
happened until near noon of the second day, when the task force engaged
a large but disorganized enemy unit at the town of Sukchon. There was
no trouble the third day as the column crossed the Chongchon River at
Sinanju and Anju, but at Pakchon, to the north, the bridge across the
Taenyong River was destroyed, and there was a two-day delay before
the column headed west toward Chongju. North Koreans offered some

resistance to the river crossing at Pakchon and, more significant, there was a sudden stiffening of enemy activity. As a result, the brigade commander concluded that the days of "rolling" were over. When the advance began again at 0800 on 28 October it was with greater caution. Lead companies investigated all likely enemy positions instead of leaving them to the follow-up units, and the column therefore moved only fifteen miles during the day.

Again on the morning of 29 October the task force resumed its march westward. The day's objective was Chongju. The Royal Australian battalion and Company D, 89th Medium Tank Battalion, led the column. The infantrymen dismounted frequently to screen suspected high ground to the flanks, and the tank battalion's liaison plane patrolled the area well ahead of the column. The liaison pilot (Lt. James T. Dickson) stopped the column several times during the morning while fighter planes made strikes against enemy tanks. About noon, as the head of the column neared the top of a high hill, Lieutenant Dickson sent a radio message to the tankers warning them of enemy tanks dug in and camouflaged on each side of a narrow pass where the road cut through a low hill. This position was at the top of the ridge ahead, beyond a narrow strip of paddy fields and about two and a half miles away over a winding and narrow road. Proceeding slowly, the leading platoon of tanks went down to the bottom of the hill to the east edge of the valley. There Lieutenant Dickson dropped a message advising them to hold up temporarily because of the enemy tanks.

After a delay of a few minutes, the tank battalion commander (Lt.Col. Welborn G. Dolvin) and the Australian infantry battalion commander arrived at the head of the column. While they were planning the next move, Lieutenant Dickson spotted what he believed to be a camouflaged tank position on the reverse slope of a low hill just beyond the next ridge ahead. The fighter planes were busy with another target, so he radioed the tankers to ask them to place indirect fire in the area. The platoon of tanks that was second in line, led by Lt. Francis G. Nordstrom, opened fire from its position on top of the hill. Nordstrom did not expect to hit anything but, after firing about ten rounds, with Lieutenant Dickson adjusting the fire, smoke started to rise from the camouflaged position. It was heavy, black smoke such as that made by burning gasoline. Lieutenant Dickson called off the firing.

Meanwhile, the battalion commanders had worked out their plan of attack. Since Lieutenant Nordstrom liked the point position where he could open the action and control it, they decided to let his platoon lead the attack. No infantrymen would accompany his tanks. The other two tank platoons, mounting infantrymen, would follow in column. This force consisted of thirteen tanks and about two companies of infantry.

Nordstrom's platoon was to head at full speed for the point where the road went through the narrow pass—a distance of about two miles. This seemed to be the most important ground since there was no apparent way to bypass it. The next platoon of tanks, under Lt. Gerald L. Van Der Leest, would follow at a 500-yard interval until it came within approximately a thousand yards of the pass, where the infantrymen would dismount and move to seize the high ground paralleling the road on the right side. The third platoon of tanks, under Lt. Alonzo Cook, with a similar force was to seize the high ground left of the road. After discharg-

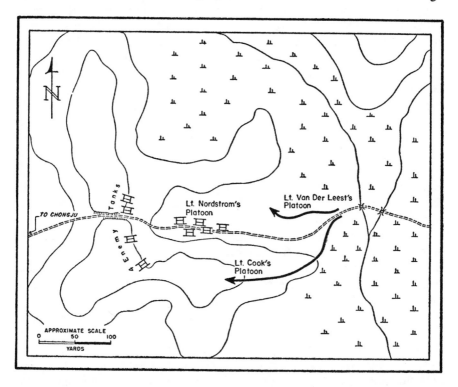

ing the infantrymen, the tank platoon leaders were to maneuver to the left and right of the road and support the advance of their respective infantry units.

The attack started with Lieutenant Nordstrom's tank in the lead. Within a hundred yards of the road cut Nordstrom noticed enemy soldiers hurriedly climbing the hill on the left of the road. He ordered his machine-gunner to open fire on them. At about the same time he spotted an enemy machine-gun crew moving its gun toward the pass, and took these men under fire with the 76mm gun. The first shell struck the ground next to the enemy crew, and the burst blew away some foliage that was camouflaging an enemy tank dug in on the approach side of the pass on the right side of the road. As soon as the camouflage was disturbed the enemy tank fired one round. The tracer passed between Nordstrom's head and the open hatch cover. In these circumstances he did not take time to give fire orders; he just called for armor-piercing shells and the gunner fired, hitting the front of the enemy tank from a distance of less than a hundred yards. The gunner continued firing armor-piercing shells and the third round caused a great explosion. Ammunition and gasoline began to burn simultaneously. Black smoke drifted east and north across the high ground on the right side of the pass, effectively screening that area. Lieutenant Nordstrom ordered the commander of the last tank in his platoon column (Sgt. William J. Morrison, Jr.) to fire into the smoke with both machine guns and cannon. At the same time other tank crews observed other North Koreans left of the pass and directed their guns against them.

Lieutenant Nordstrom did not move on into the pass itself because by this time it seemed to him that the enemy would have at least one anti-tank gun zeroed in to fire there and could thus block the pass. He remained where he was—about seventy yards from the pass with the other tanks lined up behind his. Fire on the enemy to the left of the road tore camouflage from a second enemy tank dug in on the left of the pass in a position similar to that of the tank already destroyed. Nordstrom's gunner, firing without orders, destroyed this tank with the second round. There was another violent explosion, which blew part of the enemy tank's turret fifty feet into the air.

While this fire fight was going on at the head of the column, the Australian infantrymen were attacking along the ridges on each side of the road. There was considerable firing in both areas. Lieutenant Cook's tanks, on the left side of the road, had been able to follow the infantrymen onto the hill and provide close support.

In the midst of the fighting at the head of the column, the guns in the two leading tanks jammed because of faulty rounds. At that time a shell came in toward Nordstrom's tank from the left front. Nordstrom instructed his platoon sergeant (MSgt. Jasper W. Lee) to fire in the general direction of the enemy gun until he and the tank behind him could clear their guns. This was done within a few minutes, and Nordstrom, having the best field of fire, started placing armor-piercing rounds at five-yard intervals along the top of the ridge to his left, firing on the only logical positions in that area, since he could see no enemy vehicles. Following the sixth round there was another flash and explosion that set fire to nearby bushes and trees.

The next enemy fire came a few minutes later—another round from a self-propelled gun. It appeared to have come from the right-front. It cut across Lieutenant Nordstrom's tank between the caliber .50 machine gun and the radio antenna about a foot above the turret, and then hit one of the tanks in Lieutenant Cook's platoon, seriously injuring four men. Because of the smoke it was impossible to pinpoint the enemy, so

Nordstrom commenced firing armor-piercing shells into the smoke, aiming along the top of the ridge on the right side of the road. He hoped that the enemy gunners would believe that their position had been detected, and move so that he could discover the movement. Another green tracer passed his tank, this time a little farther to the right. Nordstrom increased his own rate of fire and ordered three other tank crews to fire into the same area. There was no further response from the enemy gun and, to conserve ammunition which was then running low, Nordstrom soon stopped firing. It was suddenly quiet again except along the ridgelines paralleling the road where Australian infantrymen and the other two tank platoons were pressing their attack. No action was apparent to the direct front.

At the rear of the column, Lieutenant Cook had gone to his damaged tank, climbed in and, sighting with a pencil along the bottom of the penetration, determined the approximate position of the enemy gun. He radioed this information to Nordstrom, who resumed firing with three tanks along the top of the ridge on the right side of the road. Again he failed to hit anything. For lack of a better target he then decided to put a few rounds through the smoke near the first enemy tank destroyed. He thought the two rounds might possibly have come from this tank even though the fire and explosions made this very improbable. The third round caused another explosion and gasoline fire. With this explosion most enemy action ended and only the sound of occasional small-arms fire remained.

Shortly thereafter both Australian units reported their objectives secured. Since it was now late in the afternoon, the British commander ordered the force to form a defensive position for the night. It was a U-shaped perimeter with a platoon of tanks and an infantry company along the ridgeline on each side of the road, and Lieutenant Nordstrom's tanks between them guarding the road.

When the smoke cleared from the road cut there was one self-propelled gun that had not been there when the action commenced. It appeared that it had been left to guard the west end of the road cut and its crew, becoming impatient when no tanks came through the pass, had moved it up beside the burning tank on the right side of the road, using the smoke from this and the other burning tanks as a screen.

At 2100 that night enemy infantrymen launched an attack that appeared to be aimed at the destruction of the tanks. Lieutenant Nordstrom's 1st Platoon tanks, which were positioned near the road about a hundred yards east of the pass, were under attack for an hour with so many North Koreans scattered through the area that the tankers turned on the headlights in order to locate the enemy. The Americans used grenades and pistols as well as the tanks' machine guns. Gradually the action stopped, and it was quiet for the rest of the night. When morning came there were 25 to 30 bodies around the 1st Platoon's tanks, some within a few feet of the vehicles. At 1000 the column got under way again and reached Chongju that afternoon. This was the objective, and here the task force broke up.

★ DISCUSSION

This narrative illustrates the employment of a tank battalion as part of a task force equal in size to a reinforced regimental combat team. The task force successfully completed its exploitation mission by taking its objective, Chongju.

The action on 29 October brings out several techniques. The pilot of the liaison plane did more than see and tell. He also thought and acted. The task force's tanks gained a great advantage through reconnaissance by combining fire with aggressive action. In almost every instance the tanks located the enemy by observing the results of their friendly fire, rather than by waiting for the enemy to give away his location by drawing *his* fire.

The aggressive double envelopment against the enemy positioned around the defile near Chongju brought to bear a large part of the task force strength. Almost simultaneously the enemy was hit from three different directions. This action stands out against the background of other regimental attacks in Korea wherein only a few individuals have led the assault. Deployment for an attack takes time and coordination, and frequently it is too hurried to be well accomplished. Horatius held the bridge because his attackers could not deploy to hit him from all sides.

The use of the tanks to place indirect fire on an area target is very questionable—if artillery support is available. The target as described seems a more logical one for artillery. A good guide to follow in this or similar situations is this: Other things being equal, use supporting fire from the weapon most easily resupplied with ammunition.

No reason is given to account for the halt of the task force on the night of 29 October. Men tire and machines exhaust fuel, but a pursuit must be pressed night and day. The enemy must be denied all chances to rally, reconstitute his lines, or recover his balance.

★ NOTE

1. This account is based upon an interview with Lt. Francis G. Nordstrom, and 25th Infantry Division war diaries unit reports: 89th Medium Tank Battalion, October 1950.

In war obscurity and confusion are normal. Late, exaggerated or misleading information, surprise situations, and counterorders are to be expected.

INFANTRY IN BATTLE

5
Artillery at Kunu-ri

★ After crossing two thirds of North Korea in the fall of 1950, Eighth Army's advance to the Yalu River ended abruptly. The commander of one field artillery battalion reconnoitered for forward positions one afternoon but early the next morning, after strong enemy attacks against nearby units during the night, he received orders to select positions for a displacement to the rear. This was the beginning of a long withdrawal.

The U.S. 17th Field Artillery Battalion, an 8-inch howitzer unit, was attached to the 2d Infantry Division on 24 November after being relieved, the day before, from control of the 1st Cavalry Division. After a reconnaissance on the night of 23 November, the battalion moved into positions in the vicinity of Kujang-dong the next morning.

Kujang-dong was a bleak-looking town—a few dozen earth-colored houses along the narrow road and the single-track railway. Battery A placed its guns at the edge of the village, taking over the better buildings for sleeping quarters and for its command post.[1]

At this time Battery A had a strength of 74 of the authorized 135 men, having come overseas under-strength in August. Soon after the battery arrived in Korea, fifty Republic of Korea (ROK) soldiers were sent to Battery A and had stayed until October, when they had been released because everyone thought the war was over.

The first indication Battery A men had that the war wasn't over came on the morning of 24 November from an air observer who, while registering the No. 2 howitzer on the base point, spotted an estimated two hundred enemy soldiers. It had been a month or more since anyone had seen so many North Koreans, and no one realized that these soldiers were Chinese. The front line was not more than three thousand yards north of Kujang-dong when Battery A began firing. Expecting to continue the usual rapid northward advance, the battalion commander (Lt.Col. Elmer H. Harrelson) went forward on the morning of 25 November to select positions two miles farther north. At the same time the commander of the nearby 61st Field Artillery Battalion (a 105mm unit) selected positions in the same area. Both units were to move that afternoon, but the road was already so jammed with traffic that Division Artillery decided not to move the 8-inch howitzers until the next morning.[2] Early that night Chinese troops waded the Chongchon River and attacked in force, hitting units of the 23d Infantry Regiment and overrunning the new positions of the 61st Field Artillery Battalion. At 2300 some of the men from the 61st straggled into the area of Battery A, having left their position with neither equipment nor howitzers. One man was barefoot. The commander of Battery A (Capt. Allen L. Myers) put everyone on an alert basis for the night, although the Chinese did not penetrate that far.

After daybreak, 26 November, the commanding general of the 2d Infantry Division Artillery ordered Colonel Harrelson to pull back several miles. While the 61st Battalion attacked to recover its howitzers and equipment, Harrelson selected positions to the rear. The narrow supply road was still so jammed with vehicles, however, that it was late that night before Battery A received the march order, and it was 2330 before the battery pulled onto the road and started south, moving under blackout conditions. The chief of section of the last howitzer in the column put his hand on the shoulder of the man driving the tractor to indicate that he wanted the driver to slow down through the town of Kujang-dong. The driver, thinking that the section chief wanted him to turn left, turned down a small side street. There was a delay of five or ten minutes while the crew turned the tractor and howitzer around, knocking down several buildings in the process. This section was now separated from the rest of the column and it was impossible to catch up because of the solid line of vehicles but Captain Myers had taken his chiefs of section with him when he selected the position and the men now knew where to go.

Captain Myers's new position was in a stream bed near the road to Kunu-ri. Three howitzer sections arrived first; then the maintenance, wire, kitchen, and radio sections; then the fourth gun section; and finally, the local security detail. The temperature was near zero and there was a strong wind as the crews put the guns into firing position. Battery A fired without registering, using average corrections furnished by the fire direction center. On 27 November, while the infantry regiments of the 2d Division and some of the artillery units were experiencing heavy enemy attacks, Battery A had a comparatively quiet day although it was too cold for the

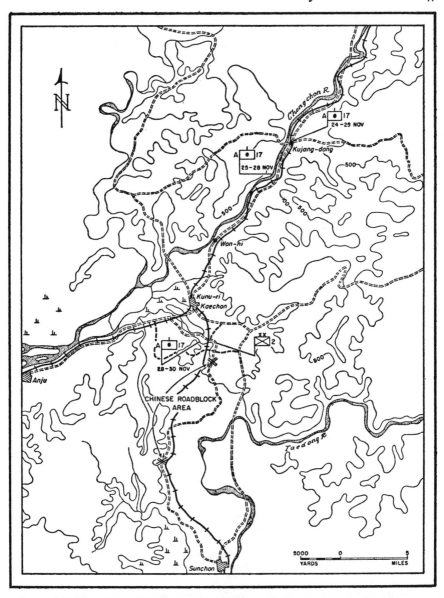

men to sleep. They sat huddled around gasoline stoves when they had no fire missions. All men whom Captain Myers could spare from the firing sections were needed either for outpost duty or for hauling ammunition from Kunu-ri, twenty-five to thirty miles away. The narrow road, follow-ing the curves of the Chongchon River, was better suited to the native ox-carts than to the heavy trucks that now jammed it, moving only a few miles an hour.

Enemy pressure increased throughout the division's area and at 2200 that night, Colonel Harrelson received orders to again displace to the rear. By 0745 the following morning, 28 November, when Battery A march-ordered, front-line infantry units had fallen back until the artillerymen could hear the sound of small-arms fire. Captain Myers heard that an ROK division west of the 2d Infantry Division had collapsed, exposing the division's right flank. This time Myers moved his battery approximately five miles south, where he put the howitzers in position near the road but, at 1230, with the battery laid and ready to fire in the new position, he was ordered to close station and march-order, again moving south. By this time all units of the 2d Division were moving back.[3]

Battery A now went into position southwest of Kunu-ri in a large field along the division's supply road. The first part of the night was quiet and the men had a chance to sleep some, but the battery began getting fire missions and commenced shooting in a northerly direction two hours before daylight, 29 November.

Several incidents occurred during the day that indicated the situation was fast becoming critical. Early in the morning Colonel Harrelson received instructions to look for new positions along the route of withdrawal to Sunchon.[4] Earlier, however, a report reached 2d Division headquarters indicating that the enemy had established a roadblock several miles south on the road to Sunchon. Officers at the division's command post accepted this information calmly, but sent a patrol to investigate and, a little later that morning, ordered the Reconnaissance Company out to open the road. Meanwhile, the reconnaissance for new positions was held up until afternoon when, as officers at division headquarters expected, the Reconnaissance Company would have eliminated the enemy roadblock on the Kunu-ri–Sunchon road.[5] About mid-morning, Captain Myers received orders to haul the ammunition he needed from Kunu-ri because the ammunition dump there was going to be destroyed. And during the day the three 105mm howitzer battalions and the 155mm howitzer battalion of the 2d Division passed by the gun position of Battery A, all headed south.

Colonel Harrelson, Captain Myers, and the other battery commanders undertook that afternoon to reconnoiter for positions on the Sunchon road, expecting it to be open. It wasn't. Vehicles were jammed on and near the road for several miles south of Kunu-ri, and occupants of some vehicles returning from the south claimed the road was cut, that it was impossible to get through.[6] Captain Myers and his party returned to the battery position at dark while Colonel Harrelson went to Division Artillery's command post for a briefing on the general situation. There he learned the 2d Division was confident it would be able to open the road. He was told to fire his regular missions during the night. If the road were open by morning of 30 November, the 17th Field Artillery Battalion would withdraw over that road, taking its place at the head of the column of artillery battalions, since the 8-inch howitzers were considered to be the most valuable pieces and the hardest to replace.[7] If the roadblock were not cleared by morning— and if the division did not issue another order—the battalion was to pull out by another road west to Anju and then south toward Pyongyang. Colonel Harrelson received this information between 2200 and 2300. Since the division's command post was being attacked at that time, he realized that the situation could change abruptly.[8]

The direction of fire, which was north on the morning of 29 November, gradually shifted east during the day. That evening, with the howitzers laid on an azimuth of 1600 mils, Battery A started firing charge 7 at a range of eighteen thousand yards. By morning on 30 November the cannoneers were using charge 1 at a range of thirteen hundred yards. Because of the critical situation Colonel Harrelson, calm but anxious to keep the battery informed, held three battery commanders' calls during the night. At the call held at 0400 on 30 November he outlined three possible plans of action: to return to Kunu-ri and put a large ammunition trailer across the road to block traffic long enough to get the battalion's vehicles into the solid column of traffic and move the battalion west through Anju; to go south on 2d Division order when the roadblock was opened; if these failed, he proposed that the battalion stay and fight until it was forced to destroy all equipment and fight its way south as a battalion. Harrelson preferred to take the road to Anju since his battalion had followed that road when it moved north and was familiar with it. However, soon after this meeting Colonel Harrelson was called to Division Artillery's command post and there learned that, by division order, his battalion would withdraw over the road to Sunchon. During the night of 29–30 November the military police told the division's provost marshal that the road to Anju was also cut by the Chinese. At the same time, IX Corps, of which the division was a part, directed the 2d Division to use the Sunchon road since the road from Anju south was already burdened with three divisions.[9]

Soldiers continued to straggle through and past Battery A's position during the early morning of 30 November. Some were ROK soldiers and some were from the 2d Division or from another nearby U.S. division. Soon after daylight a tank officer stopped at Battery A's position and told Captain Myers that all infantry units to the north had withdrawn. He said he had some tanks in the rear that could help the artillerymen if necessary. This was not an accurate report but, as a precaution, Myers assigned zones for direct fire to each of the gun sections. Even as the situation was, the cannoneers could see the shell bursts from their gun positions.

Colonel Harrelson met his battery commanders again at 0800 on 30 November and told them of the decision to use the road to Sunchon even though the road leading west to Anju appeared to be still open. The 2d Division, he said, had ordered the 9th Infantry Regiment to attack south and destroy the enemy roadblock. The 9th Infantry, however, had suffered such heavy casualties during its last three days of fighting that it had an attacking force of only four hundred or five hundred men when it started south toward the critical area early that morning. By 0900 it became apparent at division headquarters that this force was too weak to destroy the roadblock, and the 38th Infantry was ordered to help.[10]

At 0930 Colonel Harrelson called Captain Myers with instructions to march-order and move as a fighting column. Myers at first interpreted this to mean he should destroy all equipment, but before he did so he called his battalion commander again and learned that Colonel Harrelson wanted the tractors and howitzers to go first, then the wheeled vehicles with the rest of the equipment. He wanted the tops and windshields down, machine guns mounted, and the men equipped to fight as infantrymen if necessary.[11] By batteries, the order of march was: B, A, Headquarters, Service, C. Within Battery A the four gun sections left first; then the tractor pulling the large ammunition trailer, the Diamond-T four-ton ammunition truck, and the ¾-ton executive truck. The rest of the wheeled vehicles followed.

Moving southward at an average rate of five miles an hour, Battery A passed three of the 2d Division's organic artillery battalions—all still in position and firing. It appeared to members of Battery A that the guns were laid to fire in several directions. About noon the column stopped when Battery A's vehicles were near a deserted quartermaster supply dump that had belonged to the U.S. 25th Infantry Division. Here the men loaded up on quartermaster supplies, especially overcoats, which many of them lacked. Near the supply dump a hundred or more soldiers, American and South Korean, were lying on the ground trying to sleep. A captain was in charge of them. There was a two-hour delay at the dump while the remaining fighting force of two infantry regiments attempted to reduce the enemy positions at the roadblock. At about 1400 the column started moving again, and the infantrymen by the supply dump climbed up on Battery A's vehicles. Vehicles were closed up bumper to bumper on the dry road which, having been graded by U.S. engineers, was wide enough for two-way traffic in most places. Low hills lay on both sides of the thousand-yard-wide valley.

The day was cold. The men were tired and tense. After proceeding haltingly for a mile and a half or two miles, the battery's vehicles passed between enemy machine guns firing from opposite sides of the road and the men scrambled for the ditches. Friendly airplanes strafed the hills along the road, occasionally quieting the guns. When they did, the column would get under way until another gun fired or until vehicles ahead came under enemy fire. After passing several enemy machine guns, all located between two hundred and three hundred yards from the road, the column stopped again and this time failed to move until almost dark. Military police patrolled the road in jeeps, doubling the column to locate the trouble.

During the halt a large number of South Korean soldiers came across the enemy-occupied hills on the left side of the road and joined the column. They were badly disorganized and some were without weapons.

Meanwhile, Colonel Harrelson, fearing that his battalion would be stranded in the center of the roadblock through the night, made plans to pull his vehicles off the road and form a perimeter, but at dusk the vehicles began moving again. About this time a halftrack mounting a twin 40mm came past the column and took a position at the head of Battery A. It fired at all suspected enemy positions, often getting air-bursts by aiming at the trees. Many of the South Korean soldiers climbed on the vehicles as they started forward.

After dark drivers used only blackout lights, and it was difficult to distinguish the many vehicles abandoned by the road from other vehicles in the column. The communications chief (Sgt. Preston L. Bryson) was driving the executive truck and pulled up behind a jeep in which he could see two men. After waiting for several minutes, he realized both men were dead and then pulled around the jeep. There were twenty-five to thirty vehicles abandoned along the seven-mile stretch that was under enemy fire.

The main difficulty occurred at the southern end of the roadblock. A two-lane concrete bridge had been destroyed, forcing the withdrawing column to use a bypass and to ford the stream which, at the time, was several feet deep. The bypass approach from the north was in good condition, but the southern exit was up terraced rice paddies, the first terrace being very difficult to maneuver. After fording the stream the driver of the first tractor in Captain Myers's column found his path blocked by two ¾-ton trucks and one 2½-ton truck that were stuck and abandoned. None of the abandoned vehicles belonged to the 17th Field Artillery Battalion.

The battalion S3 (Major Joseph J. Prusaitis) came back and instructed Captain Myers to uncouple the first tractor and pull the vehicles out of the bypass. The lead tractor belonged to the 2d Section (Sgt. Harrington D. Hawkins) which uncoupled it just as two tanks drove up the road from the south with their lights on. The beams of the headlights fell on the men working in the bypass. Immediately several enemy machine guns opened fire and tracer bullets flashed all around the artillerymen. Mortar rounds began falling nearby. Shouting, Captain Myers made the men get off the vehicles nearby. The battery executive (Lt. Donald D. Judd) was standing in the road when the lights shone on him. A Chinese rifleman thirty feet away was aiming at Judd when one of the cannoneers killed the enemy soldier. After this action flared up the tanks turned their lights off and began firing at the enemy. Thinking that the tanks had come to pull the abandoned vehicles away, Captain Myers instructed Sergeant Hawkins to couple up again and proceed.

Meanwhile, on the north side of the destroyed bridge, MSgt. Judge

Shanks, driving the next howitzer, looked across and saw the tank on the south side of the bridge. Not realizing there was a gap in the bridge, he pulled up on the north approach where he was forced to halt. The following vehicle stopped a few feet behind him and the rest of the column was jammed up to the rear. This caused another difficult delay before the 8-inch howitzer and prime mover could be backed up and run through the bypass.

The bypass was the end of the roadblock. At 2130 the last of the men of Battery A cleared the obstacle and saw the lights come on at the head of the column. There were stragglers and wounded men on the trailers, howitzers, fenders, and hoods of the vehicles, and three ¾-ton trucks had been turned into ambulances. The artillerymen had passed the bodies of at least four hundred American or other friendly troops that were lying by the road.[12] Battery A had eight men wounded while running the roadblock, none killed. It lost four 2½-ton trucks, three ¾-ton trucks, the kitchen trailer, and the supply trucks of which one was abandoned because of mechanical failure. For the battalion the equipment losses amounted to twenty-six vehicles and a howitzer from Battery B, which overturned and killed eight ROK soldiers who were riding on it.

The artillery battalions and other units of the 2d Division that followed were not so fortunate. Soon after Colonel Harrelson's battalion cleared the bypass, an M6 tractor pulling a 155mm howitzer stalled in the middle of the ford, effectively blocking the route of withdrawal. All vehicles north of the ford were abandoned and the personnel walked out.

★   NOTES

1. Unless otherwise noted, this narrative is based upon an account written in Korea by Major Edward C. Williamson. Major Williamson interviewed members of the 17th FA Battalion and prepared a manuscript, "Action at Kunu-ri: The 17th Field Artillery Battalion."

2. 2d Division: G3 journal, entry 1328, 25 November 1950.

3. *Ibid.;* see messages for 28 November 1950.

4. 2d Division Artillery: S3 journal, message 0730, 29 November 1950.

5. Lt.Col. Maurice C. Holden, letter to Major Roy E. Appleman, 26 February 1952.

6. Holden, *op. cit.,* describes the traffic jam.

7. Holden, *op. cit.*

8. Lt.Col. Elmer H. Harrelson, in an interview by the author.

9. Holden, *op. cit.;* also Harrelson, *op. cit.* The U.S. 24th Infantry and 1st

Cavalry Divisions, and the 1st ROK Division, were withdrawing over the Anju–Pyongyang road.

10. Holden, *op. cit.*

11. Harrelson, *op. cit.*

12. Colonel Harrelson indicates that this figure is conservative (Harrelson, *op. cit.*).

6

Chosin Reservoir

★ It was bitter cold. The temperature was below zero. The wind howled. Snow fell—a snow so dry that dust from the road mixed with it in yellowish clouds that swirled about the column of trucks. Tundra-like, bleak, and without vegetation in most places, the land was depressing.

Huddled together in the back of the trucks, the men of the 1st Battalion, 32d Infantry, stomped their feet on the truck beds in futile attempts to keep their limbs from becoming stiff and numb. Most of them wore long woolen underwear, two pairs of socks, a woolen shirt, cotton field trousers over a pair of woolen trousers, shoepacs, pile jacket, wind-resistant reversible parka with hood, and trigger-finger mittens of wool insert and outer shell. To keep their ears from freezing they tied wool scarves around their heads underneath their helmets. Still the cold seeped through. Occasionally the entire column ground to a halt to permit the men to dismount and exercise for a few minutes.[1]

Lt.Col. Don C. Faith commanded the 1st Battalion, 32d Infantry. As part of the 7th Infantry Division and of X Corps (Maj.Gen. Edward M. Almond), the battalion was moving from Hamhung north to relieve marines on the east shore of Chosin Reservoir and then to continue the attack to the Yalu River. A man could take even stinging, stiffening cold if it meant the end of a war. And that was how things looked on this 25th day of November 1950. In fact, just before Faith's battalion left Hamhung some of the men had listened to a news broadcast from Tokyo describing the beginning of a United Nations offensive in Korea designed to terminate the war quickly. Originating in General of the Army Douglas MacArthur's headquarters, the report predicted that U.S. divisions would be back in Japan by Christmas. It had been cheering news.[2]

Having assembled three divisions at the east coast port of Hungnam at the end of October, General Almond had launched his X Corps on an offensive with the objective of reaching the Manchurian border as soon as possible.[3] By the third week of November the corps was scattered across an area of more than four thousand square miles of bare, bleak, and rugged mountains. The 1st Marine Division, attacking along both sides of Chosin Reservoir, was more than fifty miles inland. One regiment of the 7th Division—the 17th Infantry—had gone more than a hundred miles north of Hungnam and had reached the Yalu River on 21 November.[4] Other units of that division were separated by straight-line distances of seventy or eighty miles. Road distances, tortuously slow, were much longer. North Koreans had offered only slight resistance against X Corps advances, but the obstacles of terrain and weather were tremendous.

Passing engineer crews working on the twisted, shelf-like road notched into the side of precipitous slopes, the truck column bearing Colonel Faith and his men northward at last reached Hagaru-ri at the south end of Chosin Reservoir. Several Marine Corps units were located in Hagaru-ri. The truck column passed a few tents and small groups of marines huddled around bonfires.[5] When the road forked, Colonel Faith's column followed the right-hand road, which led past the few desolate houses in Hagaru-ri toward the east side of the reservoir.

At least one or two men from each company were frostbite casualties late that afternoon when the battalion closed into defensive positions a mile or so north of Hagaru-ri. The night was quiet. There were warm-up tents behind the crests of the hills and the men spent alternate periods manning defense positions and getting warm.

The morning of 26 November was clear and cold. Since the marines still occupied the area, Colonel Faith waited for more complete orders, which had been promised. Toward noon, the assistant commander of the 7th Division (Brig.Gen. Henry I. Hodes) arrived at Faith's command post with more information on the planned operation. Having flown to Hagaru-ri by light aircraft, he had driven north by jeep. Additional 7th Division units, he explained to Colonel Faith, were then en route to Chosin Reservoir. The commander of the 31st Infantry Regiment (Col. Allan D. MacLean) was to arrive soon to take command of all units on the east side of the reservoir. He was bringing with him his own 3d Battalion, his Heavy Mortar Company, his Intelligence and Reconnaissance Platoon, a detachment of medical personnel, and the 57th Field Artillery Battalion. The last-named unit would be short one of its firing batteries but would have with it Battery D, 15th AAA Automatic Weapons Battalion—a unit equipped with halftracks mounting quadruple caliber .50

machine guns (M16s) and dual 40mm guns (M19s).[6] General Hodes said
the Marine regiment would move on the following day to join the rest
of the 1st Marine Division in an attack aimed at securing another important road northwest from Hagaru-ri. The mission of MacLean's task
force, and thus of Colonel Faith's battalion, was to secure the important
road running along the east side of the reservoir and thence north to the
Manchurian border.[7]

When Colonel MacLean arrived with his staff later that evening, he
stated his intentions of attacking north as soon as his task force arrived.
He approved Colonel Faith's plan to take over the northernmost defensive
position as soon as the marines vacated it the next morning.[8]

Monday, 27 November, was another clear, cold day. Marine trucks
were on the road soon after dawn shuttling troops south. By noon, when
the road was clear again, Colonel Faith moved his battalion north. The
rest of Colonel MacLean's force arrived that afternoon, moving into
position about three or four miles south of Faith's battalion.

As night fell on 27 November, the first order of business was defense, although a continuation of the northward drive the marines had
begun was planned for the next day. Lending greater force to common
knowledge that Chinese forces in undetermined strength were roaming
the mountains in the vicinity of Chosin Reservoir, the marines had told
Colonel Faith that on the day before several Chinese prisoners had revealed
the presence of three fresh divisions operating in the area of the reservoir.
Their mission, the prisoners had said, was to sever the American supply
route.[9] The marines also told Faith's men that on the previous night, in
this same location, a Chinese patrol had pulled a marine from his foxhole,
disarmed him, and beaten him.

With this in mind, Colonel Faith placed his companies in a perimeter
that lay across the road facing north, with the right flank bent south to
face mountains that loomed high to the east. During the late afternoon the
companies dug in their positions and cut fields of fire through some
scrub brush on the hills. After breaking through eight or ten inches of
frozen earth, the digging was easy. There were no stones in the ground.
Colonel Faith set up his command post in a few farm houses in a small
valley less than a thousand yards behind the front lines. It got dark
early, still bitterly cold. For an hour or two after dark there was the sound
of shell bursts around the perimeter since forward observers had not
completed the registration of artillery and mortar defensive fires before
dark. For another hour or two, until after 2100, it was quiet.

The battalion adjutant, having driven a hundred and fifty miles that
day from division headquarters, arrived with two weeks' mail. A few
minutes later an officer from Colonel MacLean's headquarters brought
the operation order for the attack scheduled for dawn the next morning.
Colonel Faith called his company commanders, asking them to bring

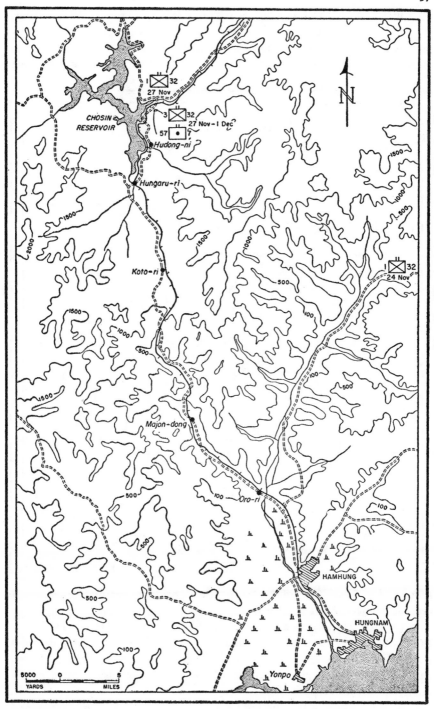

their mail orderlies and to report to his command post for the attack order.

The enemy attacked while the meeting was in progress. Probing patrols came first, the first one appearing in front of a platoon near the road. When the friendly platoon opened fire Company A's executive

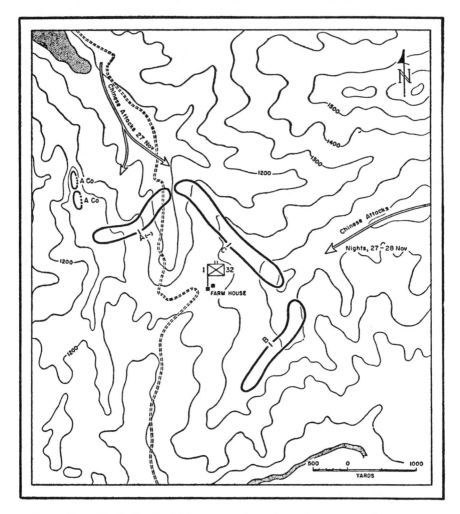

officer (Lt. Cecil G. Smith), suspecting that the enemy force was a reconnaissance patrol sent to locate specific American positions, tried to stop the fire. He ran up and down the line shouting: "Don't fire! Don't fire!" But by the time he succeeded, the enemy force had evidently discovered what it needed to know and had melted away into the darkness. In the meantime, enemy patrols began to repeat this pattern at other points along the defensive perimeter.

A few minutes after midnight the patrolling gave way to determined attack. While one Chinese company struck south along the road, another plunged out of the darkness from the east to strike the boundary between the two rifle companies that were east of the road.

The defensive perimeter began to blaze with fire. In addition to directing steady mortar and small-arms fire against Colonel Faith's battalion, the Chinese kept maneuvering small groups around the perimeter to break the line. As one enemy group climbed a steep ridge toward a heavy machine gun operated by Cpl. Robert Lee Armentrout, the corporal discovered he could not depress his gun enough to hit the enemy. He then picked up his weapon, tripod and all, cradled it in his arms, and beat off the attack.

As the night wore on not every position along the perimeter held as well. Within two or three hours after they first attacked, the Chinese had seized and organized the highest point on the two ridgelines that had belonged to the two companies on the east side of the road. Loss of this ground seriously weakened the defense of both companies, and also permitted the enemy to fire into a native house where Capt. Dale L. Seever had set up his command post. Forced to vacate, he moved his Weapons Platoon and command group to the front line to help defend what ground he had left. On the extreme right flank the Chinese forced two platoons out of position. On the left side of the road they circled wide around the left flank and seized a mortar position.

Wire communications with Colonel MacLean's headquarters and with the 57th Field Artillery Battalion went out soon after the attack started. After establishing radio communication, which was never satisfactory, Colonel Faith learned that the Chinese were also attacking the other units of MacLean's task force. This explained why the artillery, involved with the more immediate necessity of defending its own position, was unable to furnish sustained support to Faith's battalion.[10]

Colonel Faith's battalion was still in place when daylight came on 28 November, but there were serious gaps in the line. Although ordered to launch his attack at dawn, when the time came to carry out the order Colonel Faith had his hands full trying to hang onto his perimeter and recover the ground lost during the night. The night attack had been costly in casualties and morale. When it moved to Chosin Reservoir, Faith's battalion had about ninety per cent of its authorized strength plus 30 to 50 ROK soldiers attached to each company. Morale had been good.[11] Although casualties during the night had not been alarmingly high, a disproportionately high number of officers and noncoms had been put out of action. In Company A, for instance, when Lt. Raymond C. Denchfield was wounded in the knee, his company commander (Capt. Edward B. Scullion) set out to temporarily take charge of Denchfield's platoon. An enemy grenade killed Scullion. Colonel Faith then sent his assistant S3 (Capt. Robert F. Haynes) to take command of Company A. He was killed by infiltrators before he reached the front lines. Colonel Faith telephoned the executive officer (Lieutenant Smith) and told him to take command of the company.

"It's your baby now," Faith told him.

The strength and determination of the enemy attack was also a blow to morale. It now appeared to Faith's men that, in addition to the severe weather, their troubles were to be compounded by fresh enemy troops. The cold weather was bad enough, especially as there were no warm-up tents within the perimeter. During the night, when they had not been engaged in beating off enemy attacks, the men could do nothing for relief but pull their sleeping bags up to their waists and sit quietly in their holes watching for another attack, or for morning. The light machine guns did not work well in the cold. This was especially true during the night when the temperature dropped sharply. The guns would not fire automatically and had to be jacked back by hand to fire single rounds. The heavy machine guns, however, with antifreeze solution in the water jackets, worked all right.

Similar attacks had fallen against the perimeter enclosing Colonel Mac-Lean's force four miles to the south of Faith's battalion. Chinese had overrun two infantry companies during the early morning and got back to the artillery positions before members of two artillery batteries and of the overrun companies stopped them. After confused and intense fighting during the hours of darkness, the enemy withdrew at first light. Both sides suffered heavily.[12]

Colonel MacLean had another cause for concern. Soon after arriving in that area the night before, he had dispatched his regimental Intelligence and Reconnaissance Platoon to patrol the surrounding area. Twelve hours after the platoon had set out, no member had returned.[13]

Colonel Faith tried all day to recover the ground lost during the night. The most critical loss was the prominent knob at the boundary of the two companies east of the road. Lt. Richard H. Moore led his platoon in counterattacks on 28 November and succeeded in recovering all but the important knob itself. Repeatedly, Moore got his platoon to the bottom of the knob only to have the Chinese—many of whom were firing American-made weapons—drive it back again. The friendly counterattacks were greatly aided by mortar fire and by very close and effective air support by carrier-based Corsairs. There were planes in the air most of the day. Front-line observers communicated with the planes by the regular assault-wire lines to battalion headquarters, where a Marine tactical air control officer (Capt. Edward P. Stamford) relayed the instructions to the pilots. The planes made some passes so close to friendly troops that several targets were marked with white phosphorus grenades thrown by hand. More frequently the infantrymen used rifle grenades to mark their targets.[14] In spite of these efforts, the Chinese managed to hold the important knob.

Late in the afternoon both Lieutenant Moore and the battalion sergeant major were put out of action by the same burst from an American caliber .45 Thompson submachine gun. One bullet killed the sergeant. Another one struck Moore squarely on the forehead, raised a bump and dazed him for a short time, but did not otherwise hurt him. Unable to recover the main terrain feature within its perimeter, Company C organized a reverse-slope defense directly in front of the knob.

Sixty or more casualties gathered at the battalion aid station during the day. By evening about twenty bodies had accumulated in front of the two-room farm house in which the aid station was operating. Inside, the building was crowded with wounded; a dozen more wounded, some wearing bandages, stood in a huddle outside.

During the afternoon of 28 November a helicopter landed in a rice paddy near the battalion's command post buildings. General Almond (X Corps commander), on one of his frequent inspections of his front lines, stepped out of the craft. He discussed the situation with Colonel Faith. Before leaving, General Almond explained that he had three Silver Star medals in his pocket, one of which was for Colonel Faith. He asked the colonel to select two men to receive the others, and a small group to witness the presentation. Colonel Faith looked around. Behind him, Lt. Everett F. Smalley, Jr., a platoon leader who had been wounded the night before and was awaiting evacuation, sat on a water can.

"Smalley," said Colonel Faith, "come over here and stand at attention."

Smalley did so. Just then the mess sergeant from Headquarters Company (Sgt. George A. Stanley) walked past.

"Stanley," the colonel called, "come here and stand at attention next to Lieutenant Smalley."

Stanley obeyed. Colonel Faith then gathered a dozen or more men —walking wounded, drivers, and clerks—and lined them up behind Smalley and Stanley.

After pinning the medals to their parkas and shaking hands with the three men, General Almond spoke briefly to the assembled group, saying, in effect: "The enemy who is delaying you for the moment is nothing more than remnants of Chinese divisions fleeing north. We're still attacking and we're going all the way to the Yalu. Don't let a bunch of Chinese laundrymen stop you." [15]

Unfolding his map, General Almond walked over and spread it on the hood of a nearby jeep and talked briefly with Colonel Faith, gestured toward the north, and then departed. As the helicopter rose from the ground, Colonel Faith ripped the medal from his parka with his gloved hand and threw it down in the snow. His operations officer (Major Wesley J. Curtis) walked back to his command post with him.

"What did the General say?" Curtis asked, referring to the conversation at the jeep.

"You heard him," muttered Faith; "remnants fleeing north!" [16]

Lieutenant Smalley went back to his water can. "I got me a Silver Star," he remarked to one of the men who had observed the presentation, "but I don't know what the hell for!"

That afternoon Colonel MacLean came forward to Colonel Faith's battalion. Toward evening, however, when he attempted to leave, he was stopped by a Chinese roadblock between the two battalions, thus confronting him with the grim realization that the enemy had surrounded his position. He remained at the forward position.

Just before dark, between 1700 and 1730, 28 November, planes struck what appeared to be a battalion-sized enemy group that was marching toward the battalion perimeter from the north, still two or three miles away. The tactical situation, even during the daytime, had been so serious that many of the units did not take time to carry rations to the front line. When food did reach the soldiers after dark, it was frozen and the men had no way to thaw it except by holding it against their bodies. By this time most of the men realized the enemy was mounting more than light skirmishes, as they had believed the previous evening.

"You'd better get your positions in good tonight," one platoon leader told his men that evening, "or there won't be any positions tomorrow." [17]

As darkness fell on 28 November, Colonel Faith's battalion braced itself for another attack. The most critical point was the enemy-held knob between the two companies east of the road. Lt. James G. Campbell (a platoon leader of Company D) had two machine guns aimed at the knob, and between his guns and the Chinese position there was a five-man rifle squad. Lieutenant Campbell was particularly concerned about this squad. He was afraid it was not strong enough to hold the position.

Enemy harassing fire, fairly constant all day, continued to fall within the battalion perimeter after dark. It had been dark for three or four hours, however, before the enemy struck again, hitting several points along the perimeter. As expected, one enemy group attacked the vulnerable area east of the road. Lieutenant Campbell heard someone shout and soon afterward saw several figures running from the knoll held by the five-man squad. In the darkness he counted five men and shot the sixth, who by then was only ten feet from his foxhole. Expecting more Chinese from the same direction, he shouted instructions for one of his machine-gun crews to displace to another position from which it could fire upon the knoll that the five men had just vacated. At that moment Lieutenant Campbell was knocked down. He thought someone had hit him in the face with a hammer, although he felt no pain. A mortar fragment about the size of a bullet had penetrated his cheek and lodged in the roof of his mouth. He remained with his gun crews. After the first Chinese had been driven back, enemy activity subsided for about an hour or two.

While this fighting was taking place, General Almond was flying to Tokyo at General MacArthur's order. The corps commander reported to General MacArthur at 2200, 28 November, and received orders to discontinue X Corps' attack and to withdraw and consolidate his forces for more cohesive action against the enemy.[18]

Five hours after this meeting, at about 0300, 29 November, Colonel Faith's executive officer (Major Crosby P. Miller) went to the front-line companies with orders from Colonel MacLean to prepare at once to join the rest of his force four miles to the south. Because of the enemy road-block separating the two elements of his task force, Colonel MacLean ordered Faith to abandon as much equipment as necessary in order to have enough space on the trucks to haul out the wounded, and then to attack south.[19] All wounded men—about a hundred by now—were placed on trucks that formed in column on the road. Because of the necessity of maintaining blackout, it was not practical to burn the vehicles, kitchens, and other equipment to be left behind.

When the withdrawal order reached the rifle platoons, the plan for withdrawing the battalion segment by segment collapsed as the men abruptly broke contact with the Communists, fell back to the road, and assembled for the march. Enemy fire picked up immediately since the movement and the abrupt end of the firing made it obvious to the Chinese that the Americans were leaving.

Colonel Faith directed two companies to provide flank security by preceding the column along the high ground that paralleled the road on both sides for about two miles. Movement of the 1st Battalion column got under way about an hour before dawn, 29 November. Because Captain Seever (CO, Company C) had been wounded in the leg the day before, he instructed one of his platoon leaders (Lt. James O. Mortrude) to lead the company. Slipping and stumbling on the snow-covered hills, Mortrude and the rest of the company set out along the high ground east of the road. Company B was on the opposite side. Mortrude could hear the vehicles below, but could see nothing in the dark. He encountered no enemy. The column moved without opposition until, at the first sign of daylight, it reached the point where the road, following the shoreline, turned northeast to circle a long finger of ice. The Chinese roadblock was at the end of this narrow strip, and here enemy fire halted the column. The battalion's objective, the perimeter of the rest of MacLean's task force, was now just across the strip of ice and not much farther than a mile by the longer road distance.

Halting the vehicular column, Colonel Faith sent two companies onto a high hill directly north of the strip of ice with orders to circle the roadblock and attack it from the east. At the same time, he told Lieutenant Campbell to set up his weapons on a hill overlooking the enemy roadblock. Carrying two heavy machine guns and a 75mm recoilless rifle, Campbell's group climbed the hill and commenced firing at the general roadblock area. From this hill he and his men could see the friendly perimeter on the opposite side of the narrow strip of ice, and to the south beyond that they could see enemy soldiers. A hundred or more Chinese were standing on a ridgeline just south of the friendly force. About a dozen Chinese, in formation, marched south on the road. They were beyond machine-gun range, but the recoilless rifle appeared to be effective on the ridgeline.

Down on the road, Colonel Faith's column suddenly received fire from the vicinity of the friendly units across the finger of ice. Believing that the fire was coming from his own troops, Colonel MacLean started across the ice to make contact with them and halt the fire. He was hit four times by enemy fire—the men watching could see his body jerk with each impact—but he continued and reached the opposite side. There he disappeared and was not seen again.

It now became evident that the fire was Chinese. Colonel Faith assembled as many men as he could and led them in a skirmish line directly across the ice. As it happened, a company-sized enemy force was preparing to attack positions of the 57th Field Artillery Battalion when Faith's attack struck this force in the rear. Disorganized, the Chinese attack fell apart. Faith's men killed about sixty Chinese and dispersed the rest. In the meantime, the two rifle companies approached the enemy force manning the roadblock. Now surrounded itself, the roadblock force also fell apart and disappeared into the hills. With the road open, the column of vehicles entered the perimeter of the other friendly forces.[20]

After a search for Colonel MacLean failed to discover any trace of him, Colonel Faith assumed command and organized all remaining personnel into a task force. Friendly forces, although consolidated, still occupied a precarious position. During the afternoon Faith and his commanders formed a perimeter defense of an area about 600 by 2,000 yards into which the enemy had squeezed them. This perimeter, around a pocket of low, slightly sloping ground, was particularly vulnerable to attack. Except for the area along the reservoir, Colonel Faith's task force was surrounded by ridgelines, all of which belonged to the Chinese. There were firing positions on a couple of mounds of earth within the perimeter and along the embankments of the road and single-track railroad that ran through the area. Several Korean houses, all damaged, stood within the perimeter. There were many Chinese bodies on the ground, one of which wore a new American field jacket that still had its original inspection tags.[21] Rations were almost gone. Ammunition and gasoline supplies were low. The men were numbed by the cold. Even those few who had managed to retain their bedrolls did not dare fall asleep for fear of freezing. The men had to move their legs and change position occasionally to keep their blood circulating. Automatic weapons had to be tried every fifteen to thirty minutes to keep them in working order.

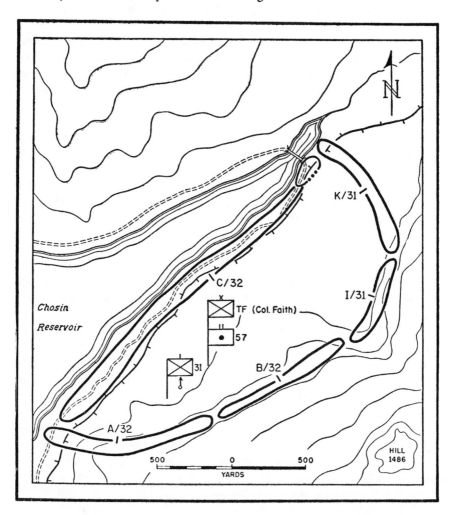

Three factors prevented the situation from being hopeless. First, airdrops were delivered on the afternoon of 29 November. The first drop landed on high ground to the east, and friendly forces had to fight to get it. They recovered most of the bundles, and captured several Chinese who had also been after the supplies. A second drop went entirely to the Chinese, landing outside the perimeter to the southwest. A third drop was successful. One airload consisted of rations, the other of ammunition.

The second factor was the Marine tactical air support, which constantly harassed the enemy with napalm, rockets, and machine-gun fire. Throughout 29 and 30 November the black Corsairs hit the enemy—even during the night between the two days, when they operated by bright moonlight. Pilots later reported that so many enemy personnel were in the area, they could effectively drop their loads anywhere around the perimeter.

The third factor was the hope that friendly forces would break through the Chinese from the south and effect a rescue. There was talk that the assistant commander of the 7th Division (General Hodes) had even then formed a task force and was attempting to join them. This was true.

Colonel MacLean had asked for help the day before (28 November) when he realized he was surrounded. In a message to X Corps he had asked that his 2d Battalion, then at Hamhung awaiting orders from corps, be dispatched to him at once, even if it had to fight its way north.[22]

Although corps failed to act promptly upon MacLean's request, it did form a task force from several small units then located at Hudong-ni, a small lumber town about a third of the distance north between Hagaru-ri and Colonel MacLean's force. Under command of General Hodes, this task force started north at mid-morning, 28 November, but a strong enemy force halted it just north of the village, and forced it to withdraw.[23]

The 2d Battalion, 31st Infantry, meanwhile waited for orders. Late on the afternoon of the 28th, corps ordered it to set up a blocking position at Majon-dong, a third of the distance from Hamhung to Hagaru-ri. It was to move by rail, with its trucks following by road. A little later corps changed the orders. The 2d Battalion was to move by rail to Majon-dong the next morning. From there X Corps would furnish trucks to haul the battalion north to help Colonel MacLean. The battalion arrived at Majon-dong and spent the entire day waiting for X Corps trucks. None came. When the battalion's own trucks arrived, as part of the initial plan for establishing a roadblock in the village, X Corps ordered them off the road. Because of confusion at X Corps headquarters, the battalion's own trucks were not released to it, even though the promised X Corps trucks did not arrive.[24] Thus, two entire days passed without progress in providing relief for Colonel MacLean's surrounded battalions. It was while his 2d Battalion waited at Majon-dong that Colonel MacLean disappeared at the enemy roadblock.

Finally, on the morning of 30 November, the relief battalion got under way. Before it had gone halfway to Hagaru-ri, it came under enemy attack itself, and did not reach Koto-ri until the following morning. By then, the road between Hagaru-ri and Hamhung was threatened by the enemy and it became necessary to divert the 2d Battalion to help protect the entire corps withdrawal route, and it was therefore held in Koto-ri.[25]

Ten miles above Hagaru-ri, Colonel Faith's task force beat off enemy probing attacks that harassed his force during the night of 29–30 November. The Chinese concentrated on the two points where the road entered the perimeter, and on the south they succeeded in overrunning a 75mm recoilless rifle position and capturing some of the crew. There were no determined attacks, however, and the perimeter was still intact when dawn came. It was another cold morning. The sky was clear enough to permit air support. Inside the perimeter, soldiers built fires to warm themselves and the fires drew no enemy fire. Hopefully, the men decided they had withstood the worst part of the enemy attack. Surely, they thought, a relief column would reach the area that day.

A litter-bearing helicopter made two trips to the area on 30 November, carrying out four seriously wounded men. Fighter planes made a strike on high ground around Task Force Faith, and cargo planes dropped more supplies, some of which again fell to the enemy. As the afternoon wore on, it became apparent that no relief column was coming that day. Colonel Faith and Major Curtis organized a group of men to serve as a counterattack force to repel any Chinese penetration that might occur during the coming night. As darkness settled for another sixteen-hour-long night, commanders tried to encourage their troops: "Hold out one more night and we've got it made." [26]

On 30 November, again beginning about 2200, the Chinese made another of their dishearteningly regular attacks. From the beginning it showed more determination than those of the two previous nights, although it did not appear to be well coordinated, nor concentrated in any one area. Capt. Erwin B. Bigger (CO, Company D), in an attempt to confuse the Chinese, hit upon the idea of firing a different-colored flare every time the enemy fired one, and blowing a whistle whenever the enemy blew one.[27]

Soon after midnight, when the enemy attack was most intense, a small group of Chinese broke into the perimeter at one end. Faith sent his counterattack force to patch up the line. From then until morning there were five different penetrations, and as many counterattacks. One of the penetrations, just before first light on 1 December, resulted in enemy seizure of a small hill within the perimeter, thus endangering the defenses. Battalion headquarters called Company D to ask if someone there could get enough men together to counterattack and dislodge the Chinese.

Lt. Robert D. Wilson, a platoon leader, volunteered for the job. "Come on, all you fighting men!" he called out. "We've got a counterattack to make."

During the night Lieutenant Wilson had directed mortar fire, but the ammunition was gone by this time. Assembling a force of 20 or 25 men, he waited a few minutes until there was enough light. His force was short of ammunition—completely out of rifle grenades and having only small-arms ammunition and three hand grenades. Lieutenant Wilson carried a recaptured tommy gun. When daylight came the men moved out, Lieutenant Wilson out in front, leading. Near the objective an enemy bullet struck his arm, knocking him to the ground. He got up and went on. Another bullet struck him in the arm or chest.

"That one bit," he said, continuing. A second or two later, another bullet struck him in the forehead and killed him.

SFC Fred Sugua took charge and was in turn killed within a few minutes. Eventually, the remaining men succeeded in driving the Chinese out of the perimeter.[28]

Even after daylight, which usually ended the enemy attacks, the Chinese made one more attempt to knock out a 75mm recoilless rifle that guarded the road. In about two-platoon strength, they came up a deep ditch along the road to the south. Lieutenant Campbell rushed Corporal Armentrout forward to plug the gap with his machine gun. Hit by a mortar round the night before, the water jacket on the machine gun was punctured and, after several minutes, the gun jammed. Armentrout sent his assistant back for the other heavy machine gun, the last good one in the section. With it, and by himself, Corporal Armentrout killed at least twenty enemy soldiers and stopped the attack.[29]

At 0700, 1 December, as Lieutenant Campbell was telling the battalion S4 (Capt. Raymond Vaudrevil) that everything was under control, a mortar shell landed ten feet away and knocked him down. Fragments sprayed his left side, and wounded two other men. Someone pulled Campbell under a nearby truck, then helped him to the aid station. The aid-station squad tent was full; about fifty patients were inside. Another thirty-five wounded were lying outside in the narrow-gauge railroad cut where the aid station was located.

Dazed with shock, Lieutenant Campbell lay outside about half an hour. Colonel Faith appeared at the aid station, asked all men who could possibly do so to come back on line.

"If we can hold out forty minutes more," the Colonel pleaded, "we'll get air support."

There was not much response. Most of the men were seriously wounded.

"Come on, you lazy bastards," Faith said, "and give us a hand."

That roused several men, including Campbell. Because he could not walk, he crawled twenty yards along the railroad track and found a carbine with one round in it. Dragging the carbine, Campbell continued to crawl to the west. He collapsed into a foxhole before he reached the lines, and waited until someone helped him back to the aid station. This time he got inside for treatment. The medical personnel had no more bandages. There was no more morphine. They cleansed his wounds with disinfectant, and he dozed there for several hours.

As it was everywhere else in the perimeter, the situation at the aid station was most difficult. Near the medical tent a tarpaulin had been stretched over the railroad cut to shelter additional patients, and other wounded were crowded into two small Korean huts. Company aid men, when they could, assisted the medical officer (Capt. Vincent J. Navarre) and three enlisted men who worked continuously at the aid station.

Two thirds of the No. 2 medical chests were lost during the withdrawal from the first positions. The jeep hauling them had simply disappeared. Thus, most of the surgical equipment was gone. Aid men improvised litters from ponchos and field jackets. One splint set was on hand, however, and there was plenty of blood plasma. The aid station had one complete No. 1 chest. When bandages were gone, aid men used personal linens, handkerchiefs, undershirts, and towels. They gathered up parachutes recovered with the airdropped bundles, using white ones for dressings and colored ones to cover the wounded and keep them warm. Sgt. Leon Pugowski of the Headquarters Company kitchen had managed to save two stoves, coffee, and some cans of soup. He set the stoves up in the aid station, and the seriously wounded got hot soup or coffee.

Task Force Faith had been under attack for eighty hours in sub-zero weather. None of the men had washed or shaved during that time, nor eaten more than a bare minimum. Frozen feet and hands were common. Worst of all, the weather appeared to be getting worse, threatening air support and aerial resupply. Few men believed they could hold out another night against determined attacks.

Captain Seever (CO, Company C) sat on the edge of a hole discussing the situation with Major Curtis (battalion S3). An enemy mortar shell landed 10 to 15 feet away and exploded without injuring either of them. Seever shrugged his shoulders.

"Major," he said, "I feel like I'm a thousand years old." [30]

A single low-flying Marine fighter bomber appeared over the surrounded task force about 1000 on 1 December. Establishing radio contact with the tactical air control party, the pilot stated that if the weather improved as forecasted, he would guide more tactical aircraft into the area shortly after noon. He also stated that there were no friendly forces on the road between Faith's perimeter and Hagaru-ri.

Colonel Faith decided to try to break out of the perimeter and reach Hagaru-ri in a single dash rather than risk another night where he was. He planned to start the breakout about 1300 so that it would coincide with the air strike. He ordered the artillery batteries and the Heavy Mortar Company to shoot up all remaining ammunition before that time and then to destroy their weapons. He placed the 1st Battalion, 32d Infantry, in the lead, followed by the 57th Field Artillery Battalion, the Heavy Mortar Company, and the 3d Battalion of the 31st Infantry. Half-track vehicles of Battery D, 15th AAA Automatic Weapons Battalion, were interspersed throughout the column. To minimize danger from enemy attack, Colonel Faith wanted the column to be as short as possible —only enough vehicles to haul out the wounded. All other men would walk. Vehicles, equipment, and supplies that could not be carried, or that were not necessary for the move, he ordered destroyed. The men selected twenty-two of the best vehicles—2½-ton, ¾-ton and ¼-ton trucks—and lined them up on the road. They drained gasoline from the other vehicles and filled the tanks of the ones they were going to take. Then they destroyed the remaining vehicles with white phosphorus or thermite grenades.

About noon someone roused Lieutenant Campbell and said, "We're going to make a break for it."

He and the other wounded men—several hundred of them by this time—were placed in the vehicles. They lay there for about an hour while final preparations for the breakout attempt were made. Enemy mortar shells began dropping in the vicinity.

Colonel Faith selected Company C, 32d Infantry, as advance guard for the column. Lieutenant Mortrude's platoon, the unit least hurt, was to take the point position for the company. Supported by a dual 40mm half-track, this platoon would clear the road for the vehicle column. Lieutenant Mortrude, who was wounded in the knee, planned to ride the half-track. Company A, followed by Company B, would act as flank security east of the road. There was no danger at the beginning of the breakout from the direction of the reservoir, which was to the west.

Friendly planes appeared overhead. Mortrude moved his platoon out about 1300. Lieutenant Smith led out Company A. The men of these units had walked barely out of the area that had been their defensive perimeter when enemy bullets whistled past or dug into the ground behind them. At almost the same time, four friendly planes, in close support of the breakout action, missed the target and dropped napalm bombs on the lead elements. The halftrack in which Mortrude planned to ride was set ablaze. Several men were burned to death immediately. About five others, their clothes afire, tried frantically to beat out the flames. Everyone scattered. Disorganization followed.

Up to this point, units had maintained organizational structure, but suddenly they began to fall apart. Intermingling in panic, they disintegrated into leaderless groups of men. Most of the squad and platoon leaders and the commanders of the rifle companies were dead or wounded. Many of the key personnel from the battalions were casualties. Capt. Harold B. Bauer (CO, Headquarters Company), Major Crosby P. Miller (battalion executive officer), Major Curtis (battalion S3), Capt. Wayne E. Powell (battalion S2) and Lt. Henry M. Moore (Ammunition and Pioneer Platoon leader) had all been wounded. The same was true of the important noncoms. No one had slept for several days. One thought drove the men: they had to keep moving if they were to get out. Even those who were not

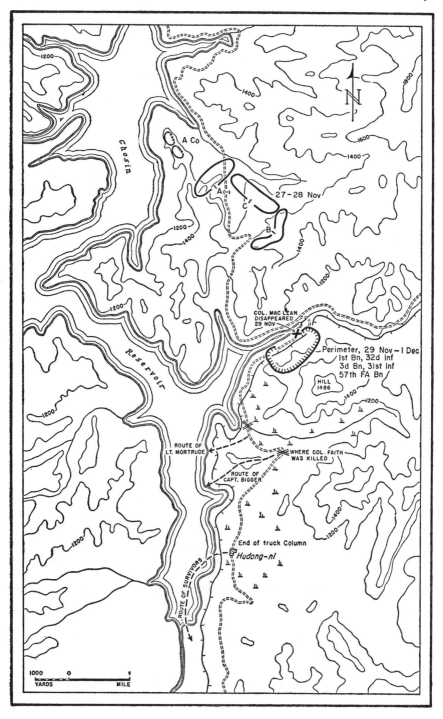

wounded were strongly tempted to lie down and go to sleep; but they knew they would be lost if they did.

Lieutenant Mortrude gathered ten men around him and proceeded to carry out his orders. Firing as they advanced, they dispersed twenty or more enemy soldiers who fled. As they ran down the road screaming obscenities at the enemy, Mortrude and his men encountered several small Chinese groups, which they killed or scattered. One such group was putting in communication lines. Another was repairing a wrecked jeep. Out of breath and hardly able to walk on his wounded leg, Mortrude and those men still with him reached a blown-out bridge two miles or more south of the starting point. Attracting no enemy fire, they stopped there to rest and wait for the column. A little later a Company A platoon leader (Lt. Herbert E. Marshburn, Jr.) came up with a group of men and joined them. Together they crossed under the bridge and moved to the east, then south, to reconnoiter. Enemy fire came in from the high ground to the northeast. Most of the men fell to the ground to take cover. Lieutenant Mortrude wondered why the vehicles were not coming down the road, since he had expected the column to follow closely. As he lay on the slope of the ridge, a bullet struck him in the head and knocked him unconscious.

The main body of the column, meanwhile, waited until Colonel Faith could reorganize it. Since Company C and part of Company A were disorganized by the burning napalm, he ordered Company B to take the lead and to advance with marching fire to the blown-out bridge. The vehicular column moved slowly down the road, keeping abreast of Company B, which was sweeping the high ground. Air cover was continuous.

It was mid-afternoon or later when the truck column stopped at the blown-out bridge where it was necessary to construct a bypass over the rough and steep banks of the stream. A half-track towed the trucks across while the able-bodied men with the column took care to prevent them from overturning. In the middle of this tediously slow process, Chinese riflemen began firing at the trucks and men. One truck—the one in which Lieutenant Campbell was lying—stalled in the middle of the stream bed. Enemy fire struck some of the wounded men in the truck. Campbell, figuring it would be better for him to get out and move under his own power, crawled out of the truck. He started walking up the ditch toward the lead vehicles, which had stopped again a third of a mile ahead. After he had gone about two hundred yards enemy riflemen began shooting at him, forcing him to the ground. He discovered his head was clear now, and the feeling of weakness had vanished. Although his leg and side pained him, and although his cheek and mouth were swollen from the wound he had received three days before, he felt pretty good. When a ¾-ton truck came by after about twenty minutes, he got on it. He never did learn what happened to the truck he had left.

Back at the blown-out bridge the column moved forward as fast as the halftrack could drag the trucks through the bypass. The battalion motor officer (Lt. Hugh R. May) stood in the road supervising the operation. He appeared to be unconcerned about the enemy fire, which remained heavy as long as there were men and trucks at the roadblock. It was late in the afternoon before the last truck was across.[31]

When Lieutenant Mortrude regained consciousness on the slope of the ridge, he noticed friendly troops moving up the hill in the area south of the blown-out bridge. An aid man (Cpl. Alfonso Camoesas) came past and bandaged his head. Then Mortrude stumbled across the ridgeline, passing many American dead and wounded on the slope. Dazed and in a condition of shock, he followed a group of men he could vaguely see ahead of him. The group went toward the reservoir and walked out onto the ice.

While all of this was taking place, another enemy roadblock halted the lead trucks in the column at a hairpin curve a half mile beyond the blown-out bridge. At least two machine guns and enemy riflemen kept the area under fire. Colonel Faith, a blanket around his shoulders, walked up and down the line of trucks as he organized a group to assault the enemy who were firing from positions east of the road. Each time he passed his jeep in the center of the column he fired several bursts from the caliber .50 machine gun mounted on it. Heavy enemy fire also came from the west side of the road, from the direction of the reservoir. This fire raked the truck column, hitting the wounded men in the trucks. Darkness was not far off. Colonel Faith was desperately anxious to get his column moving and the wounded men out before the Chinese closed in on them. He got some wounded into the ditch to form a base of fire and then organized several groups to assault the enemy positions.

One group of men, under Captain Bigger (CO, Company D), was to clear out the area between the road and the reservoir. Colonel Faith instructed the S2 of the 1st Battalion, 32d Infantry (Major Robert E. Jones), to gather all available men and move them onto the high ground south of the hairpin curve, while he himself organized another group to move onto the high ground just north of the roadblock at the hairpin curve. They would then attack from opposite directions at the same time.[32]

Captain Bigger, blinded in one eye by a mortar fragment and wounded in the leg, supported himself on a mortar aiming stake and waved his group up the hill, hobbling up himself. Like Captain Bigger, the majority of his group was walking wounded.

It was almost dark when Major Jones and Colonel Faith, each with a hundred men or less, launched their attacks against the roadblock and knocked it out. Colonel Faith, hit by grenade fragments, was mortally wounded. A man next to him, hit by fragments of the same grenade, tried to help him down to the road, but was unable to do so. Some other men came by, carried him down to the road, and put him in the cab of a truck.[33]

Colonel Faith's task force, which had started to break up soon after it got under way that afternoon, now disintegrated completely because those men who had commanded the battalions, companies, and platoons were either dead or wounded so seriously they could exercise no control. The task force crumbled into individuals, or into groups of two or ten or twenty men. Major Jones, with the help of several others, took charge of the largest group of men remaining—those who stayed to help with the trucks carrying the wounded. Enemy fire had severely damaged the truck column. Several trucks were knocked out and blocked the column, and others had flat tires. The time was about 1700, 1 December, and it was almost dark.

Those who were able, now removed all wounded men from three destroyed 2½-ton trucks which blocked the column, carried the wounded to other trucks, and then pushed the destroyed vehicles over the cliff toward the reservoir. Someone shouted for help to gather up all men who had been wounded during the roadblock action. For half an hour the able-bodied men searched both sides of the road. When the column was ready to move again the wounded were piled two deep in most of the trucks. Men rode across the hoods and on the bumpers, and six or eight men hung to the sides of each truck. After re-forming the truck column with all operating vehicles, Major Jones organized as many able-bodied and walking wounded men as he could—between a hundred and two hundred men—and started south down the road. The trucks were to follow.[34]

The group of men that had gone with Captain Bigger, after having run the Chinese off of the high ground on the west side of the road, found that there were still enemy soldiers between it and the road. Rather than fight back to the road, Bigger led his men west and south to the reservoir shore, and then out onto the ice. Another group of about fifteen men, including Lieutenant Smith (who had commanded Company A), Lt. Richard H. Moore (one of his platoon leaders), and Lieutenant Barnes (an artillery forward observer), after knocking out one of the enemy machine guns on the same side of the road, watched Captain Bigger and his men heading toward the ice. They debated what they should do. They could see the trucks stalled along the road. They were out of ammunition. Deciding there was no reason to go back, they continued toward the reservoir ice. A group of 15 or 20 Chinese, trying to head them off, came as far as the reservoir bank and fired at them without effect. One enemy soldier, however, did follow them out on the ice to bayonet a man who had fallen behind. Six men of this group, including Smith, were wounded or had frostbitten feet.

Lieutenant Campbell stayed with the column of trucks following the men with Major Jones. Just before leaving the last roadblock position, Campbell happened to meet his platoon sergeant (MSgt. Harold M. Craig). Craig was wounded in the middle of his back and was about to throw away his carbine and rely on his bayonet. Figuring that he would have to make a break for it as soon as darkness came, Craig felt his carbine would encumber him. Campbell gladly accepted the carbine. It had a "banana clip" in it, with thirty rounds. As the trucks moved forward he found one with a place on the side to which he could cling. There were five other men clinging to the same side. It was a ragged and desperate-looking column of men and vehicles. Those following Major Jones had little semblance to a military unit. Without subordinate leaders, without formation or plan, they were a mixture of the remnants of all units, a large percentage being walking wounded. About 15 of the original 22 trucks were left.

A mile or two beyond the roadblock two burned-out tanks partly blocked the road and delayed the column until men could construct a bypass. Beyond that, the column made steady but slow progress for another mile or so. Some of the men began to believe they were safe. There were stragglers along the road—men who had struck out for themselves during previous delays. Some of them swung onto the passing trucks. By this time, it was nearly 2100 and the column, having covered more than half of the approximate ten miles between the last defensive perimeter and Hagaru-ri, approached Hudong-ni, the small lumber village. As the leading truck, which was some distance ahead of the rest of the column, entered the town, Chinese soldiers opened fire and killed the driver. The truck overturned and spilled out the wounded men, a few of whom managed to work back up the road to warn the rest of the column. At this point Major Jones decided it would be advisable to get away from the road and follow the railroad tracks south. The railroad paralleled the road but was closer to the reservoir shoreline. Some of the men followed him.[35]

About 75 to 100 men stayed with the vehicles. An artillery officer collected all who could walk and fire a weapon, and led them forward. At the edge of the village they began to receive fire from rifles and at least one automatic weapon of an enemy unit of undetermined size. After returning the fire for a few minutes, the group returned to the vehicles. They picked up several wounded men from the overturned truck and took them back. The trucks moved a little closer to the village and halted. It was then 2200 or later, 1 December.

A group of officers and men decided they would wait where they were. Word of their situation, they argued, must surely by then have gotten through to Hagaru-ri. Aid would undoubtedly arrive soon.

They waited about an hour or so until the rear of the column began to receive small-arms and mortar fire. Then they decided to make a run for it. Lieutenant Campbell was still hanging to one of the trucks. "We'll never make it through," he thought.

As the column proceeded through the village, moving slowly, enemy fire killed the drivers of the first three trucks. The column halted and an enemy machine gun immediately raked it at point-blank range. Jumping off the tailgate of the third truck, Lieutenant Campbell scrambled for the right side of the road where an embankment separated it from a small plot of cultivated ground eight or ten feet beneath. In the darkness he could see only outlines of the trucks on the road and the flashes of a machine gun firing from a hill on the opposite side of the road. Leaning against the embankment, he fired his carbine at the machine gun's flashes. A body, an arm torn off, lay nearby on the road. The overturned truck, its wheels in the air, rested in the small field below the road. Someone pinned under it kept pounding on the truck's body. Wounded men, scattered nearby, screamed either in pain or for help. Up on the road someone kept yelling for men to drive the trucks through. Chinese soldiers closed in on the rear of the column. Campbell saw a white phosphorus grenade explode in the rear of a truck at the end of the column.

"This is the end of the truck column!" he said to himself.[36]

Someone yelled, "Look out!"

Campbell turned in time to see a ¾-ton truck coming over the embankment toward him. As he scrambled to one side, the truck ran over his foot, bruising the bones. Someone had decided to try to get the lead vehicles off the road. Pushed by the fourth, the first three trucks, without their drivers, jammed together, rolled off the embankment, and overturned. Wounded men inside were spilled and crushed. The frantic screams of these men seemed to Lieutenant Campbell like the world gone mad. He fired his last three rounds at the enemy machine gun, headed for the railroad track on the opposite side of the tiny field, and dived into a culvert underneath the railroad. It began to snow again—a fine, powdery snow.

Everyone scattered. Corporal Camoesas (company aid man) found himself in a group of about fifteen men, none of whom he knew. Carrying six wounded, the group reached the reservoir. As Camoesas walked out on the ice, he looked back. Several trucks were burning.

Lieutenant Campbell crawled through the culvert. He found a man, wounded in the leg, who could not walk. Two other soldiers came over the embankment and joined him. Dragging the wounded man, the group walked in a crouch across the rice paddy to a large lumber pile in the middle of the field. There, two more soldiers joined them. At the edge of the reservoir, three quarters of a mile away, several others joined Campbell's party. Staying close to the shoreline, the men walked on the reservoir ice. Campbell was not sure where Hagaru-ri was, but he felt they would reach it if they followed the reservoir shore.

The reservoir ice was not slippery. The wind had blown off most of the snow, leaving a rough-surfaced crust, and it was so thick that 76mm shells had ricocheted off without appreciable effect.

At a North Korean house, an ROK soldier with them asked where the marines were. He was told that American jeeps came down the road every day. Some of the group, suspicious of the North Koreans, wanted to continue across the reservoir, but Lieutenant Campbell thought he recognized the road. He led off, and the rest followed. By then, he had seventeen men with him, of whom three were armed. Two miles down the road, the group reached a Marine tank outpost, and the tankers directed them to the nearest command post, where a truck took them to a Marine hospital in Hagaru-ri. Lieutenant Campbell arrived there at 0530, 2 December. The shell fragment in the roof of his mouth began to bother him.

Individuals and other groups straggled into Hagaru-ri for several days beginning on the night of 1 December. Lieutenant Smith and those men with him, who had left the column at the second roadblock, reached a Marine supply point at Hagaru-ri about 2200 that night. A plane had dropped a note in a canteen instructing them to keep away from the shoreline and continue across the ice. A little later that night, Captain Bigger hobbled in with his group.

The men who went with Major Jones, after following the railroad tracks for some distance, had been fired on by an enemy machine gun. Many of the men took off toward the reservoir and began arriving at the Marine perimeter soon after midnight.

Most of the men who had served with Task Force Faith were left where the truck column stopped near the lumber village of Hudong-ni, or were strewn along the road from there to the northernmost position. When those few men who could move had left, the others were either captured or frozen.

PFC Glenn J. Finfrock (a machine gunner from Company D) became unconscious from loss of blood about the time the truck column came to its final halt. It was daylight on the morning of 2 December when he regained consciousness again. He moved down the road a short distance until he found several wounded men trying to build a fire by one of the trucks—the one in which Colonel Faith had been placed the previous evening. His frozen body was still in the cab. Since the truck appeared to be in good order, Finfrock and another man tried unsuccessfully to start it. As they were working on the truck some Chinese walked toward them from the village, and several of the men ran toward the ice. Others were captured. The Chinese gave morphine to several men, bandaged their wounds and, after caring for them for several days, freed them.[37]

Lieutenant Mortrude, wounded in the knee and in the head, walked to Hagaru-ri from the blown-out bridge. It was 0330 on 2 December when he reached friendly lines.

Corporal Camoesas (the aid man) and his group carrying the six wounded men, after hiding in brush near the reservoir shore in order to rest, followed the railroad track until they came to the road leading toward

Hagaru-ri. About o800 they met a Marine tank, and three hundred yards beyond were trucks and ambulances waiting to take them to the rear. All day other men made their way back to friendly lines.

On 4 December, when most of its survivors had returned, the 1st Battalion, 32d Infantry, counted only 181 officers, men, and attached Republic of Korea troops, of the original 1,053 that had begun the operation. The other battalions in the perimeter had suffered equal losses.[38]

This was not the immediate end of trouble, since the enemy still controlled much of the road between Hagaru-ri and the port city of Hungnam. But at Hagaru-ri the 1st Marine Division had a solid perimeter that included the airstrip, and there were food and ammunition and medical supplies. From Hungnam the more seriously wounded were evacuated by plane. For the others, ten days of fighting lay ahead.

★ NOTES

1. Unless otherwise noted, this account is based on a narrative prepared in Korea by Capt. Martin Blumenson. To this account the author has added some information obtained from official records, and some obtained by supplemental interviews or by letters from men who participated in the action.

2. Major Wesley J. Curtis, letter and enclosure to OCMH, 28 January 1953.

3. X Corps, command report: Special Report on Chosin Reservoir, 27 November to 10 December 1950 (hereafter cited as X Corps: Chosin Reservoir).

4. X Corps, war diary: monthly summary, 1 November to 30 November 1950; Drive to the Yalu (hereafter cited as X Corps: Drive to the Yalu).

5. Lt. James G. Campbell, in an interview by the author, 14 August 1952.

6. X Corps: Chosin Reservoir; Curtis, *op. cit.*

7. X Corps: Drive to the Yalu.

8. Curtis, *op. cit.*

9. X Corps: Chosin Reservoir.

10. Curtis, *op. cit.*

11. *Ibid.*

12. 7th Division: command report on Chosin Reservoir, 27 November to 12 December 1950; narrative section (hereafter cited as 7th Division: Chosin Reservoir).

13. Curtis, *op. cit.*

14. Campbell, *op. cit.*

15. X Corps: Chosin Reservoir (command section, General Almond's diary, 28 November 1950); Lt. Cecil G. Smith, in an interview by Capt. Martin Blumen-

son, 6 August 1950; Mrs. Erwin B. Bigger, letter to the author, 6 September 1952; Curtis, *op. cit.*

16. Curtis, *op. cit.;* Smith, *op. cit.*

17. Campbell, *op. cit.*

18. X Corps: Chosin Reservoir.

19. 7th Division: Chosin Reservoir.

20. *Ibid.* (statement of Major Robert E. Jones).

21. Campbell, *op. cit.*

22. X Corps: Chosin Reservoir (narrative section).

23. 7th Division: Chosin Reservoir (narrative section).

24. *Ibid.* (statement of Lt.Col. Reidy, CO, 2d Battalion, 31st Infantry).

25. *Ibid.*

26. Curtis, *op. cit.*

27. *Ibid.*

28. The account of this counterattack is based upon statements by Sgt. John Doritsky, PFC Royce Jensen, PFC Gainius E. Woodby, Lt. James G. Campbell, and Cpl. Edward Deland. All of these men belonged to Companies C or D, 32d Infantry.

29. Campbell, *op. cit.*

30. Curtis, *op. cit.*

31. Campbell, *op. cit.*

32. 7th Division: Chosin Reservoir (statement of Major Robert E. Jones).

33. *Ibid.*

34. *Ibid.;* Campbell, *op. cit.*

35. Jones, *loc. cit.*

36. Campbell, *op. cit.*

37. 7th Division: Chosin Reservoir (statement of SFC Willard Donovan).

38. 7th Division: Chosin Reservoir. The statement of Major Jones in this report lists the total strength of the battalion by companies on 4 December. The command report for the 32d Infantry Regiment for November provides a list of the daily strength of each battalion. The figure for 21 November was used.

The event corresponds less to expectations in war than in any other case whatever.

LIVY: HISTORY OF ROME. XXX. 10.

7

Twin Tunnels Patrol Ambush

★ During the withdrawal from northern Korea in December of 1950, U.S. Eighth Army outdistanced the pursuing Chinese and North Koreans and broke contact with the enemy. By the end of January 1951, as a result of firm orders from its commander (Lt.Gen. Matthew B. Ridgway) the army turned and took up defensive positions near the 37th parallel, and from there sent feeler patrols northward to locate the enemy again and reestablish contact.

The 24th and 2d Infantry Divisions occupied adjoining positions near the center of Eighth Army's line. Late on the 27th of January, the commanding general of U.S. X Corps directed the 2d Division to send a reconnaissance patrol northward to the vicinity of two railroad tunnels a few miles south of Chipyong-ni. It was to join forces at Iho-ri with a group from the 24th Division, after which the composite patrol would proceed to the objective.[1]

Because the order reached the divisions so late, the 24th Division was unable to make arrangements for crossing the unbridged Han River in time to effect the meeting. A patrol from the 23d Infantry (2d Division) reconnoitered the Twin Tunnels area, however, and returned to its base without incident.[2]

At 2240 on the night of the 28th, X Corps directed the 2d Division to run the same patrol on the following day, again in conjunction with a patrol from the adjoining division. This time the 2d Division was to furnish five additional jeeps to carry the men from the 24th Division, which was still unable to get its vehicles across the river.[3]

First orders concerning the patrol reached the 23d Infantry at 2300. They were passed on down to the 1st Battalion which, in turn, called Company C and gave preliminary instructions to Lt. James P. Mitchell (one of its platoon leaders), asking him to report to battalion headquarters the following morning at 0600 to get complete orders.[4]

It was still dark, the sky was clear, and the temperature was a few degrees above zero when Lieutenant Mitchell reached the S3 tent on the morning of 29 January. Here he was given the mission of making another reconnaissance of the Twin Tunnels area—by road, about thirty miles north of Company C's location—and told to make contact with the enemy, if he could, but to avoid combat with any large enemy force. He was ordered to move out as soon as possible since he was scheduled to meet the 24th Division's patrol at 1030. By 0630 Lieutenant Mitchell had returned to his company to organize his group.

Plans for the patrol were being made and changed while the members assembled. Battalion headquarters called three times between 0630 and 0800, each time adding men and weapons to the patrol. There were also difficulties and delays in securing enough vehicles and radios, both of which were acutely scarce as a result of heavy equipment losses which the 2d Division had sustained during its withdrawal from northern Korea. The 1st Battalion finally arranged to borrow three jeeps, with drivers, from another battalion of the same regiment, and extra radios from an artillery battalion. Lieutenant Mitchell had two SCR-300 radios, neither of which worked well, for communications within the patrol. To help maintain communications between the patrol and its headquarters, the regiment had arranged for an L-5 liaison plane to circle above the patrol and act as a radio relay station. It was therefore necessary to have an SCR-619 radio to communicate with the plane. To be safe, the 1st Battalion borrowed two. On the morning of 29 January, however, the artillery battalion complained because two of its radios had been damaged when loaned to the infantry the previous day, and insisted on furnishing its own operators with the radios. It was 0900 before the artillerymen reported, and the patrol was ready to get under way.[5]

Lieutenant Mitchell was in command of the patrol. As finally organized, it consisted of forty-four officers and men, most of whom were members of his Company C rifle platoon. Nine members of the patrol, including an officer, were from Company D; the others were the artillery radio operators and the drivers from the 3d Battalion. These men were mounted on two ¾-ton weapons carriers and nine jeeps, five of which were for the 24th Division men. Mitchell's men carried two BARs and either rifles or carbines, plus a 75mm and a 57mm recoilless rifle, a 3.5-inch bazooka, a 60mm mortar, and two caliber .50 and three caliber .30 machine guns mounted on the vehicles, and two light machine guns with tripod mounts.

For 20 of the 44 members of the patrol, this was their first combat action since they had joined Company C only four days before. They were

from specialist schools—listed as draftsmen, mechanics, and technicians—
and had received little training as infantrymen.

Another officer joined the patrol just before it left. Capt. Melvin R.
Stai (battalion assistant S3) went along only to be certain that Lieutenant
Mitchell's patrol met the men from the 24th Division as planned. He was
told to return to battalion headquarters after the composite patrol departed
for the tunnels.[6]

Lieutenant Mitchell, with four men in a jeep mounting a caliber .50
machine gun, made up the advance party and led the patrol by about fifteen
hundred yards. The main body, under the control of Lt. William C. Penrod
(a Company D platoon leader), followed, with intervals of at least a hundred yards between vehicles. For Korea, the road was good but movement
was slow because of heavy snow in shaded spots and patches of ice that
covered some sections of the narrow road.

The liaison plane circled above the vehicular column as far as Iho-ri
where it lost visual contact because of the haze that frequently filled the
narrow Korean valleys during the morning hours.

At 1115 the column reached Iho-ri, a small village on the east bank of
the Han River, where the patrol from the 24th Division was waiting. The
group from the 24th consisted of Lt. Harold P. Mueller and fourteen men
whom he had selected from his platoon of Company F, 21st Infantry. In
addition to rifles, the men had six BARs and a light machine gun. They had
reversible parkas which they wore with the white side out, including white
hoods over their helmets, whereas the men from the 2d Division were
dressed in fatigue clothing and field jackets. The combined patrol now
numbered 4 officers and 56 men, including Captain Stai, who decided at
Iho-ri to accompany the patrol instead of returning to battalion headquarters. It proceeded at once toward the objective, which was still approximately fifteen miles away.

The Twin Tunnels were located about three miles southeast of
Chipyong-ni and less than a mile northwest of a little village named Sinchon.
As Lieutenant Mitchell in the lead vehicle neared the objective, he passed
a large hill that rose steeply on the left (west) side of the road, dominating
the entire area. This was Hill 453. Skirting the base of the hill, the road
crossed a ford in a shallow stream and then split at the base of another,
smaller hill. One fork of the road turned right to Sinchon; the other fork
went west for several hundred yards, then turned north for another two
thousand yards where it crossed the railroad track between the two tunnels.

At the ford Lieutenant Mitchell stopped to wait for Lieutenant Mueller
and Captain Stai, who were riding in the two jeeps immediately behind.
Since the patrol was already behind schedule, Captain Stai offered to go
alone into Sinchon while the rest of the patrol went on to investigate the
tunnels, after which they would be ready to return. Accordingly, the two
lieutenants and the men with them proceeded to the railroad track, turned

their vehicles around in position to go back, and then waited near a farm house. The tunnels were not side by side, but were, instead, end to end, cutting under two steep ridges, one on each side of the road and narrow valley. On the west side the ridge rose toward the south to the hill mass of

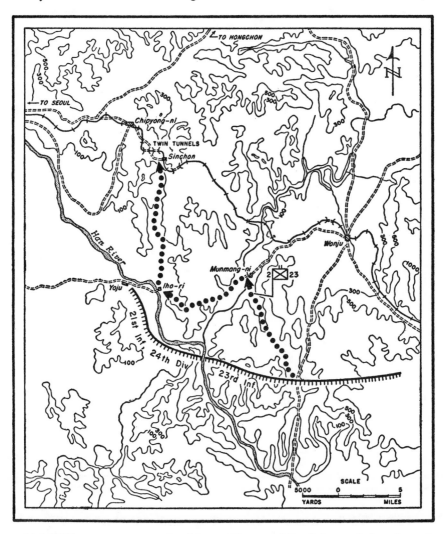

which Hill 453 was a part; the ridge on the east side of the road sloped north to Hill 333. Between these two ridges were a stream, terraced rice paddies, and scattered Lombardy poplars, all typical of the Korean landscape.

Captain Stai left his driver and vehicle by the road, walked alone toward the cluster of drab houses in Sinchon and disappeared. The time was about 1215.[7]

Trouble started within a minute or two after the two jeeps stopped by the railroad tracks. Men from the 21st Infantry patrol spotted 15 or 20 Chinese soldiers running from a small hill just north of the railroad crossing, and opened fire on them. The others of the patrol ran up to see what was happening. Soon after the first shots, ten or twelve scattered mortar rounds

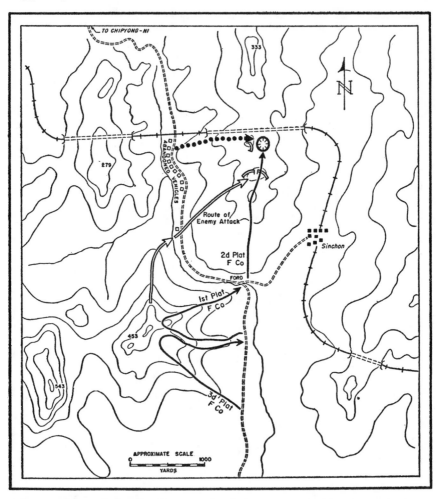

fell near the road, landing just south of the two parked jeeps and in front of the other vehicles which were now closing into the tunnels area.

At about this time the liaison plane appeared overhead again. The battalion executive officer (Major Millard O. Engen) was in the plane which, after it had turned back at Iho-ri because of ground haze, was now returning since visibility had increased. Major Engen saw the same enemy troops whom Lieutenant Mueller's men had taken under fire, as well as another company-sized group on Hill 453. He immediately reported this over the SCR-619 radio together with instructions for Lieutenant Mitchell to turn his patrol around and get out of the area at once.[8] Lieutenant Mitchell did not receive this message because of faulty radio reception.

By the time the last vehicle in the column crossed the ford near Sinchon, Mitchell also saw enemy movement to the south and suspected that his patrol had been caught in a well-planned ambush. He realized that from the fingers of Hill 453, which dominated the road and even the ditches along the road, the Chinese could see when the last vehicle of the patrol closed into the tunnels area. Hill 453 also blocked the route of retreat. Further advance of the column was stopped by enemy positions on Hill 333 northeast of the railroad crossing. Lacking radio communication with the liaison plane and also within the column, and since the ridge tips crowded so close against the road that the men in the trailing vehicles could not see ahead, the vehicles and the entire patrol bunched up in the area just south of the railroad crossing.

Lieutenant Mitchell had decided to make a run for it before the last vehicles in the column had come to a stop.

"Let's get out of here!" he shouted to the men, most of whom had dispersed to seek cover when the first mortar rounds fell. "Let's get out of here!"

Before the last vehicles to arrive could be turned around, however, the men could see Chinese soldiers running from Hill 453 down toward the ford.

In the plane overhead, Major Engen also watched the Chinese moving to cut off the patrol. He radioed new instructions, this time directing Mitchell to head for the high ground east of the road. He then left the area since it was necessary to refuel the plane. No one received this message either.

Men in the get-away jeep, which having turned around was now in the lead, opened fire with their caliber .50 machine gun, but the gun was cold and had so much oil on it that it took two men to operate it, one to jack it back and another man to fire it. It had little effect. Lieutenant Penrod tried to get the 75mm recoilless rifle in position to fire, but gave that up when he saw that the Chinese had already cut the road and that they were racing for the high ground on the east side of the road. He called back to Mitchell to say they couldn't get through.

After Captain Stai had walked off toward Sinchon, his driver followed him in the jeep for a hundred or two hundred yards and had then stopped in the single-lane road to wait. When the enemy force began running from Hill 453 toward the east side of the road, the driver left, apparently trying to join the main body of the patrol. He was shot and killed before he had gone far, the jeep overturning by the road.

When the firing commenced, Lieutenant Mueller looked at the hill on the east side of the road. Realizing they had no chance of breaking out of the ambush by following the road and, wanting to get on defensible high ground, he started up the hill, calling for his men to follow.[9]

A single, narrow ridge rose abruptly at the east edge of the road, and then extended east for nine hundred yards to the high part of the ridge. The ridge was only about four hundred feet higher than the road, and both it and the ridge leading to it were covered with low brush and, on the northern slopes, a foot of wet snow. After climbing a short distance, Lieutenant Mueller stopped to study the area through his binoculars. To the south he saw the Chinese running toward the same hill for which he was heading.

"We're going to have to get to the top of that hill," he called back to Lieutenant Mitchell. "The Chinese are coming up from the other side! This is our only chance!"

From this time on it was a race for the high ground, with the Chinese climbing the south slope of the hill from which the snow had melted.

The patrol, well equipped when mounted, was forced to abandon most of its heavy and crew-served weapons now that it was on foot. Penrod and Mitchell loaded their men with as much ammunition as each man could carry, and with the tripod-mounted caliber .30 machine gun and the 3.5-inch bazooka. Mueller's men had another light machine gun with them. The two recoilless rifles, the 6omm mortar, the five machine guns mounted on the vehicles, and the ammunition that could not be carried, were all left on the vehicles which were abandoned on the road, their engines still running.[10]

Seven of Lieutenant Mitchell's men, all from the group of replacements, stayed in the ditch by the road. They had become frightened at the outbreak of the enemy fire, had taken cover in the ditch, and refused to leave when the other men started for the high ground. All seven were killed in the same ditch later that afternoon. With Captain Stai and his driver, nine of the original sixty men were out of action. It was after 1300. The remaining fifty-one men were climbing the steep northern side of the ridge.

The climb was agonizingly slow. Since enemy soldiers were climbing the hill on the south side of the same ridge, Mitchell's men had to stay on the north, steep, snowy side. Even so, they were under fire from several enemy riflemen and an enemy machine gun located to the north. Men from the 23d Infantry were conspicuous targets since their dark clothing made them prominent against the bright snow. Much of the way they moved on their hands and knees, pulling themselves from one scrub brush to another. Enemy fire was so accurate they would often pretend that they had been hit, deliberately roll a short distance down the hill and lie quietly until the enemy rifleman shifted his fire to someone else. They did this in spite of the extreme difficulties of carrying their heavy loads up the steep, slippery ridge.

Within a short time all of the men were wet, either from the snow or from perspiration, and several of them were injured on the way up. PFC Bobby G. Hensley, who was carrying the light machine gun and tripod on his back, stumbled and fell forward over a pointed stump, breaking several ribs. Sgt. Alfred Buchanan, who was with him, carrying four boxes of ammunition, rubbed snow in Hensley's face to revive him, and had him on his feet a few minutes later when Lieutenant Penrod came along and told Hensley to throw away the bolt and leave the machine gun. Hensley said he didn't think he could make it any farther.

"You've got to make it, son," said Penrod. "Just keep climbing."

Sergeant Buchanan left the ammunition and helped Hensley part way up the hill.

Lieutenant Mitchell also became a casualty before reaching the hill. During World War II he had received an injury to his spine, which left his back and legs weakened. Three fourths of the way up the hill one of his legs became weak and numb. Mitchell slid himself along the ground for a while but finally sat down in the snow to rest. While he was sitting by the trail a jeep driver (PFC William W. Stratton) stopped and urged Mitchell to go on. Stratton was one of the recent replacements and this was his first day in combat. When Lieutenant Mitchell explained that he couldn't move for a while, Stratton offered to stay with him. Just about this time, three Chinese riflemen appeared on top of the ridge and stopped about fifteen feet from where the two men were sitting. Mitchell was hidden partially by brush. Stratton saw them first and fired seven rounds from his rifle, missing each time. Mitchell fired one round and missed. His carbine jammed then and he had to take out his bayonet and pry the cartridge from the chamber. Meanwhile, a bullet from one of the Chinese guns hit the stock of Stratton's rifle and then his hand, tearing it badly. Then the enemy gun jammed. The other two Chinese had turned their backs and appeared to be listening to someone who was shouting to them from the opposite side of the hill. Lieutenant Mitchell finally got his carbine in operation and killed all three of the enemy. The two men slid down the hill a short distance to a small gully that offered more cover from enemy fire. Hensley (the machine gunner with the broken ribs) was already sitting in this gully, having been left there by Sergeant Buchanan. The three men sat there for about a half hour.

Except for one man, the remaining forty-eight men left in the patrol reached the crest of the hill. Sgt. John C. Gardella, loaded with machine-gun ammunition, slipped in the snow and fell down a steep part of the ridge. Since he was unable to climb back at that point, he circled to the north looking for an easier route. As it happened, he went too far north and suddenly came upon several enemy riflemen and a crew operating a machine gun. He was within twenty feet of the group before he noticed it and, although he was in heavy brush at the time and had not been seen, he was afraid to move back. He lay there for the rest of the day and throughout the night.

Lieutenant Mueller and his fourteen men were the first to reach the top of the hill. Once there, they learned that it afforded little protection from the enemy guns, which both to the north and to the south were located on higher ground. The ridge, which extended south from Hill 333, was made up of several pointed peaks connected by narrow saddles. The hill Mueller's men now occupied was approximately sixty feet lower than the top of Hill 333, nine hundred yards to the north, and a little lower than another hill not more than one hundred and fifty or two hundred yards to the south. The Chinese reached the hill to the south about the same time Lieutenant Mueller occupied the center high ground. In addition to the two narrow saddles that connected Mueller's position with the enemy-held ground both to the north and to the south, there was another narrow saddle between his hill and a smaller mound of earth to the west, on the ridge that the patrol followed toward the high ground. This mound of earth was within grenade-throwing distance. All three of these saddles were under enemy fire.

The useable area on top of the hill was so small it could have been covered by a squad tent and was tilted so that it sloped toward the east side of the hill, which was so steep that there was no danger of enemy attack from that direction. However, the hilltop was too small to accommodate all of the men, so Mueller and Penrod put some of the men along the saddle toward the north. Even then, it was crowded. There were no holes and the ground was frozen too deep to allow digging.

Enemy activity commenced almost at once, with machine-gun and rifle fire coming from both the Chinese north and south positions. The activity from the south was the more serious threat for two reasons. The enemy machine gun on the southern hill, being only slightly higher than the hilltop occupied by the American patrol, fired from a flat angle. Its beaten zone, therefore, was long and almost exactly covered the hilltop. In addition, the saddle connecting the two hills was so deep that the Chinese would be able to move under the machine-gun or other supporting fire until they were within a few yards of the patrol before they would mask their own fire. This would place them within easy grenade range. Fortunately, this same path was so narrow that the Chinese would be limited to small groups for each assault. Lieutenant Mueller, realizing that this was the critical part of his perimeter, placed his machine gun to guard this approach. (The machine gun was the only one left to the patrol by this time. There were eight BARs and the 3.5-inch bazooka.) The first enemy assault was prepared by mortar fire while the Chinese moved under the machine-gun fire until they were within easy grenade range. Mueller's men stopped it just below the rim of the perimeter with the machine gun and a concentration of BAR fire. The Chinese backed away and the enemy was comparatively inactive for about twenty minutes.

Meanwhile, the three injured men—Lieutenant Mitchell and Privates Hensley and Stratton—worked their way up on the hill to join the rest of the men in the perimeter. Stratton, pleased because he thought his shattered hand would be sufficient cause for returning home, crawled around the perimeter and showed it to some of the men.

"Give me your telephone number," he said to several of them, "and I'll call your wife when I get back to California."

Soon after the initial thrust from the south, the enemy gun to the north opened fire, wounding seven men at that end of the perimeter. The men lay as still as possible to avoid this fire, except for an eighteen-year-old squad leader (Cpl. LeRoy Gibbons) who already had been wounded six times during the Korean war. Gibbons wanted to talk with Lieutenant Mitchell, who, by this time, had reached the small, flat part of the perimeter. He stood up and walked erect through a string of tracers that went past him. Several of the men yelled at him to get down.

"Aw, hell," he said, "they couldn't hit the broad side of a barn," and continued walking.

After this demonstration, Sgt. Everett Lee decided to take the enemy gun under fire. He crawled about fifteen feet farther north, saying to the other men nearby, "I'm going to get that son of a bitch." He fired two rounds to zero in his rifle, then killed two of the men operating the machine gun. Other men near him joined in the firing and the enemy gun went quiet and did not again fire. Sergeant Lee stood up and walked back to his position on the line. This relieved much of the pressure on the north end of the line and, from then on, the main enemy efforts came from the south and from the west.

Lieutenant Mueller's machine gun, the only one to reach the top of the hill, was the main strength of the defense. Five or six separate assaults were directed against the south side of the perimeter during the afternoon. Each time the men held their fire until the enemy soldiers were within close range and then directed all available fire at the narrow enemy approach route. The machine gun was effective and Mueller's chief concern was keeping it and several BARs operating at the south end of the line. Seven men firing these weapons were either killed or wounded during the afternoon, all hit in the head. When one man was hit others would pull him back by his feet and another man would crawl forward to man the machine gun.

One of the machine gunners (Cpl. Billy B. Blizzard) raised his head not more than six inches from the ground and was struck by a bullet that went through his helmet, cutting into the top of his head.

Lieutenant Mitchell noticed Blizzard's head jerk and saw the hole suddenly appear in his helmet. He yelled to him, "You aren't hurt, son. That was a ricochet."

Corporal Blizzard turned so that his platoon leader could see the blood running across his forehead. "Like hell it's a ricochet," he said.

Mueller put another man in Blizzard's place. "For God's sake," he kept saying, "we've got to keep this gun going."

During one of the attacks, a Chinese crawled close to the perimeter, stood up and fired a continuous burst from his burp gun. He hit five men, including Mueller, before one of the Americans killed the enemy soldier.[11]

When Major Engen (executive officer of the 1st Battalion) and the liaison pilot left the Twin Tunnels area to refuel their plane, they immediately reported to the 23d Infantry that the Chinese had ambushed and surrounded Mitchell's patrol. The regimental commander (Col. Paul Freeman) immediately requested an air strike, ordered the 2d Battalion to send relief to the patrol, and directed that a liaison pilot make a drop of ammunition to the patrol.

The 2d Battalion occupied a patrol base forward of the regimental line and was already about ten miles (road distance) nearer than the remainder of the regiment. The order reached the 2d Battalion commander (Lt.Col. James W. Edwards) at 1300.[12] Colonel Edwards immediately called Capt. Stanley C. Tyrrell, whose Company F had performed a similar rescue mission the day before. Even though Company F was available at once, it required a little more than two hours to assemble the vehicles, weapons, and necessary supplies for the company, which consisted of 3 other officers and 142 enlisted men. Colonel Edwards added a section of 81mm mortars, a section of heavy machine guns from Company H, and included an artillery forward observation party because its radio was necessary for communications with the liaison plane. Thus reinforced, the total strength of the force amounted to 167 officers and men.[13]

Captain Tyrrell's mission was to rescue the ambushed patrol and to recover the bodies and the vehicles. Since darkness was not far off, Colonel Edwards instructed Tyrrell to form a defensive perimeter and proceed with the mission the following morning, if he could not gain contact with the ambushed patrol that night.[14] Company F started north at 1515.

Back at the perimeter, the afternoon wore on with occasional lulls between enemy assaults. Toward late afternoon ammunition was getting scarce and the officers kept cautioning their men to use it sparingly. Medical supplies were exhausted three and a half hours after the fighting had begun.[15] More than a third of the men had become casualties, although many of the wounded men remained in the perimeter fighting.

Private Stratton (the jeep driver with the shattered hand) had taken over a BAR from another wounded man. He fired it with his left hand. During quiet periods he crawled around the perimeter telling the other men not to worry about their situation. "We'll get out of this all right," he kept saying. However, by evening few of the men there expected to get out alive.

Lieutenant Mitchell pulled his men back several feet to the rim of the hilltop. There were advantages to this move. There, the Chinese could not spot American weapons so easily, and from the new position the Americans could not see an enemy soldier until his head appeared a few feet away. This saved ammunition since the men could not fire until they could see a Chinese head. As a frozen crust formed over the snow, the men braced themselves for the heavy blow they expected as soon as the darkness was complete. Said one of the men, "I'll see you fellows down below."

The first help for the surrounded patrol members came late in the afternoon. A Mosquito plane appeared above the patrol about 1730, just before sunset. The men watched as it circled above them and then screamed with delight when the first fighter planes appeared. Altogether they were two flights of four planes each. The first planes were jets, and they came in so low the men thought they could have touched them with the tips of their bayonets. Enemy activity stopped abruptly and, for the first time that afternoon, the men could raise their heads from the ground and move around freely in their crowded perimeter. The first planes fired machine guns and rockets. The second flight carried napalm bombs that burst into orange blossoms of flame among the enemy positions. It was excellent close support, and Lieutenant Mitchell and the members of his patrol grinned with appreciation during the half hour that it lasted.

Immediately following the air strike a liaison plane came over to drop supplies to the patrol. It made four runs over the group of men, each time flying no higher than fifteen feet above their heads, so low the men could see that the pilot had pink cheeks. And because the enemy hills were so close, the plane had to cross the enemy positions at the same height. The pilot dropped thirty bandoleers of rifle ammunition, two cases of machine-gun ammunition and several belts of carbine cartridges and then, on the last run, an envelope to which was fastened a long, yellow streamer. Except for one box of machine-gun ammunition, all of this fell beyond the tiny perimeter and, now that the air strike was over, in an area that was under enemy fire. Nevertheless, several men dashed out to retrieve everything that was close.

A young soldier raced after the message, which fell well down on the eastern slope, and took it back to Lieutenant Mitchell. The message said, "Friendly column approaching from the south. Will be with you shortly." Mitchell read it and then crawled around the perimeter to show it to the rest of the men.[16]

About the same time, there was the sound of firing to the south. A few minutes later mortar rounds exploded on the top of Hill 453. Hopes of survival soared suddenly and the men shouted for joy. This, they decided, was the friendly relief column.

The airplanes left just as darkness began to set in, and Mitchell and Mueller warned their men to expect an enemy assault just as soon as it got dark. They also told the men not to yell out if they were hit because they did not dare let the Chinese know how many of the group were wounded.

Several mortar shells fell in the area, and one exploded in the center of the crowded perimeter, wounding one man seriously. The Chinese added automatic-weapons and rifle fire, building up the volume fast. There was the sound of bugles and of enemy voices and, between bursts of enemy fire, the sound of enemy soldiers walking over the crusted snow. Four men crawled forward until they could see the enemy approaching across the narrow saddle from the south. One of them, Sgt. Donald H. Larson, began yelling: "Here they come! Here they come!" They opened fire but within a few seconds all four of the men were hit. They crawled back.

Sergeant Larson pointed to his head wound—his fifth for the day— as he crawled past Lieutenant Mitchell. "That's enough for me," he said.

The situation was grim. The fire fight that had flared up in the vicinity of Hill 453 had stopped, and there was now no evidence of friendly troops nearby. Gradually, the men who had been looking anxiously toward the area from which Captain Tyrrell's men had been firing lost their hope of getting out of their perimeter. It was colder now. Their wet clothing was freezing to the ground. Several men were suffering from frostbite. More than half were casualties. Those with serious wounds had been dragged to the rear (east) part of the hilltop where they were laid on the frozen earth. The hill was so steep there that if grenades were dropped they would roll on down the hill away from the wounded men.

Those men who were less seriously wounded kept firing on the line or loading magazines for automatic rifles and carbines. One man with a large hole in his stomach loaded ammunition for an hour and a half before he died.[17] Lieutenant Mueller, who had been wounded earlier when a bullet struck his leg, was hit a second time—this time in the head—injuring his left eye. He began to see flashes of light and occasionally lost consciousness.[18]

Instead of the expected help, a second night attack hit Mitchell's patrol. It began with the usual mortar and machine-gun fire, worked up to grenade range, but again stopped a few feet from the edge of the perimeter when faced by the concentrated fire at the south end—fire from the machine gun and from several BARs. Private Stratton fired one of the automatic rifles with his left hand. When the Chinese were close, he stood on the rim of the perimeter, leveled his BAR at them and emptied the magazine. He was hit a second time, this time through the chest. Someone pulled him back toward the center of the perimeter. Soon afterwards a grenade exploded between his legs. Stratton screamed.

"For God's sake," said Mitchell, "shut up!"

"My legs have just been shot off," Stratton complained.

"I know it," the Lieutenant answered, "but shut up anyway."

Soon after this Stratton was wounded a fourth time, and died.[19]

While all of these events were taking place on the hill, Captain Tyrrell's rescue mission was progressing even though Mitchell's men could see no action. Company F had arrived in the Twin Tunnels area between 1720 and 1730—as the air strike was in progress and a few minutes before darkness. The vehicular column of eight ¾-ton trucks and thirteen jeeps, with all of the trucks and some of the jeeps pulling trailers loaded with extra mortar and recoilless rifle ammunition, followed the same road used by the patrol. While the column was en route, an observer in a liaison plane dropped a message giving the exact location of the ambushed patrol, its vehicles, and also several positions where he had observed groups of enemy soldiers in that vicinity.

Nothing important happened until the two jeeps that formed the point of the column were within one hundred or two hundred yards of the ford near which Captain Stai had disappeared earlier in the day. Two machine guns on Hill 453 opened fire on the jeeps, bringing them to a quick halt. The occupants scrambled into the ditch for protection.

Captain Tyrrell, in the third jeep, soon appeared. He dismounted and walked back toward the rest of the column while his driver, already in the ditch, called after him, "You'd better get in the ditch, Captain. The Chinks will get you."

Tyrrell walked on back toward the 2d Platoon, which was next in column. "To hell with the Chinks," he said.[20]

Deciding he could not proceed to the patrol with enemy machine gunners in his rear and riflemen on the highest hill in the area, Tyrrell hurriedly prepared to attack Hill 453. He ordered his 2d Platoon to dismount and lay down a base of fire to support an attack by the other two platoons. The 2d Platoon was firing rifles at Hill 453 within three to five minutes after the Chinese began firing. In the haze of dusk, Tyrrell sent his other two platoons toward the top of the hill, attacking up two of three spur ridges which extended generally east from Hill 453 and ended abruptly at the road. The heavy-machine-gun section was in action by the time the infantrymen started up the steep ridgeline, and before they had gone far the 81mm mortar section began firing. Captain Tyrrell told the mortar crew to plaster the hill during the attack, moving the shell bursts up the ridgeline just in front of the advancing platoons. All of this had taken place in no more than twenty minutes, and in the midst of brisk enemy fire.[21]

The first sergeant of Company F, in the meantime, had all vehicles turned around and parked in a closed column near the mortar section so that the drivers and other men not actively engaged at the time could guard both the mortar section and the vehicles.

There was no fight for the top of Hill 453; the Chinese abandoned it and fell back in front of the mortar and machine-gun fire. In fact, enemy fire fell off sharply after the first half hour, and thereafter there was negligible opposition. Darkness, however, retarded the advance, which was already difficult and tedious because of the snow and the steepness of the ridge. It took two hours or longer for the 1st Platoon—the one that attacked straight west—to gain the top of Hill 453. Once there, Captain Tyrrell told it to form a hasty perimeter for the defense of the hilltop and then send one squad south to contact the other platoon, which was coming up along the southern of the three spur ridges, thus making certain that the top of the hill was free of enemy soldiers. At 2030 these two platoons made contact.[22]

From the hill to the north came the sounds of grenade explosions and heavy firing as another enemy attack fell against Lieutenant Mitchell's patrol.

Having secured Hill 453 and eliminated the threat from his rear, Tyrrell was ready to go ahead with his original mission. His 2d Platoon, which had been in support so far, was on the road and ready to head straight north toward the surrounded patrol just as soon as the rest of the company could be maneuvered into place to support the attack. By radio Captain Tyrrell ordered one of the platoons on Hill 453 to return to the road by the most direct route, and told the other one to move northeast to a point approximately two thirds of the way down the northernmost of the three spur ridges from that hill mass. When this platoon reached a position from which it could support the 2d Platoon by fire, it was to hold in place. He also sent the heavy-machine-gun section up the northern ridgeline to join the platoon that was to form the base of fire.[23]

This re-positioning of his force required time, and in the meanwhile Tyrrell went to the area of his 2d Platoon to work out the complete plans for its advance and to make certain that all men of the platoon knew of the movements of the other platoons so that units of his company would not get into a fire fight among themselves. Having done this, he walked off to choose new positions east of the road for the heavy mortars, which he intended to displace forward. It was, by this time, 2100 or later.

While Tyrrell was thus engaged, he heard a voice coming from the direction of Sinchon: "Hey, are you GIs?" It sounded like an American voice.

Captain Tyrrell called back, "Who are you?" and received an answer that they were three wounded Americans.

Returning to the road, he alerted the platoon there to the possibility of some incident occurring on its right flank, moved a squad into position about a hundred yards east of the road and then, with his runner and radio operator, walked forward toward the direction from which the sound of the voice had come. They stopped at a ditch and Tyrrell called for one man to come forward to be recognized. Someone answered, claiming they could not come forward separately since two of them were wounded—one seriously—and could not walk alone. Tyrrell, by this time reasonably certain that they were Americans, told them to come forward together. It was so dark that Tyrrell could distinguish objects only a few yards away and although he could see nothing, he could hear the three men stumbling through the crusted snow. He saw them first when they were only a few yards away, halted them, and asked who they were.

The three men explained that they were members of Mitchell's patrol. They had escaped from the perimeter and had made their way down the steep east side of the hill to the railroad tracks, which they had followed south. All of them appeared to be excited and suffering from exhaustion. One was bleeding badly. Tyrrell told them to get into the ditch with him and remain quiet while he listened for the sound of any enemy soldiers who, he thought, might have followed them. The six men sat quietly. There was no sound anywhere in the area, only darkness and stillness. After several minutes of waiting, they returned to the road and the area of the 2d Platoon.[24]

Everyone else in the patrol, according to the three men who reached Company F, was dead. They described the last attack which ended with Chinese swarming over their perimeter, shooting and throwing grenades. Only the three of them had escaped and there was nothing on the hill now, they claimed, but "hundreds of Chinese." Although Captain Tyrrell questioned them in detail, they were emphatic in stating that the entire patrol had been overrun and all members had been killed.[25]

The last fire fight on the hill had ended abruptly after what seemed to Tyrrell like a half hour of heavy fighting. He now decided to wait until morning before continuing, since his battalion commander had told him that if he could not make contact with the patrol before dark, to form a defensive perimeter until morning to prevent falling into an enemy trap or getting into a fire fight with friendly troops. He advised his platoon leaders of the change in plan.[26]

Ten or fifteen minutes later the leader of the 1st Platoon (Lt. Leonard Napier), which was moving down the northern ridge from Hill 453 with the mission of establishing the base of fire for the next attack, called his company commander by radio.

"If you had talked with a man who just came into my position," he told Tyrrell, "you wouldn't believe the patrol was wiped out."

This was Lieutenant Mueller's aid man who had run out of medical supplies during the afternoon and had left the perimeter after dark to try to get back to the vehicles where he hoped to find more supplies. For some unaccountable reason, he had gone too far south and there encountered Napier's platoon. Captain Tyrrell, questioning the medic over the radio, learned that the patrol was still holding at the time he left, even though three fourths of the men were casualties.[27]

At once, Tyrrell issued new orders for his 2d Platoon (Lt. Albert E. Jones) to head north up the end of the long ridge toward the ambushed patrol. In the path of this platoon were three high points on the same ridge-line. Moving as quietly as possible, without preparatory or supporting fires, Lieutenant Jones and his platoon started forward, experiencing only the difficulties of moving and maintaining contact over steep terrain. They could hear another fire fight starting at the perimeter. They reached the first knob an hour later. The next knob ahead was the one from which most of the Chinese attacks had originated. Beyond that was the slightly lower knob where the patrol itself was located. There was no firing going on at the time Jones's 2d Platoon arrived at the southernmost knoll. Afraid that he might be walking into an ambush with his own platoon, he halted and then decided to go forward with one squad while the rest of his men formed a defensive perimeter.[28]

Several hours had passed since Company F had done any firing. To the surviving members of Mitchell's patrol there was no evidence of the promised rescue. Enemy attacks, however, continued. Between first darkness and about 2100, the enemy made four separate assaults, all of them against the south end of the perimeter. It was the last of these that Captain Tyrrell had heard end abruptly while he was waiting for two of his platoons to get into position. Like the others, this attempt was preceded by heavy machine-gun and rifle fire with a few men making the final assault. It was broken up by Cpl. Jesus A. Sanchez, one of Lieutenant Mueller's men from 21st Infantry. Sanchez loaded two BAR magazines, waited until the Chinese were almost upon them, then jumped up and forward a few feet, and emptied both magazines at the Chinese. He ran back and lay down again.

There was respite for an hour before the enemy struck again, this time as Lieutenant Jones's platoon began moving north. For this assault the Chinese shifted to the small mound just west of Mitchell's hill, and attacked from that direction. Ten or fifteen enemy soldiers crawled up under the mortar and machine-gun fire and attempted to overrun the American position. Since Lieutenant Mueller's machine gun was still guarding the south end of the line, five men with rifles and automatic carbines waited until the Chinese were at the rim of their perimeter, then fired at full rate for a minute or less. There was another brief lull before the Chinese made one more assault. This time three enemy soldiers succeeded in getting into the perimeter where they caused considerable confusion in the darkness. One Chinese soldier stood erect among Lieutenant Mitchell's men.

"Get the son of a bitch!" one of them yelled.

Several men fired at once, killing him. They killed another one who appeared immediately afterwards. A third Chinese walked up to within a few feet of SFC Odvin A. Martinson (Mueller's platoon sergeant) and fired at him with a burp gun. Sergeant Martinson, who already had been wounded five times that day, fired back with a pistol. Neither of them hit the other. PFC Thomas J. Mortimer, who was lying on the ground immediately behind the Chinese soldier, raised up and stuck a bayonet into his back as someone else shot him from the front. Sergeant Martinson picked up the body and threw it out of the perimeter.

"I don't want them in here," he said, "dead or alive."

The time was now 2230. There were between 27 and 30 wounded men in the perimeter, including those who were unable to fight, and several others, like Martinson, who had been wounded but were able to keep fighting. Lieutenant Mueller, having become conscious again, kept experiencing flashes of light in front of one eye. Ammunition was nearly gone, the effective strength of the patrol was low, and several doubted if they could hold off another attack. A few of the men wanted to surrender.

"Surrender hell!" said Sergeant Martinson who was, by this time, thoroughly angry.

Two red flares appeared toward the west and thereafter it was quiet. The patrol members waited for a half hour or longer while nothing happened. Then they heard footsteps again, the same sound of men approaching over frozen snow. This time the sound came from the south again. When the footsteps sounded close, Lieutenant Mitchell's men opened fire.

"GIs!" someone below yelled. "Don't shoot! GIs!"

For several seconds no one spoke or moved. Finally Corporal Sanchez called down, "Who won the Rose Bowl game?"

There was silence again for a few seconds until someone below called, "Fox Company, 23d Infantry, by God!"

Lieutenant Jones and his squad from Company F moved on up, following the same snow-beaten path over which the Chinese attacked during the afternoon and evening. Sanchez, the BAR man, stood up.

"We're relieved, fellows!" he yelled. "We're relieved!"

The others who could also stood up and, from then on, they disregarded the Chinese who had, apparently, moved back for the night.

A thin moon came up and furnished a little light, which made the evacuation of the wounded men easier. Nevertheless, it required more than three hours to move everyone off of the hill. Corporal Sanchez took charge of the top of the hill and supervised the evacuation from that end, searching the hill to be certain no living men were left behind, and emptying the pockets of the dead.[29]

Some of the men whose wounds were not serious complained about the cold and the hardships of walking over the difficult terrain in the dark, but those men who were wounded seriously expressed only their gratitude, and tried to help themselves. Sergeant Martinson, with five bullet wounds, left the litters for the other men and hobbled out with two other men. Private Hensley, who broke several ribs while climbing the hill at the beginning of the action and had received help himself at that time, now helped carry another man down the hill. It was 0330, 30 January, before Company F men had carried down all surviving members of the patrol. Captain Tyrrell gave the word to move out and the column started south with one platoon of Company F marching ahead of the column and another following on foot behind the trucks.[30]

The sun came up as the column reached Iho-ri.

★ DISCUSSION

An army is a team. It is composed of many subordinate teams, called organizations or units, which make up the whole. An army operates by teamwork.

Only under extreme circumstances should subordinate units be broken up and teamwork jeopardized.

The patrol to the Twin Tunnels area was not a team. It had a rifle platoon, three drivers from another battalion, radio operators from an artillery battalion, attached heavy-weapons men, fourteen men from a platoon of another division, and an extra captain. Eleven All Stars do not make a football team until they have worked together. Fifty-six men and four officers do not make a patrol.

Security for a motorized patrol may be provided by speed, by regulated movement, by reconnaissance and observation to the front and flanks, and by the use of a proper formation. Either this account lacks detail or the patrol commander depended almost entirely on speed. No mention is made of movement by bounds from one position of observation to another. No patrols or individuals were sent out from the column to reconnoiter. No system of observation from within the column is described. The patrol leader—more courageously than wisely—is a part of the sole security element—four men in a jeep a hundred yards ahead of the main body.

It is doubtful, although the patrol followed the same route as a patrol on the preceding day, that the Chinese had prepared an ambush. A more probable explanation is that the patrol blundered into Chinese forces moving into or through the area. By any standards an organized ambush when sprung should have placed more immediate and more destructive fire on any inclosed patrol. If the enemy is to be credited with skillfully executing an ambush he must be criticized for permitting his prey to escape. If the enemy had not prepared an ambush, then he must be commended for his prompt and vigorous reaction.

In spite of the organizational handicap facing the patrol leader, he had almost unanimous support in his obviously good plan to break out of an awkward position. Only unity of effort and courageous leadership saved the patrol until a well-coordinated and skillfully executed attack by the Company C *team* relieved it.

★ NOTES

1. 23d Infantry Regiment: S2 journal, entry 22, 27 January 1951; 23d Infantry Regiment: special report, Patrol Ambush and Rescue Action, 29 January 1951 (hereafter cited as 23d Infantry: Patrol Ambush).

2. 23d Infantry: Patrol Ambush.

3. 2d Infantry Division: G3 journal and file, entry 107, 28 January 1951.

4. Unless otherwise mentioned, the account of the Twin Tunnels patrol action is based upon interviews by the author with the following officers and men who participated in the action: Lt. James P. Mitchell, Lt. William G. Penrod, PFC Bobby G. Hensley, Cpl. Billy B. Blizzard, PFC Thomas J. Mortimer, PFC Bernard L. Dunlap, and Sgt. John C. Gardella.

5. Major Millard O. Engen: comments and notes. Major Engen was executive officer of the 1st Battalion, 23d Infantry, at the time of the patrol action.

6. Engen, *op. cit.*

7. An enemy radio broadcast made in March or April 1951 mentioned a Capt. Melvin R. Stai, claiming he was a prisoner of the Chinese Communists.

8. Engen, *op. cit.*

9. Statement of Lt. Harold P. Mueller. Lieutenant Mueller and his men reached the top of this hill some time before the men from the 23d Infantry.

10. Although several reports indicate these vehicles were destroyed before they were abandoned, Lieutenants Mitchell and Penrod, in Twin Tunnels interviews, say they were not destroyed then, and that the engines were left running since they thought there was a possibility that they might later escape and need the vehicles. The next day (30 January) the 2d Division requested and got an air strike to destroy the vehicles. See Capt. William G. Penrod, letter to the author, 6 May 1953; also 2d Division: G3 journal and file, entry 36, 30 January 1951.

11. Lt. Harold P. Mueller, letter to the author, 30 January 1952.

12. The narrative of the action of Company F, 23d Infantry, is based on an account by Lt.Col. James W. Edwards, CO, 2d Battalion, "Patrolling at Twin Tunnels," and upon two letters from Major Stanley C. Tyrrell to Major Leonard O. Friesz, dated 5 March and 9 September 1952. These letters were written in answer to questions submitted by OCMH.

13. Statement of Lt.Col. James W. Edwards.

14. Tyrrell, *op. cit.*, 5 March 1952.

15. Mueller, *op. cit.*

16. Statement of Lt. Harold P. Mueller.

17. Mueller, *op. cit.*

18. *Ibid.*

19. In order that his family may not suffer unnecessary anguish, "Stratton" has been substituted for the real name of this brave soldier.

20. Edwards, *op. cit.*

21. Tyrrell, *op. cit.*, 9 September 1952.

22. *Ibid.*

23. *Ibid.*

24. *Ibid.*

25. Tyrrell, *op. cit.*, 5 March and 9 September 1952.

26. *Ibid.*

27. *Ibid.*

28. Edwards, *op. cit.*, p. 11.

29. Mueller, *op. cit.*

30. Tyrrell, *op. cit.*, 9 September 1952.

*It appears that it is as necessary to provide sol-
diers with defensive arms of every kind as to in-
struct them in the use of offensive ones. For it is
certain a man will fight with greater courage and
confidence when he finds himself properly armed
for defense.*

VEGETIUS: MILITARY INSTITUTIONS OF THE ROMANS

8

Chipyong-ni

★ Chipyong-ni was defended because the commanding general of Eighth Army (Lt.Gen. Matthew B. Ridgway) decided to make a
stand there against the Chinese Communists. In the chronology of Korean
battles, the fighting for Chipyong-ni followed the withdrawal from northern Korea at the end of 1950, a brief Eighth Army offensive that began on
5 February 1951, and a full-scale Chinese counteroffensive that struck a
week later.

The 23d Regimental Combat Team made the decisive defense of
Chipyong-ni on 13 and 14 February 1951. This action followed the patrol
ambush and the subsequent battle for the Twin Tunnels area—some high
ground three miles southeast of Chipyong-ni. After the Twin Tunnels
operation, the 23d Infantry Regiment (2d Infantry Division) proceeded
on the afternoon of 3 February to the town of Chipyong-ni and set up a
perimeter defense. Chipyong-ni was a small crossroads town half a mile
long and several blocks wide, situated on a single-track railroad. Besides
the railway station there were several other brick or frame buildings in the
center of the town, but most of the buildings were constructed of the usual
mud, sticks, and straw. At least half of the buildings were already reduced
to rubble as the result of previous fighting in the town.

Encircling Chipyong-ni were eight prominent hills that rose to an
average height of 850 feet above the rice paddies and buildings in the
valley. These hills provided excellent defensive positions, but to have occupied
them would have stretched the front-line defensive positions along 12 miles
of ridgelines and formed a perimeter with a 3- to 4-mile diameter. Instead,

the regimental commander (Col. Paul L. Freeman) stationed his infantry-men on lower ground around a tight perimeter about a mile in diameter. On three sides of the town the line followed small hills; on the northwest section the infantrymen dug their holes across a half-mile strip of rice paddies.

During the ten days after going into position at Chipyong-ni, Colonel Freeman's regiment dug in and strengthened its positions. The 37th Field Artillery Battalion (attached to the regiment) arrived on 5 February. Battery B, 82d Antiaircraft Artillery Automatic Weapons Battalion, joined the regiment, adding six M16 and four M19 flakwagons to the defense of the town. Several days later Battery B, 503d Field Artillery Battalion (a 155mm howitzer unit), was attached to reinforce the fires of the 37th Field Artillery Battalion.[1]

The infantry companies dug in their machine guns, registered their mortars, sowed antipersonnel mines, and operated daily patrols to the en-compassing high ground. The regimental Heavy-Mortar Company divided the fires of its platoons and sections among the sectors of the perimeter, the artillery registered on all probable avenues of enemy approach, and all units established good communications lines. There was time to coordinate the infantry, artillery, and air support into an effective combat team.[2]

This narrative describes the fighting for Chipyong-ni that occurred in that sector of the 2d Battalion's perimeter defended by Company G, 23d Infantry. As it happened, the howitzers of Battery B, 503d Field Artillery Battalion, were in position at the bottom of Company G's hill so that the artillerymen were drawn into the same battle. The commander of the 2d Battalion (Lt.Col. James W. Edwards) placed all three of his rifle companies on the front line to cover the sector assigned to his battalion. This was the south rim of the perimeter. Within the companies, two company com-manders committed their three rifle platoons. The other company (F), to which Colonel Edwards assigned the center and smallest sector, manned its part of the line with only two platoons, leaving its support platoon as the battalion reserve.[3]

The narrow supply road leading southwest from Chipyong-ni went under the railroad on the south edge of the town and then, within a third of a mile, passed two embankments of red clay where the road cut through the two ends of a U-shaped hill. Company G started at the second of these two road cuts and extended left (east) along the southern side of the U. It was not much of a hill—only a couple of contour lines on the map. In-fantrymen could climb the smooth hump of earth in a few minutes. The 1st Platoon of Company G held the right end of the hill next to the road cut. The 3d Platoon had the center position (the highest part of the hill) and extended its line left to the bend of the U. The 2d Platoon was down in the rice paddies between the 3d Platoon and Company F.[4]

Men from the two platoons on the hill dug their holes just over the top of the forward slope. The positions restricted the fields of fire somewhat but provided good observation, especially for the 3d Platoon, which could see all areas to the south except for a dead spot in a dry creek bed just in front of its right flank.

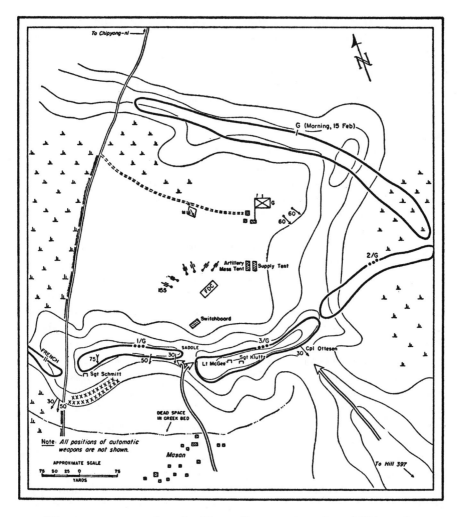

There were two other significant features near the 3d Platoon's area. At the foot of the hill and just beyond the dry creek bed was a cluster of 15 or 20 buildings that made up the village of Masan. The second feature was a narrow spur of ground that formed a link between the 3d Platoon's hill and a large hill mass to the south. The 2d Platoon in the rice paddies lacked satisfactory observation but had good fields of fire across the flat land to its immediate front.

In addition to its own Weapons Platoon, Company G's supporting weapons included a section of 75mm recoilless rifles, a section of heavy machine guns from Company H, and a platoon of 81mm mortars which was dug in near the edge of the town and had a forward observer stationed with Company G. There were also forward observers from the regimental Heavy-Mortar Company and from the 37th Field Artillery Battalion with Company G. During the daytime men from the 75mm recoilless rifle section manned their weapons, but at night they replaced them with two caliber .50 machine guns to prevent having their positions disclosed at night by the back-blasts of the recoilless rifles.[5]

The Ammunition and Pioneer Platoon set up two fougasses (drums of napalm), the first on the road just south of the road cut, and the second in the rice paddies in front of the 2d Platoon. The 1st Platoon, which was next to the road, also strung barbed-wire entanglements across the road and in front of its position. There was not enough wire available to reach across the company front.[6] Colonel Edwards supervised the siting of all weapons, and the digging of the holes which he insisted be of the standing type and deep enough for good cover.

When Battery B, 503d Field Artillery Battalion, arrived, its 155mm howitzers went into position in the small bowl formed by the U-shaped ridge of which Company G occupied one side. The howitzers were laid by platoon to support the east, north, and west sectors of the regimental perimeter. To the rear of the howitzers, the artillerymen set up a tent for the fire direction center (FDC) personnel. Behind that, near the bottom of Company G's hill, were several other tents for the mess and supply sections. A liaison officer from the 37th Field Artillery Battalion to Battery B (Capt. John A. Elledge), and the commander of Company G (Lt. Thomas Heath) worked out a plan for joint defense of the sector. This plan provided for the use of the artillery's machine guns on the front line and, if necessary, the use of some artillerymen as riflemen while skeleton crews manned the howitzers. The two officers also set up an infantry-artillery machine-gun post in the road cut with a six-man crew to operate two machine guns—one caliber .50 and one caliber .30. This road cut was also the dividing line between Colonel Edwards's 2d Battalion sector and that of the French Battalion (a regular battalion of the 23d Infantry).

In the meantime, while the 23d RCT built up its defenses, an Eighth Army general offensive got under way on 5 February with X Corps, in the center of the line, attacking to make a double envelopment of the town of Hongchon, an important enemy build-up area. The attack moved slowly until the night of 11 February, when the Chinese launched a full-scale counteroffensive with two columns driving south aimed at the towns of Hoengsong and Wonju in X Corps' sector.[7] The vigorous enemy attack drove through two ROK divisions and turned the United Nations' attack into a withdrawal that rolled the front lines south between 5 and 20 miles.[8] Before the Chinese attack, the front lines of X Corps were well ahead of

Colonel Freeman's Chipyong-ni perimeter, but as the units went south, sometimes fighting through enemy roadblocks, Chipyong-ni became a conspicuous bulge on the left of the corps' line.

At the 23d Infantry's perimeter, the usual patrols for the daylight hours of 13 February reported increased enemy activity crowding close to Chipyong-ni on three sides—north, east, and west. The Air Force observation plane operating with the RCT reported enemy groups moving toward the perimeter from the north and east. Observers called for artillery fire against those enemy columns within reach, while the tactical air control party directed forty flights of aircraft against other enemy groups beyond artillery range.[9]

Another indication of enemy strength and dispositions came from the 2d Division's Reconnaissance Company. Reinforced by a rifle company, it was ordered on the morning of 13 February to patrol the road from Iho-ri straight north to Chipyong-ni—a distance of 15 to 18 miles. Even on this road there were Chinese in sufficient strength to halt this force and turn it back.[10]

Faced with this growing threat of encirclement, Colonel Freeman wanted to give up his positions and go back to Yoju, fifteen miles south. The commander of X Corps (Maj.Gen. Edward M. Almond) flew into Chipyong-ni by helicopter at noon on 13 February and discussed with Colonel Freeman the advisability of such a withdrawal—a move that had the approval of the corps and division commanders. At noon Colonel Freeman recommended that his regiment go south on the following morning (14 February). However, within an hour and a half after General Almond returned to his command post to relay this recommendation to General Ridgway, Colonel Freeman changed his mind and his recommendation. The report from the 2d Division's Reconnaissance Company describing enemy opposition to movement on the main supply road south convinced Freeman that it would be better to leave as soon as possible, and he presented his request to division headquarters. In the meantime, however, General Almond had submitted the original recommendation and request—to leave Chipyong-ni on the following morning—to General Ridgway. General Ridgway adamantly refused permission to abandon Chipyong-ni.[11]

Colonel Freeman immediately started to strengthen his position. He asked for air strikes and airdrops for the next day, set up a secondary perimeter to be manned at night by a company of engineers, positioned his tanks near the outer perimeter, and ordered all gaps mined or blocked by lanes of machine-gun fire.[12] During the early part of the evening of 13 February, Colonel Freeman called his unit commanders together to warn them that the movement of enemy troops probably meant that they would soon be surrounded and attacked by the Chinese.

"We'll stay here and fight it out," he said.[13]

The early part of the evening was quiet. At Battery B's position Lt. Robert L. Peters was sitting in a tent writing a letter. The battery executive (Lt. Randolph McKinney) went to bed after having decided to remove his shoes but to sleep in his clothes in case troubled started. Most of the men of Battery B were inexperienced replacements who had joined the battery after the action at Kunu-ri, where more than half of the men and all equipment had been lost. Before Lieutenant Peters finished his letter he heard a burst of fire from what seemed like several thousand yards away. He stepped outside to look. To the southwest he could see what appeared to be six torches along a trail leading from a large hill. In a short time the machine-gunners in the road cut opened fire at figures they could distinguish moving across the rice paddies to the south. Peters called back to Lieutenant McKinney: "Get up, McKinney; this is *it!*"

On the east end of Company G's sector, PFC Donald E. Nelson and Pvt. Jack Ward (members of the 2d Platoon) were sitting in their foxhole in the rice paddy arguing over which one of them had to stay awake during the first part of the night. The company was required to be on a fifty per cent alert at all times, which meant that one man in each foxhole had to be awake while the other slept. Suddenly they heard the sound of digging. It sounded as if it were several hundred yards away.

Soon after this, two squads of Chinese soldiers attacked the center of Company G's line, hitting its 3d Platoon (Lt. Paul J. McGee). One of these enemy squads crawled along the spur of ground that led to the center of the 3d Platoon's position. The enemy threw three grenades at a machine gun manned by Cpl. Eugene L. Ottesen, and then opened with rifles. Corporal Ottesen began firing his machine gun. The other enemy squad, two hundred yards to the west, taking advantage of the dead spot in the dry creek bed, climbed the hill and attacked the 3d Platoon at the point where it joined the 1st Platoon. It was about 2200 when the first firing broke out.

Hearing the firing, PFC Herbert G. Ziebell awakened his foxhole buddy (PFC Roy F. Benoit) and said: "There's some firing going on. Get up and get ready."

Ziebell did not fire immediately because he could see nothing to shoot, and he was afraid the flash of his rifle would draw enemy fire. Along the line other men heard the firing and sat in the darkness waiting for the attack.

When Lieutenant McGee heard Corporal Ottesen's machine gun open fire he immediately telephoned his company commander (Lieutenant Heath). He then called his squad leaders by sound-powered telephone and informed them of the attack. In order to conserve ammunition, he ordered his men to fire only when they could see the enemy. Apparently making only a probing attack, the enemy withdrew after a few minutes. Except for some firing by the 2d Platoon, there was a lull for about an hour.

Around 2300 a Chinese squad worked up close to the center of the 3d Platoon. An enemy tossed a grenade in the hole of one of Lieutenant McGee's squad leaders (Cpl. James C. Mougeat), wounding him.

Corporal Mougeat crawled out of his hole and, shouting, "Lieutenant McGee, I'm hit!" started west along the hilltop toward the platoon's command post, twenty yards away.

The enemy threw several grenades at him, one of which knocked his rifle from his hand and tore off the stock. Fortunately for Mougeat, two men from his squad shot the Chinese. Recovering his damaged rifle, Corporal Mougeat ran on to the command post. There Lieutenant McGee calmed him down, and Mougeat decided to return to his squad.

"I'm not hit bad," he said.

Lieutenant McGee was watching several men about twenty yards below the platoon's position. One of them called his name.

"Who is that?" he asked a BAR man beside him.

"It's a Chink," the BAR man said.

McGee tossed a grenade down the hill. The explosion apparently wounded the enemy soldier who rolled down the slope. Lieutenant McGee borrowed the BAR and killed him.

Main activity near Battery B's position centered around the machine guns at the road cut. As soon as these began firing, one of the artillery officers (Lt. John E. Travis) and his machine-gun sergeant (Cpl. William H. Pope) grabbed several boxes of ammunition and went to the road cut. The rice paddies in front of these machine guns were completely covered with snow. On previous nights when Travis had gone there to check the position, that area had been smooth and white, but now there were lines of dark forms moving across the fields. They were barely visible in the dark but appeared plainly when illuminating flares hung over the area.

Lieutenant Travis and Corporal Pope had been at the outpost position only a short time when a mortar shell exploded in the cut, killing the two men closest to them, and wounding six, including Travis and Pope. Travis headed for the fire direction center tent and began yelling for some men to help—six to man the machine guns and another six to carry back the wounded.

Captain Elledge (the liaison officer) gathered up ten men and told them to follow. Enemy mortar shells were also falling in the battery's area at this time so that the artillerymen, most of whom were in action for the first time, were reluctant to leave their holes. Five of the men followed Captain Elledge; the others dropped off on the way and went back to their foxholes. When they reached the outpost position, the caliber .50 machine gun was jamming, so Captain Elledge and PFC Leslie Alston returned for another gun, carrying one of the wounded men back as they went. They then made several trips between the battery's position and the outpost, carrying ammunition out and wounded men back.

These two machine guns fired steadily for several hours, although no close action developed until about 0200 on 14 February when a platoon-sized group of Chinese made an attack against the French Battalion just to the right of the machine-gun outpost. The enemy soldiers formed one hundred or two hundred yards in front of the small hill which the French occupied, then launched their attack, blowing whistles and bugles, and running with bayonets fixed. When this noise started, the French soldiers began cranking a hand siren they had, and one squad started running toward the Chinese, yelling and throwing grenades far to the front and to the side. When the two forces were within twenty yards of each other the Chinese suddenly turned and ran in the opposite direction. It was all over within a minute. After this incident it was relatively quiet in the rice paddies near the road cut.

The firing battery, meanwhile, kept up a normal volume of harassing and interdiction fire, and also fired an illuminating round every five minutes for the sector on the opposite side of the regimental perimeter. The gun sections had L-shaped trenches near their howitzers where the men stayed until Lieutenant Peters or Lieutenant McKinney called out a fire mission.

During the night the enemy, signalling with whistles and horns, launched four separate attacks against Lieutenant Heath's company. Most of the action fell against the 3d Platoon. Toward morning the artillery battery commander (Lt. Arthur Rochnowski) sent twenty men up to help on Company G's line.

At first light on the morning of 14 February, there were Chinese near the front line in front of the 3d and the 1st Platoons, although only three enemy soldiers actually reached it. One of these was killed and the other two captured soon afterward. Five or six Chinese remained near the road cut machine-gun outpost until daylight, then tried to crawl back across the rice paddies. At the limiting point between the 1st and the 3d Platoons, which had been under enemy pressure for several hours, a small group withdrew, leaving 12 or 15 bodies on the south slope of the hill. The platoon sergeant of the 3d Platoon (Sgt. Bill C. Kluttz), in a foxhole next to the one occupied by Lieutenant McGee, spotted several Chinese in the creek bed just in front. He fired several times at them. Suspecting the presence of other Chinese, Lieutenant McGee ordered him to have the rocket launcher fired into the creek bed. Sergeant Kluttz fired the launcher himself. The rocket hit a tree, making an air burst over the creek bed. About forty Chinese came out of the creek bed and began running across the rice paddies in front of the 1st Platoon, which opened fire on them. By the time it was completely light, all enemy activity had stopped.

During the day of 14 February, the artillerymen and infantrymen rebuilt their defenses in preparation for another attack. At 0900 Lieutenant McGee took out a patrol which captured 5 Chinese hiding in a culvert and 7 others who were wounded and lying in the rice paddies south of the company's position. McGee counted 18 enemy bodies. Near Masan, he walked up to a small haystack. Near it was an abandoned enemy machine gun. As a wounded Chinese raised up in the haystack to shoot the platoon leader, Sergeant Kluttz shot and killed the enemy soldier. Another Chinese, although handicapped by a badly wounded leg, was still trying to operate a Soviet burp gun when Cpl. Boleslaw M. Sander killed him.

Captain Elledge and several other artillerymen set out to examine the area around the battery's position. Eight hundred yards west of the machine guns in the road cut, there was a house that Captain Elledge decided should be destroyed before the Chinese could occupy it if they attacked that night. Since the house was visible from the howitzer position, the 5th Section (Sgt. James Webb) took it under direct fire, using white phosphorus shells. After the third round the house began burning, and about fifteen enemy soldiers ran from it across the flat ground. The two machine-gunners and men from the French Battalion killed eight of them; the other Chinese escaped.

During the day the artillerymen dug new and deeper holes and personnel trenches around the howitzers, since they found many of the holes they had dug unsatisfactory during the first night's attack. The battery commander also relaid his howitzers so that, instead of the usual two platoons of three howitzers each, they were laid in pairs. The two howitzers on the left were laid on an azimuth of 5,600 mils, the center laid on 6,400 mils, and those on the right were laid on 800 mils. The normal volume of harassing fires was scheduled for the night of 14 February, about 250 rounds for the battery.

During the afternoon the commander of Company G (Lieutenant Heath) went over to Battery B's fire direction tent to work out plans with Lieutenant Rochnowski and Captain Elledge for the defense of the company and battery position. After the experience of the night before, all were confident of being able to hold if the enemy renewed his attacks. They decided the Chinese were most apt to attack the center of the company's front—the highest part of the perimeter where Lieutenant McGee's 3d Platoon was situated—and to reinforce that area as much as possible. Lieutenant Rochnowski agreed to set up three outpost positions and two BAR teams on the 3d Platoon's right flank near the saddle directly behind his battery. This was in addition to the two machine guns the artillerymen manned on the front line. If it became necessary, he offered to send some of his artillerymen up to fight with Heath's men. Rochnowski planned to send half of the men from one platoon up on the hill first; if more were needed he would then split up the other platoon and thereby contribute a total of about forty men. Skeleton crews would continue to fire the howitzers.

During the day the 23d RCT received twenty-four airdrops of ammunition. There were also several air strikes, including three south of the

Chipyong-ni perimeter where there appeared to be increased enemy activity. Inside the perimeter enemy mortar rounds fell intermittently.

Company G had a quiet day. Hot meals were served. Some of the men thought that perhaps the Chinese had withdrawn. That hope disappeared soon after dark. First, flares appeared in the southern sky; then followed the sound of bugles. After about half an hour or longer, while the men of Company G waited tensely in their holes, a small enemy group opened fire on the machine gun in the center of Lieutenant McGee's platoon, wounding the gunner. The previous night the enemy had opened the fighting by firing on the machine gun. A squad-sized group of Chinese was trying to reach Corporal Ottesen's gun by working along the spur connecting the 3d Platoon's hill with the enemy-held Hill 397 to the south. An enemy machine gun fired overhead cover for the small force. Enemy flares popped in front of the company, and the firing built up rapidly into a furious and noisy fight with the strongest enemy thrusts apparently aimed at the center of the 3d Platoon and at the saddle between it and the 1st Platoon. Tracers arched over the artillery's gun position.

Down at Company G's kitchen tent members of the mess crew heard the firing. They had neglected to dig foxholes and now the closest and best protection was the garbage pit. Eight men crowded into it. None of them made any funny remarks about the odor. An artilleryman with no protection of his own set out looking for any unoccupied foxhole. He finally found one with a man stretched out in the bottom, and jumped in.

"There ain't no room in this hole," the first man said; "not for nobody."

"No room hell!" said the second man. "We'll make room!"

Up on the hill two squads succeeded in penetrating the front line at the left end of the 1st Platoon, occupying several foxholes next to the saddle. The line was further weakened when these Chinese, having gained a foothold on the hill, planted pole charges in two of the 1st Platoon's holes; the resulting explosions killed four men. The enemy, now in control of the left side of the 1st Platoon's sector, set up a machine gun and started firing across the area of Lieutenant McGee's 3d Platoon. The leader of the 1st Platoon had his command post in a hut a short distance from another hut being used by the company commander. Without informing Lieutenant Heath, the leader of the 1st Platoon remained in his hut after the fighting started and did not join his platoon on the hill. He did maintain wire communication with his platoon sergeant (Sgt. Donald R. Schmitt) on the hill.

Because of the fire coming from the 1st Platoon's area, Lieutenant McGee began to suspect that platoon had lost some foxholes in its sector. He called the company commander on the telephone.

"Heath," he asked, "is the 1st Platoon still in position?"

Heath at once called the leader of the 1st Platoon, who in turn called Sergeant Schmitt on the hill. Schmitt was on the right end of the 1st Platoon's position, next to the road cut, still holding and unaware that the enemy had taken the opposite end of the platoon position. He claimed the line was still solid. Lieutenant Heath relayed the information to McGee.

Lieutenant McGee, however, still had his doubts. He and his platoon sergeant (Sergeant Kluttz) shouted over to the 1st Platoon area, "Anyone from the 1st Platoon?"

There was no answer.

Activities in his own area now took up Lieutenant McGee's interest as enemy soldiers overran one of his own foxholes. On the right flank of his platoon's sector, next to the saddle, he could see four Chinese soldiers with shovels strapped on their backs crawling on their hands and knees. They were about fifteen feet above and behind a hole occupied by the squad leader on the platoon's right flank.

By this time the sound-powered telephone line to the squad leader was out, so McGee shouted across to him: "There are four of them at the rear of your hole. Toss a grenade up and over."

A burst from a machine gun in the 1st Platoon's area—one now manned by the enemy—prevented the squad leader from standing up to lob the grenade. Lieutenant McGee and the other occupant of his foxhole (Pvt. Cletis Inmon, a runner), firing a BAR and rifle, respectively, killed the four enemy soldiers. The time was now about 2200.

The right-flank squad leader's troubles were not yet over. Lieutenant McGee looked down the slope and saw a group of Chinese crawl out of the dry creek bed and start up the hill toward the squad leader's hole.

McGee called to him, "About fifteen or twenty of them are coming up to your right front."

With the enemy-manned machine gun firing frequent short bursts over his hole, the squad leader did not want to stand up high enough to see and fire at the enemy. Although Lieutenant McGee and Inmon kept firing at the Chinese, they could not stop them, and the enemy continued to crawl up toward the squad leader's hole, which was on the 3d Platoon's right flank next to the saddle. The Chinese began throwing potato-masher grenades toward the hole, which the squad leader shared with two other men. The squad leader and one of the other men—a sergeant—climbed out, ran to McGee's hole, and jumped in on top of him and Inmon. The sergeant was hit on the way over. The enemy then threw a satchel charge into the hole they had just left and killed the man who had remained there.

With these men on top of him, Lieutenant McGee could neither see nor fire. "Get the hell out of here, and get back with your squad!" he yelled.

The squad leader did not budge, and McGee repeated the order. The squad leader then jumped out and was immediately shot through the shoulder. Lieutenant McGee called for a litter team, and the two men—the sergeant and the squad leader—were evacuated under fire.

By this time other enemy soldiers had started crawling up the slope toward Lieutenant McGee's position. One of them threw three grenades at McGee before the lieutenant killed the Chinese with a BAR he had taken from one of his men who had just been hit. The BAR was jamming on every tenth round. Lieutenant McGee used his pocket knife to extract the case. Finally he dropped the knife and was unable to find it in the dark. Quickly, he abandoned the automatic rifle and tried to fire his carbine at a Chinese who had crawled up to within ten feet of his hole. As the enemy soldier raised up on his knees, McGee pulled back the bolt to load the carbine, but at this critical moment the cold oil on the mechanism stopped the bolt from going home, and the weapon would not fire. McGee grabbed the operating handle and slammed the bolt in, fired four rounds at the Chinese, killing him. Men in nearby holes killed three other enemy soldiers who got close to Company G's front line.

It was now close to 2300. Lieutenant McGee needed help. Since wire communications were out, he ordered his platoon runner (PFC John N. Martin) to return to the company's command post and inform Lieutenant Heath that the platoon urgently needed men, ammunition, and litter teams.

After receiving this request, Lieutenant Heath stepped outside and shouted over to the artillery fire direction center asking Lieutenant Rochnowski for help up on the hill. The battery commander, in turn, called to his sections. In a few minutes fifteen artillerymen assembled. The runner (Martin) led them up toward the 3d Platoon's hill. As they crossed the crest of the hill the enemy opened fire on them. Lieutenant McGee watched with a sinking sensation as a mortar round killed one and wounded another, and the rest of the reinforcing group turned and ran back down the hill. Martin then returned to the rear area to guide the company's wire team, which was carrying ammunition up to the platoon.

Lieutenant Heath stopped the artillerymen at the bottom of the hill, re-formed them, and led them back up the hill himself. By this time, fighting on the hill had erupted into a frenzy of firing, with the enemy in full possession of that sector of Company G's line near the saddle. Near the top of the hill Lieutenant Heath's group fell apart again, the men running hard toward the bottom. With his men all gone, Heath started back after them. He was angry, and was yelling so loudly the men in the fire direction center tent could hear him. Halfway down the hill he stopped and stood there yelling for more help, ordering the men to return and re-form their line. When they didn't, he ran on to the bottom.

Heath grabbed a couple of the men by their clothing, yelling: "Goddammit, get back up on that hill! You'll die down here anyway. You might as well go up on the hill and die there."

Tracers from the enemy machine gun stretched along the hilltop like red beads. Flares popped overhead. The area was alternately dimly lighted and dark—as if someone were turning street lights on and off. When the artillerymen tried to find cover, Lieutenant Heath ran back and forth yelling and pulling at the men to persuade them to stand up and move. It was now between midnight and 0100 on 15 February.

Captain Elledge heard Lieutenant Heath calling for help. He went out in the gun park and yelled for men to help fight. The inexperienced artillerymen responded slowly. Captain Elledge went around the howitzers, pulled several men from their holes and, with a force of about ten men, set out for the left flank of the area still held by the 1st Platoon. Reaching the forward slope of the hill he found the caliber .30 machine gun there was silent; its three-man crew had been killed. Elledge stationed three men in the machine-gun pit and spread the others along the hill, then examined the machine gun. It was binding, apparently having been hit. There was no ammunition. Captain Elledge put the machine gun on his shoulders and ran down the hill with it, after telling his men there that he would bring another one back immediately. He exchanged the damaged gun for an extra caliber .50 machine gun of Battery B. With it and a box of ammunition, he returned to the hill. He set up the weapon, turned it over to the three men, and then continued along the ridge, moving to the right toward the road cut. He wanted to see what the situation was.

Positions still manned by the 1st Platoon were a few yards down the forward slope of the hill, below Captain Elledge. Toward the west end of the hill he heard some odd noises, and stopped beside a three-foot-high grave mound near the top of the hill. Nearby were several men whom he suspected were Chinese. He could not see them, but he could hear them making low whistling sounds, like an owl, probably as a signal to other enemy soldiers. He waited there on his hands and knees, listening. In a few moments he could hear someone crawling over the crusted snow. Raising to look over the mound, he came face to face with an enemy soldier who was also peering over the mound. Captain Elledge was holding his carbine in his right hand. It was set to operate on automatic and was pointed in the general direction of the Chinese. He pulled the trigger and hit the man in the chest. Right behind this Chinese was another whom Captain Elledge shot through the head. A third enemy soldier threw a small "ink bottle" grenade which exploded and hit Elledge in the shoulder. With his arm numb, and figuring he was badly hit, Elledge slid on down the hill and went back to the battery's mess tent.[14]

Soon after 2200, Lieutenant Heath's main line of resistance began to break up when the enemy seized and held part of the 1st Platoon's sector. The three hours that followed were filled with fighting as intense and as frantic as any in which the infantrymen had participated. Although the entire regimental perimeter was under attack, it appeared then that the main effort was directed against Company G. And within that company, the 1st and 3d Platoons were standing athwart the two routes by which the enemy tried to reach the top of Company G's hill. One of these routes followed the spur that led from Hill 397 into the center of the 3d Platoon;

the other route ran from the dead space in the creek bed to the saddle at the boundary between the 3d and 1st Platoons. Loss of this saddle early in the night seriously weakened the company's defenses, especially when the leader of the 1st Platoon, not knowing that the enemy had wrested these foxholes from his men, claimed to be in possession of the area for an hour or two after the enemy had been firing the American machine gun from there. This gave the enemy ample time to organize the saddle before the Americans counterattacked.

Lieutenant Heath used all the supporting fire he could get. He had mortar fire from his own light mortars, the 81mm weapons from Company H, and some help from the regimental Heavy-Mortar Company. The explosions from these shells, most of which fell in the area immediately south of Company G, sounded almost humdrum. The 37th Field Artillery Battalion shelled the slope of Hill 397 1,500 yards south of Company G. Enemy mortar shells fell on the north side of the hill, among Battery B's 155mm howitzers, and on the French Battalion across the road. At frequent intervals illuminating flares appeared in the sky, and one time a plane dropped three large parachute flares which hovered in the sky above Battery B. They burned for thirty seconds or longer, turning the natural bowl from which the battery was firing into a large room flooded with bluish light. By this time the Chinese had a machine gun operating in the saddle and swung it toward the howitzers, raking the area.

Up on the hill the main weapons were small arms, grenades and explosive charges. The Chinese were fighting for each foxhole, receiving heavy casualties, but also taking some of the holes on Lieutenant Heath's front line and killing and wounding men from Company G and Battery B. The walking wounded slid down the hill and gathered at the building used as the company's command post or at one of the tents set up by the artillerymen, or walked toward the medical clearing station in Chipyong-ni.

Lieutenant Heath, realizing that the enemy now held the saddle and the flank of both the 1st and the 3d Platoons, tried unsuccessfully to form a counterattack force from the artillerymen. Several groups of artillerymen were fighting determinedly, including a caliber .50 machine-gun crew and individuals along the line. But those men Heath tried to build into a counterattacking force were the artillerymen who had been on the front line and left when heavy fighting commenced, or others who had avoided getting into combat in the first place.

After the first three attempts to reach the top of the hill failed, Lieutenant Heath went to the artillery commander for more men, and then organized his line for another counterattack.

"We're going up that goddam hill or bust," he kept yelling.

While Heath struggled to hold his men together and counterattack, McGee's 3d Platoon gradually lost more men and foxholes. The enemy machine gun, firing from a position in the former sector of the 1st Platoon, sent a bullet through the left eye of Private Inmon (the platoon runner in McGee's foxhole). He started shouting: "I'm hit in the face! I'm hit in the face! Get me back off this hill!"

Blood spurted from his eye as the platoon leader tried to calm him down. Lieutenant McGee told him to lie down. "I can't take you out now," he said. He shouted across to his platoon sergeant for the medic. "Inmon's been hit."

Within a few minutes the aid man came over and bandaged Inmon's head. Lieutenant McGee wanted Inmon to keep on firing his rifle but the wounded man said he could not see well enough, so McGee asked him to load clips for his carbine while he fired.

The 3d Platoon's strongest weapon was Corporal Ottesen's machine gun located in the center of its sector. It fired along the spur over which the enemy crawled toward Company G's line, and enemy soldiers had tried repeatedly to silence it. Some time after midnight two enemy soldiers managed to flank Ottesen's hole and tossed in two grenades, knocking out the gun. Corporal Ottesen became missing in action.

No longer hearing the machine gun, Lieutenant McGee called to his platoon sergeant (Sergeant Kluttz) who was between him and the gun.

"What's happened to the machine gun?" he asked. "It's quit firing."

Sergeant Kluttz told him the position had been overrun and that Chinese were coming through between Corporal Ottesen's squad and Cpl. Raymond Bennett's squad. Bennett's squad, holding the left flank of the platoon, had not been attacked. McGee called him on the sound-powered telephone and ordered him to shift several men over to fill the gap left by the knocked-out machine gun. He also sent his other runner (PFC John Martin) to find Lieutenant Heath and ask for ammunition and for replacements to fill the empty holes along his defensive line. Heath, in turn, called Colonel Edwards, who immediately sent a squad from Company F's uncommitted platoon to bolster Company G's line.[15]

While this squad was on the way, Corporal Bennett succeeded in closing the gap where Corporal Ottesen's machine gun had been. A group of Chinese was still trying hard to seize that part of the hill. There was a bugler in the group whom Bennett shot as he tooted his second note. In the melee, however, Corporal Bennett was hit by a hand grenade which blew off part of his hand. Then a bullet hit him in the shoulder, and shortly thereafter a shell fragment struck him in the head. The sound-powered telephone went out, and Lieutenant McGee lost contact with Bennett's squad.

It was nearly 0200 when Sgt. Kenneth G. Kelly arrived with a squad from Company F's support platoon. This squad had the mission of recovering the part of Company G's line that had fallen to the enemy, especially the saddle between the two platoons. Sergeant Kluttz guided the men west toward the enemy-occupied foxholes and immediately started a fire fight that wounded or killed the entire squad from Company F within ten minutes.[16] After killing two Chinese who fired burp guns at him but missed, Sergeant Kluttz returned to tell Lieutenant McGee what had happened.

"Lieutenant," he said, "we've *got* to stop them!"

The enemy attack continued without let-up. It was not one calculated to overrun the entire hill but a persistent, gnawing assault that progressed from one hole to the next. The Chinese held most of the holes on that part of the hill between the road cut and the saddle, and those on the right flank of the weakened 3d Platoon. Then, between 0200 and 0300, the 2d Platoon, which was not under heavy fire, pulled back its right flank from its position in the rice paddies, thus breaking contact with Lieutenant McGee's platoon and taking away a machine gun that had been supporting the 3d Platoon. Only a few men from the 3d Platoon were left.

Lieutenant McGee shouted over to Sergeant Kluttz to ask how Corporal Bennett's squad was making out.

"I think three or four of them are still left," the Sergeant answered.

McGee's platoon was low on ammunition and Sergeant Kluttz was having trouble with the machine gun he was firing.

Growing discouraged, Lieutenant McGee called to his platoon sergeant, "It looks like they've got us, Kluttz."

"Well," Sergeant Kluttz called back, "let's kill as many of these sons of bitches as we can before they get us."

Once in possession of part of Company G's hill, the Chinese fired into the bowl-shaped area among the artillery and mortarmen, causing several casualties. The leader of the 4th Platoon (Lt. Carl F. Haberman) moved his mortars to a ditch a hundred yards or more to the rear. He then set out to find men to help retake the hill and eliminate the enemy fire. He walked into a squad tent filled with artillerymen.

"Hell," he said, "a squad tent won't stop bullets."

Haberman persuaded five or six men to accompany him. They went outside with him but none would climb the hill.

Some time between 0230 and 0300 Company G lost the rest of its hill. Sergeant Schmitt and the remainder of the 1st Platoon came down from the west end of the company's sector. In the center of the company's front, Sergeant Kluttz's machine gun jammed. He and Lieutenant McGee decided to try to get out. They called to the other men, threw what grenades they had left, and climbed over the crest of the hill. Lieutenant McGee and five other men, all who were left from the 3d Platoon, walked on down the hill.

Lieutenant Heath called his battalion commander (Colonel Edwards) to report the loss of his company's position. Since a break occurring anywhere around the small regimental perimeter was serious, Colonel Edwards ordered a counterattack and promised to send help. His battalion reserve now consisted of the support platoon of Company F less the squad that had been lost while attacking the saddle. After ordering this platoon to move to Company G's area, Edwards appealed to Colonel Freeman (CO, 23d Infantry) for more help. Colonel Freeman was fixed no better for reserve strength. An attached Ranger company constituted his reserve, but because of another severe enemy thrust at his 3d Battalion, Colonel Freeman was reluctant to commit his entire reserve in Company G's area. He agreed to furnish one platoon from the Ranger company and a tank.[17]

Since so few of Company G's men were left, Colonel Edwards decided to put one of his battalion staff officers (Lt. Robert Curtis) in command of the two platoons. Curtis set out to meet the Ranger platoon and guide it into position.

While these two platoons were on the way, Lieutenant Heath attempted to form a defensive line along a four- or five-foot rib of ground that crossed the center of the bowl-shaped area just behind the artillery position. At the fire direction center several artillerymen were firing an illuminating mission when they heard Heath's voice outside. Heath was now speaking in a normal voice as he stationed one of his men on the new defensive line.

"We'll form our line right along here," he explained to the man, "just back of this tent."

The artillerymen looked at one another for a few seconds.

"I guess it's time to get out of here," one of them said.

They pulled a blanket over two wounded men who lay on the ground, and prepared to leave. Just then the telephone rang. It was the S3 of the 37th Field Artillery Battalion inquiring about the illuminating mission he had requested.

"Where the hell are my flares?" he asked.

"Excuse me, sir," answered the artilleryman, "but our position is being overrun."

He dropped the telephone, followed the others outside, and crossed to the opposite side of the road in front of the howitzers. A three-foot-high embankment there afforded good protection. Other artillerymen were already behind it. The artillerymen did not abandon their howitzers; they could still cover the battery's position by fire.

Lieutenant Curtis, with the platoon from Company F and the Ranger platoon, reached Company G about 0330.[18] Lieutenant Curtis took command of the two platoons but immediately encountered trouble from the commander of the Ranger company. The latter officer had come with the platoon from his company. He claimed that the platoon, being a part of regimental reserve, was to take orders only from the regimental commander. Curtis immediately called his battalion headquarters to explain the situation to Colonel Edwards, who solved the problem by putting another staff officer—this time a captain—in command of the composite force.

It was between 0345 and 0400, 15 February, when Capt. John H. Ramsburg left the long, tin-roofed building that housed the battalion's command post and set out for Company G's area. Except for Company G's sector where there was brisk firing, the regimental perimeter was relatively quiet at the time. A quarter of a mile beyond the railroad tracks Ramsburg turned left, following a trail that led from the road to the house where Lieutenant Heath had established his command post.

Along the trail there was a quad caliber .50 halftrack. An hour or two before the crew with the vehicle had accidentally run into a ditch, nearly tipping the halftrack over. Unable to get it into firing position, the crew had abandoned the weapon and vehicle. Lieutenant Curtis was standing near the halftrack. There was enough light in the area for Captain Ramsburg to recognize him at a distance of ten or fifteen feet.

"Christ, John," Lieutenant Curtis said, "but I'm glad to see you here! I can't do anything with these Rangers."

He went on to explain that the commander of the Ranger company objected to having a platoon from his company attached to another unit, to having it participate in a counterattack, and that he refused to take orders from anyone but the regimental commander.

Captain Ramsburg went first to Lieutenant Heath's command post where he called Colonel Edwards in order to report that he and both platoons were at the position. He then talked with the commander of the Ranger company to establish his position as commander of the infantry units in that sector.

At the time the few men left from Company G and those from the platoons from Company F and the Ranger company were all mixed together—just a line of bodies on the ground firing against the hill to discourage the enemy from attempting a further advance. Captain Ramsburg had the platoon leaders separate their units and sort out the artillerymen whom he sent across the road where most men from the battery had assembled. Since none of Company G's communications facilities was working at the time, Captain Ramsburg asked Lieutenant Curtis to send men to Chipyong-ni for more radios. He then asked Lieutenant McGee to have the mortars moved closer to the line of departure so that he could call out orders to the crew.

In the meantime, the two platoon leaders re-formed their men. There were 36 men in the platoon from the Ranger company, 28 in the platoon from Company F. In addition, there were 6 or 7 mortarmen, 2 machinegun crews, and 4 or 5 men left from Company G. To the two platoon leaders he outlined his plan: following a short mortar concentration, the two machine guns would commence firing at the top of the ridge and over the heads of the attacking men who were to move on Captain Ramsburg's signal. The Ranger platoon, on the right, was to attack the hill formerly held by the 1st Platoon of Company G, while the platoon from Company F was to assault Lieutenant McGee's former position.

It was still dark when a man returned with three SCR-536 radios—one each for Captain Ramsburg and his two platoon leaders. The enemy was fairly quiet at the time and had not interfered with organizing the attack. After testing the radios and getting all men in position on the line of departure, Captain Ramsburg called for mortar fire. The first round, fired from a range of not more than 150 yards, landed squarely on the crest of the ridge.

"That where you want 'em?" one of the mortarmen asked.

"That's exactly right," Captain Ramsburg yelled back. "Now go ahead and sweep the hill in both directions."

He asked for a five-minute concentration. The mortarmen doubted that their ammunition would last that long. After two or three minutes, Captain Ramsburg signalled for machine-gun fire. The two guns went into action, but after a few bursts enemy mortar rounds landed nearby, and both the friendly mortars and the machine guns had to cease firing. Eight or ten rounds landed between the line of departure and the mortar crews about twenty yards behind it. The explosions wounded at least six men, including the leader of the platoon from Company F.

The commander of the Ranger company, thinking that friendly rounds were falling short, called for the mortar crews to cease firing. The shouting interfered with efforts to get the attack under way. Captain Ramsburg became angry. He ordered the Ranger commander to gather up and evacuate his wounded men, hoping thereby to get rid of the commander as well as the wounded men.

The platoon sergeant took command of the platoon from Company F, the machine guns opened fire again, and Captain Ramsburg signalled for the jumpoff.

"OK, let's go!" he shouted.

The men stood up, commenced firing, and walked forward through crusted snow which, in the low ground in front of the hill, was knee-deep in places. In a minute or two the advancing line, with Captain Ramsburg moving in the center, started up the hillside, the Rangers in the lead since men from that platoon, all yelling loudly, pushed their attack fast.

Several enemy mortar rounds and a few grenades exploded on the slope of the hill. In the middle of the attack, two guns located near the French Battalion's hill fired into the Ranger platoon. The guns appeared to be either automatic rifles or light machine guns, but Captain Ramsburg could not tell if the French were firing by mistake, or if Chinese soldiers had set up guns in that area. Nor did he later learn who was firing. The first burst was a long, steady one—a solid string of light from the gun to the Ranger platoon. After that there were short bursts for a minute or longer while Captain Ramsburg and several other men, believing this to be friendly fire, screamed to have it stopped. Several Rangers were wounded by this fire.

Just before the attack jumped off, Lieutenant Curtis had gone to each of the three tanks in that area to tell the tankers of the counterattack plans, and to warn them not to fire without orders. He had just returned when the machine gun fired into the Ranger platoon. One of the tank crews, having apparently decided the machine gun firing from the French Battalion's hill was friendly and the Rangers were enemy, disregarded orders and also opened fire, aiming the tank's caliber .50 machine gun at the Ranger platoon. While Captain Ramsburg yelled at the tankers, Lieutenant Curtis raced back and halted the machine gun, which had fired for 20 or 30 seconds, only long enough to sweep across the hill once. Besides creating more confusion, this caused additional casualties among the Rangers, the remaining ones of whom, by this time, were near the top of their hill still yelling among themselves.

Another gun—this one definitely manned by the Chinese—had meanwhile opened fire into the left flank of the platoon from Company F, causing serious damage in that area. The gun was in the rice paddies near the place where the 2d Platoon of Company G had been, and gave the attacking force its first indication that friendly troops had vacated that position. The commander of Company F spotted the tracers from this enemy gun and directed mortar fire at it but was unable to knock it out. As he afterward learned, the Chinese crew had been there long enough to dig in and provide overhead protection for the gun.

Captain Ramsburg, occupied with the machine-gun fire hitting the right flank of his line, did not know of the trouble the platoon from Company F was experiencing on the opposite end. Lieutenant Curtis succeeded in silencing the tank's fire. Several men from the Ranger platoon were already on top of their objective shouting for help.

"We're on top!" they yelled. "Come on up! Get some men up here!"

Other members of that platoon were still climbing the hill, but a third or more were casualties by this time, the result of either friendly or enemy fire.

A grenade exploded beside Captain Ramsburg just as the tank's fire ended and he turned to go on up the hill. A fragment struck him in the foot. At the moment he was holding a caliber .45 submachine gun in his right hand and at first he thought that, in his anger and excitement over the machine-gun fire from his own tanks, he had squeezed too hard on the trigger and shot himself through the foot. He wondered how he would explain the accident to Colonel Edwards. He then realized his gun was on full automatic and, had he pulled the trigger, it would have fired several times. He also recalled seeing a flash and decided he had been hit by a grenade fragment. He removed his glove and sat down to examine his foot. The two machine-gun crews came by on their way to the top of the hill where they were to relocate their guns. A little later Lieutenant Heath came up the hill and stopped where Ramsburg was sitting.

"What happened to you?" Heath asked. He was supposed to stay at the bottom of the hill and collect any stragglers who might congregate in that area. He was to go up on the hill later, after it was secured.

Captain Ramsburg explained that he was not seriously wounded, that he had only one or two broken bones in his ankle. Lieutenant Heath offered to take charge of the attack for the time being. Slinging Ramsburg's radio over his shoulder, Heath proceeded up the hill.

After resting for several minutes, Captain Ramsburg started on up the hill. He had hobbled a few yards when a soldier came down, dragging another man by a leg. Captain Ramsburg stopped the soldier because he did not want an able-bodied man to evacuate a wounded man, thereby losing two men because of one casualty. The soldier explained that he was wounded also and, to prove it, turned around to show one arm which was badly shot up and appeared to be hanging only by a piece of flesh. Captain Ramsburg waved him on.

"Who's the man you're dragging?" he asked as the soldier moved on.

"It's the Lieutenant," the soldier answered; "Lieutenant Heath. He got it in the chest."

After talking with Captain Ramsburg, Heath had gone on to the crest of the hill, and there had come face to face with a Chinese soldier. Heath reached for the carbine slung on his shoulder but it was entangled in the strap on the radio which he had just taken from Captain Ramsburg. Before he could get his carbine, the enemy soldier had shot him through the chest, causing a serious, but not fatal, wound. About the same time the Ranger platoon leader was killed.

The American counterattack did not force the enemy from the top of the ridge but, instead, for a brief time the opposing forces occupied the same ground, fighting in the darkness. Casualties were heavy.

Several other wounded men slid down the hill. Within a few seconds, four or five more appeared and, when Captain Ramsburg stopped them, they explained the Chinese had recaptured the hill, that no soldiers from Company F or the Rangers were left there, and that they could hold out no longer. Ramsburg followed them to the foot of the hill. The counterattack was ended.

At the mortar position Captain Ramsburg met Lieutenant Curtis. "Get as many men as you can possibly gather up," he told Lieutenant Curtis, "and get them on this hump to hold off the damned Chinese if they come over the hill."

Of the 28 men in the platoon from Company F, 22 were wounded during the brief attack; 1 became missing in action; only 5 were unhurt.[19] The Ranger platoon suffered casualties equally as heavy. Many of the walking wounded had already gone down the road into Chipyong-ni; there were 18 or 20 wounded men congregated near the farm house used as the command post, and others at the artillery supply tent. There were few effective men left, but Lieutenant Curtis stationed those he could find near the command post to guard it.

Although men from both platoons claimed no friendly troops remained on the hill, Lieutenant Curtis decided to make a search for survivors and with another man started up the slope, heading toward an area where he heard the sound of men digging. It was still dark, although in the sky there was the first indication of approaching daylight. As the two men reached the top of the ridge an enemy soldier suddenly jumped up in front of them and sounded a bugle call. A dozen or more enemy soldiers ran toward the bugler. Lieutenant Curtis and his companion thought the Chinese had heard them, but no firing followed the alarm. They backed away. On the way down they came across three wounded soldiers who said they were the last men on the hill from the platoon from Company F. Nevertheless, after helping them back to the command post shacks, Lieutenant Curtis returned—this time alone—to search the remainder of the area where the attacking platoons had been. He found only Chinese.[20]

When Curtis got back to the cluster of command post buildings, he discovered that what was left of the friendly defensive organization in that area was falling apart. The commander of the Ranger company, having returned from evacuating the men wounded at the outset of the counterattack, kept yelling, "We can't hold here; let's get out of here!"

Captain Ramsburg had reported the failure of the counterattack to Colonel Edwards who had, meanwhile, secured the remainder of the Ranger company to help regain the lost section of the perimeter. He told Captain Ramsburg to hang on, that help was on the way.[21] However, by this time no able-bodied riflemen were left. Even the men Lieutenant Curtis had left to guard the command post had gone. Up on the hill, Chinese began firing rifles into the bowl-shaped area. With only wounded men left, Captain Ramsburg finally gave the order for everyone to move back to the hill that formed the other end of the horseshoe, to a ridge just south of the railroad tracks.[22]

While these events were taking place, the artillery liaison officer (Captain Elledge) had undertaken to get the quad .50 halftrack back in operation. Abandoned earlier in the night by its crew, it was in a ditch near the trail leading from the road to the command post. About the same time that Captain Ramsburg's counterattack got under way, Captain Elledge had persuaded a tank crew to help pull the halftrack onto the road again. In the first place, Elledge wanted to get the halftrack turned around so that he could fire the machine guns; in addition, it blocked the trail leading to the command post buildings and thereby interfered with the evacuation of some of the wounded men. Half an hour later—after Captain Ramsburg's counterattack had fallen back—Elledge had the halftrack operating under its own power and had tested the small engine that drove the traversing mechanism for the quadruple-mounted machine guns. He went off to get permission to fire from the infantrymen. At the command post, Captain Ramsburg had just given the order to pull out.

"Go ahead and fire," he told Captain Elledge. "No one's left up there." [23]

Captain Elledge returned to the quad .50 and swept the length of the enemy-held hill. The tank commander (MSgt. Andrew Reyna) appeared at that time to ask for help in recovering sixteen wounded men—artillerymen and infantrymen—who had been left at Battery B's supply tent near the foot of the hill and directly under the enemy's guns. While Captain Elledge kept pounding the enemy hilltop with fire from his four machine guns, Sergeant Reyna and his crew drove the tank under the fire to the base of the hill, carried the wounded men from the tent, piled them on the tank, and returned.

Captain Elledge had been firing so steadily that, in the first gray light of the morning, artillerymen across the road could see heat waves shimmering above the four guns.[24] Elledge scanned the area, looking for targets. He noticed several enemy soldiers standing on the hill between the saddle and the road cut, and suddenly realized they were preparing to fire a 75mm recoilless rifle that the 1st Platoon of Company G had left there. It was aimed directly at him. Captain Elledge could see daylight through the tube. He watched as the Chinese shoved a round into the breech, then he quickly turned his machine guns in that direction and destroyed the enemy crew.[25]

Two wounded men had been left under a blanket in the fire direction center tent. While one tank, firing from the road, covered the rescue, PFC Thomas S. Allison and PFC Isaiah W. Williams (both members of the artillery wire section) drove a ¾-ton truck to the tent, loaded the two wounded men onto it, and backed out again.

Lieutenant Curtis urged the remaining wounded men to start walking toward Chipyong-ni, then ran to the road to tell the artillerymen that the infantrymen were pulling back.

"You're the front line now," he told them.

The artillerymen, concerned about the safety of their howitzers, decided to stay behind the road embankment where, by fire, they could keep the Chinese out of their battery's position. Two tanks on the road separating the artillerymen from their howitzers regularly fired short machine-gun bursts into the blackened, chewed-up top of the hill.

At the command post only nine wounded men were left—not counting Captain Ramsburg, who stayed behind to supervise the withdrawal. All nine were seriously wounded and waiting for litters and a vehicle to carry them to the battalion's aid station. They were lying on the ground near the straw-roofed buildings. As Lieutenant Curtis returned to the command post, a bugle sounded and he saw 10 or 12 Chinese soldiers coming down the highest hill—the one originally defended by Lieutenant McGee's platoon. Curtis pointed out the enemy to the wounded men.

"If you fellows don't leave now," he told them, "you'll never leave. There aren't enough men left to protect you."

All nine men left, somehow or other moving with only the help they could give one another or get from Lieutenant Curtis, who followed them, heading back to the new defensive position.[26]

Only two men—both sergeants—remained at the command post with Captain Ramsburg. The sergeants pulled out the telephones and the three men started toward Chipyong-ni, moving across the frozen rice paddies. Before they had gone far, however, an enemy machine-gunner fired at them. They broke into a run. Captain Ramsburg, disregarding his broken ankle which was now stiff and sore, sprinted the entire distance to the new hilltop.

The quad .50—still manned by Captain Elledge—and the three tanks pounded the enemy hill with machine-gun fire. One of the artillery officers yelled for a gun crew to man a howitzer, and half a dozen men scrambled over the road embankment and dashed to one of the 155mm howitzers. Turning it around, they fired six white phosphorus shells that blossomed into white streamers of smoke and fire along the hillside. At such close range, the sound of the propelling charge and the sound of the shell burst were barely separated.[27]

At the new position, Captain Ramsburg joined the survivors of the ten-hour enemy attack, as well as the remaining two platoons of the Ranger company attached to Colonel Edwards's battalion. All of the men experienced a feeling of relief when daylight came on 15 February, because the enemy soldiers usually withdrew then. This time, however, the Chinese did not withdraw. They conducted a determined defense against an attack made by the Ranger company and Company B, supported by air strikes, artillery, and tanks, and directed by Colonel Edwards. It was evening before the enemy was defeated and withdrew.

Several inches of snow fell during the night of 15–16 February, covering several hundred Chinese bodies on the hill originally defended by Lieutenant Heath's Company G. At Chipyong-ni, the Chinese suffered their first defeat since entering the Korean war.

★ DISCUSSION

If the commander of an attacking force disregards casualties, he will usually be able to attain at least local successes. The commander of defending troops faced with such an opponent must be prepared to limit any such successes. He holds the shoulders of any penetration. He uses supporting fires and positions in depth to blunt, slow down, and finally to stop the spearhead of the attack. Once the penetration has been contained, the defending commander then counterattacks to eliminate it.

A counterattack plan is based on the answers to these questions: When?

Where? How many? Prematurely launched counterattacks meet the enemy head on, before the enemy attack has lost its impetus, and before the enemy has been softened by fire. Tardy counterattacks meet the enemy intrenched and reinforced. Thus, ill-timed counterattacks—no matter how gallantly executed—often fail. Terrain and the disposition of the enemy within the penetration probably will dictate where the counterattack should strike. But a knowledge of all the many factors that go to make up both the enemy and friendly situation is necessary to determine the strength of the counterattack. The entire reserve should not be committed to action unless necessary. Nor should "a boy be sent to do a man's job."

Some highlights of the action at Chipyong-ni bear emphasizing by repetition.

Note that Company G was first alerted to an attack by the sound of digging. Note also the use of the machine gun to replace the recoilless rifle at night—a move that not only kept the rifle blast from disclosing the position but also used the available personnel to the maximum with a weapon much better suited to the requirements of close-in night fighting.

The reprehensible actions of some of the men of Battery B, 503d Field Artillery Battalion, cannot be attributed to inexperience alone. Few men will perform well when they are formed into an impromptu group of individuals to do an unfamiliar job. The infantry squad needs teamwork and an interdependence within itself—attributes that must reach the maximum in assault combat. An infantry squad will fight its best only when each member has confidence in all other members and in the commanders and leaders over it. Twenty artillerymen who have not demonstrated to one another their individual abilities as infantrymen and who are placed under the leadership of a stranger cannot be expected to behave with distinction. Captain Elledge, who obviously enjoyed the fight, is of a type that occurs not very often. If artillerymen are to be used as infantry, they must be so trained and so organized.

★ NOTES

1. 2d Division Artillery: S3 journal, entry J6, 110910, February 1951.

2. 2d Division, command report: 23d Infantry Regiment, February 1951, appendix 1, section D.

3. Lt.Col. James W. Edwards, "The Siege of Chipyong-ni" (unpublished manuscript on file in OCMH), p. 1.

4. Edwards, *op. cit.* (sketch maps of these positions prepared by Colonel Edwards, battalion commander at the time of the action, on file in OCMH). Unless otherwise noted, that part of this account describing the actions of Company G, 23d Infantry, is based upon a manuscript by Major Edward C. Williamson ("Chipyong-ni: Defense of South Sector of 23d Regimental Combat Team Perimeter by Company G, 13–15 February 1951"), prepared in Korea from

interviews with personnel of the battalion. That part describing the activities of Battery B, 503d FA Battalion, is based upon interviews by the author with key personnel of the battery, and upon several with Capt. John A. Elledge, 37th FA Battalion.

5. Edwards, *op. cit.*, pp. 15–16.

6. Edwards, *loc. cit.*

7. X Corps: command report, February 1951 (narrative section). See also map 2 in that report.

8. *Ibid.* See also map 4 in that report.

9. 2d Division, command report: 23d Infantry Regiment, February 1951.

10. X Corps: command report, February 1951 (Inclosure 1, "Battle of Chipyong-ni"); hereafter cited as X Corps: Chipyong-ni.

11. For details on the question of holding Chipyong-ni, see X Corps: Chipyong-ni; 2d Division: G3 journal, entry J79, 131422 February, entry J80, 131428 February, and entry J56, 131055 February 1951.

12. X Corps: Chipyong-ni.

13. Statement by Capt. John A. Elledge.

14. Capt. John A. Elledge, in an interview by the author upon which this account is based.

15. Edwards, *op. cit.*, p. 29.

16. Edwards, *loc. cit.*

17. Edwards, *op. cit.*, p. 30.

18. Capt. John H. Ramsburg, in an interview by the author. Unless otherwise noted, the account of the second counterattack to retake Company G's sector is based upon that interview. For more details on the difficulties created by the commander of the Ranger company, see Edwards, *op. cit.*, and Lt. Robert Curtis, letter to the author, 22 July 1952.

19. Lt. Donald O. Miller, letter to Major Roy E. Appleman, 18 October 1951.

20. Curtis, *op. cit.*

21. Ramsburg, *op. cit.*

22. *Ibid.*

23. Ramsburg, *op. cit.*, Elledge, *op. cit.*

24. *Ibid.*

25. Elledge, *op. cit.*

26. Curtis, *op. cit.*

27. Ramsburg, *op. cit.*

9

Task Force Crombez

★ While the 23d Regimental Combat Team, surrounded by Chinese Communists at Chipyong-ni, braced itself for the second night of the siege, a regiment of the 1st Cavalry Division set out on a sort of rescue mission: to drive through enemy lines, join the encircled unit and give it all possible assistance. Specifically, it was to open the road for supply vehicles and ambulances.[1]

On 14 February 1951, the 5th Cavalry Regiment was in corps reserve when the commanding general of U.S. IX Corps (Maj.Gen. Bryant E. Moore) alerted it for possible action. It was midafternoon when he first telephoned the regimental commander (Col. Marcel G. Crombez) warning him to make plans for an attack along the road running from Yoju to Koksu-ri and then northeast into Chipyong-ni—a road distance of fifteen miles.[2] Another force, attacking along the better and more direct road to Chipyong-ni, had been unable to make fast enough progress because of heavily entrenched enemy forces along its route.

Immediately relaying the warning order to subordinate units, Colonel Crombez organized a task force.[3]

In addition to the three organic infantry battalions of the 5th Cavalry, he included a medical company, a company of combat engineers, two battalions of field artillery of which one was equipped with self-propelled howitzers, two platoons of medium tanks, and an attached company of medium tanks.[4] The last named—Company D, 6th Tank Battalion—was not a part of the 1st Cavalry Division, but happened to be located closer than any other available tank company. General Moore attached Company D

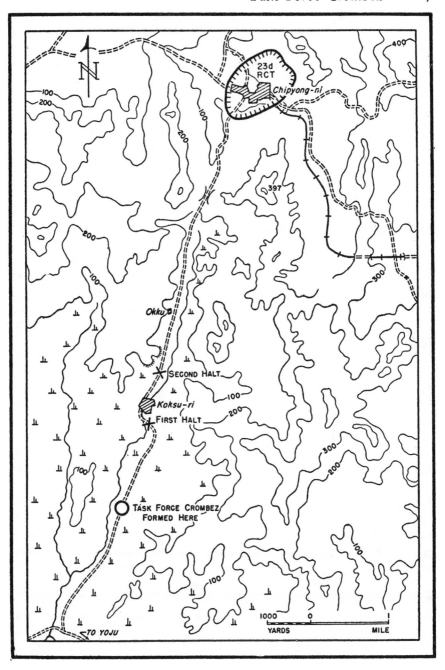

to the 5th Cavalry and ordered it to get under way within thirty minutes to join that unit. Company D was on the road twenty-eight minutes later. At 1700 that afternoon, the corps commander again called.[5]

"You'll have to move out tonight," he told Colonel Crombez, "and I know you'll do it." [6]

In the darkness, trucks and vehicles formed a column along the narrow, rutted road, snow covered and patched with ice. Moving under blackout conditions and in enemy territory, all units except the two artillery battalions crossed the Han River and advanced approximately half of the distance to Chipyong-ni. About midnight the regimental column halted at a destroyed bridge where units formed defensive perimeters while combat engineers rebuilt the structure.[7]

At daylight on 15 February, the 1st Battalion jumped off again—this time on foot. Its mission was to seize a terrain feature on the right which dominated the road for several miles to the north. When the battalion was engaged after moving a hundred or two hundred yards, Colonel Crombez sent the 2d Battalion to attack north on the left side of the road. Within an hour or two a full-scale regimental attack was in progress. Two artillery battalions supported the action, lifting their fire only for air strikes. Chinese resistance was firm. Observers in airplanes reported large enemy forces north of the attacking battalions.[8]

The advance lagged throughout the morning. Sensing that the enemy offered too much opposition for the infantry battalions to be able to reach Chipyong-ni by evening, Colonel Crombez decided that only an armored task force would be able to penetrate the enemy-held territory.[9] With corps and division headquarters pressing for progress, Colonel Crombez separated the tanks—a total of twenty-three—from his regimental column, and organized an armored task force. The tanks came from Company D, 6th Tank Battalion, and Company A, 70th Tank Battalion. He also ordered a company of infantrymen to accompany the tanks in order to protect them from fanatic enemy troops who might attempt to knock out the tanks at close range. This task fell to Company L, 5th Cavalry Regiment.[10] In addition, four combat engineer soldiers were ordered to go along to lift any antitank mines that might be discovered. The engineers and the infantrymen were to ride on top of the tanks.[11]

While the tanks maneuvered into position, Colonel Crombez reconnoitered the road to Chipyong-ni by helicopter. It was a secondary road even by Korean standards: narrow, with mountain slopes on the left side and flat rice paddies on the right, except at a deep roadcut a mile south of Chipyong-ni where, for a short distance, steep cliffs walled both sides of the road.

Meanwhile, the Company L commander (Capt. John C. Barrett) and the commander of Company D, 6th Tank Battalion (Capt. Johnnie M. Hiers), worked out the plans at company level. The two officers agreed that when the tanks stopped, the troopers would dismount, deploy on both sides of the road, and protect the tanks and the engineers who might be lifting mines. When the tank column was ready to proceed, Captain Hiers would inform the tankers by radio; the tankers, in turn, would signal the troopers to remount.[12]

The M46 tanks of the 6th Tank Battalion were placed to lead the 70th Tank Battalion's M4A3 tanks because the M46s mounted 90mm guns, could turn completely around in place (an important consideration in the mountainous terrain traversed by a single and narrow road), and had better armor protection than the M4A3 tanks, which mounted only 76mm guns.[13]

Original plans called for a separate column of supply trucks and ambulances to follow the tanks. Colonel Crombez, however, doubted if such a column could get through. He decided to proceed with only the armored vehicles. When the road was clear and suitable for wheeled traffic, he would radio instructions to the supply vehicles and ambulances. By radio he informed the commanding officer of the 23d RCT that he was coming, but without the supply trains.

"Come on," the commander of the encircled force answered; "trains or no trains." [14]

Just before the task force left, the commander of the 3d Battalion, 5th Cavalry (Lt.Col. Edgar J. Treacy, Jr.) arranged for a 2½-ton truck to follow the rear of the tank column and pick up any wounded men from Company L. The Company L commander (Captain Barrett) issued instructions that any troopers who became separated from the tank column were to make their way back to friendly lines if possible, or wait near the road, utilizing the best available defensive positions, until the tanks returned from Chipyong-ni later in the day.[15]

About 1500 Captain Barrett mounted his company on the tanks in the center of the column, leaving four tanks at each end of the column bare. The four engineer soldiers rode on the second tank in the column. Thus, 15 tanks carried 160 Company L infantrymen.[16] The infantry platoon leaders selected one man on each tank to fire the caliber .50 machine gun mounted on its deck. Captain Barrett rode on the sixth tank in line, along with ten enlisted men and Colonel Treacy who, at the last minute, decided to accompany the task force.[17]

Planes strafed and bombed enemy positions along the route of march before the armored column took off. The two infantry battalions maintained strong pressure to keep the Chinese occupied and to prevent them from drawing off any strength to throw against the task force. With Colonel Crombez riding in the fifth tank, the mile-long column got under way at 1545 on 15 February.[18] Liaison planes circled overhead, maintaining contact with the advancing tanks.[19]

The task force, with fifty-yard intervals between tanks, proceeded about two miles—until the lead tank approached the village of Koksu-ri.

All of a sudden, enemy mortar shells began exploding near the tanks, and enemy riflemen and machine gunners opened fire on the troopers exposed on the decks. Just then the lead tank stopped at a bridge bypass on the south edge of Koksu-ri, and the entire column came to a halt.[20] The tankers turned their guns toward Chinese whom they could see clearly on nearby hills and opened fire with their machine guns and cannons. Several troopers, wounded by the first bursts of enemy fire, fell or were knocked from the tanks. Others left the tanks, not so much to protect them as to take cover themselves.[21] Colonel Crombez directed the tank fire.

"We're killing hundreds of them!" he shouted over the intertank communications.

After a few minutes, however, feeling that the success of the task force depended upon the ability of the tanks to keep moving, Colonel Crombez directed them to continue.[22]

Without warning, the tanks moved forward. The troopers raced after the moving tanks but, in the scramble, thirty or more men, including two officers of Company L, were left behind. The truck following the tanks picked up three wounded men who had been left lying near the road. This truck, however, was drawing so much enemy fire that other wounded men preferred to stay where they were. After both officers in the group were wounded by mortar fire, MSgt. Lloyd L. Jones organized the stranded men and led them back toward their own lines.[23]

There was another halt just after the column passed through Koksu-ri, and again the infantrymen deployed. Against the intense enemy fire the tankers and infantrymen fired furiously to hold the enemy soldiers at some distance. For the second time, the tanks began moving without notifying the infantrymen, and again many Company L men were unable to remount. Some troopers were deployed 50 or 75 yards from the road and the tanks were going too fast to remount by the time the men got back to the road.[24] Less than seventy men were left on the tanks when Task Force Crombez moved out after the second halt.[25] Another large group of men was left to seek cover or to attempt to rejoin friendly units south of Koksu-ri. Several men from this group, including the commander of the 3d Battalion (Colonel Treacy) are known to have become prisoners of the Chinese.[26]

Captain Barrett was unable to remount the tank upon which he had been riding, but he did manage to climb on the fifth or sixth tank behind it.

During the next three or three and a half miles there were several brief halts and almost continuous enemy fire directed against the column whether it was halted or moving. Several times, in the face of heavy enemy fire, tank commanders inquired if they should slow down or stop long enough to shell and silence the Chinese guns. Although enemy fire was causing many casualties among the troopers who remained on the tanks, Colonel Crombez, speaking in a calm and cool voice over the radio network, each time directed the column to continue forward.[27]

Task Force Crombez, in turn, maintained a volume of rifle, machine-gun, and cannon fire that, throughout the six-mile attack, could be heard by members of the infantry battalions still in position at the task force point of departure. Much of this fire was directed only against the bordering hills, but there were also definite targets at which to aim—enemy machine guns, bazooka teams, and individual Chinese carrying pole or satchel charges. Even though it was difficult to aim from moving tanks, the remaining troopers kept firing—at Chinese soldiers who several times were within fifty yards of the road. On one occasion Captain Barrett shot and killed three enemy soldiers who, trotting across a rice field toward the tanks, were carrying a bangalore torpedo.[28]

Because of the intense enemy fire on the road, Colonel Crombez decided that wheeled traffic would be unable to get through. When he had gone about two thirds of the way to Chipyong-ni, he radioed back instructions to hold up the supply trucks and ambulances and await further orders.[29]

The Chinese made an all-out effort to halt Task Force Crombez when the leading tanks entered the deep roadcut south of Chipyong-ni. For a distance of about 150 yards the road passed between steep embankments that were between 30 and 50 feet high. And on each side of the road at that point were dominating hills, the one on the right (east) side of the road being Hill 397 from which the Chinese had launched several of their attacks against the Chipyong-ni perimeter. There was a sudden flare-up of enemy fire as the point tank (commanded by Lt. Lawrence L. DeSchweinitz) approached the cut. Mortar rounds exploded on and near the road. SFC James Maxwell (in the second tank) spotted an enemy soldier carrying a bazooka along the top of the embankment at the roadcut. He immediately radioed a warning to Lieutenant DeSchweinitz, but before he got the call through a bazooka round struck the point tank, hitting the top of the turret and wounding DeSchweinitz, the gunner (Cpl. Donald P. Harrell), and the loader (Pvt. Joseph Galard). The tank continued but without communication since the explosion also destroyed its radio.[30]

The four members of the engineer mine-detector team rode on the next tank in line (Sergeant Maxwell's). They clung to the tank as it entered the zone of intense enemy fire. An antitank rocket or pole charge exploded on each side of Maxwell's tank as it entered the pass and one of the engineers was shot from the deck, but the vehicle continued, as did the next tank in the column.[31]

Captain Hiers (tank company commander) rode in the fourth tank that entered the road cut. Striking the turret, a bazooka round penetrated the armor and exploded the ammunition in the ready racks inside. The tank started to burn. The men in the fighting compartment, including Captain Hiers, were killed. Although severely burned, the driver of the tank (Cpl. John A. Calhoun) gunned the engine and drove through the cut and off the road, thus permitting the remainder of the column to advance.[32] It was later learned that this tank was destroyed by an American 3.5-inch bazooka which had fallen into enemy hands.[33]

With the enemy located at the top of the cliffs directly overlooking the task force column and throwing satchel charges and firing rockets down at the tanks, close teamwork among the tankers became particularly necessary for mutual protection. As each of the remaining tanks rammed through the cut, crews from the tanks that followed and those already beyond the danger area fired a heavy blast at the embankments on both sides of the road. This cut down enemy activity during the minute or less required for each tank to run the cut. The enemy fire did, however, thin out the infantrymen riding on the tanks and, at the tail of the task force, flattened a tire on the 2½-ton truck that had been gathering up the wounded infantrymen who had either fallen or been knocked from the tanks. The driver had been hit near Koksu-ri as he was putting a wounded infantryman on the truck. Another wounded man (SFC George A. Krizan) drove after that and, although he was wounded a second time, continued driving until the truck was disabled at the roadcut. A few of the wounded men managed to get to one of the last tanks in the column, which carried them on into Chipyong-ni. The others, surrounded by the enemy, became missing in action.[34]

Meanwhile, within the perimeter of the 23d RCT at Chipyong-ni, the 2d Battalion was fighting off stubborn and persistent enemy attempts to overrun the sector shared by Company G, 23d Infantry, and Battery A, 503d Field Artillery Battalion, on the south rim of the perimeter. Late in the afternoon of 15 February, after twenty hours of uninterrupted fighting, the battalion commander managed to send four tanks a short distance down the road leading south beyond the regimental defense perimeter with the mission of getting behind the Chinese and firing into their exposed flank and rear. Ten or fifteen minutes of firing by the four tanks appeared to have suddenly disrupted the Chinese organization. Enemy soldiers began running.

Just at that moment, tanks of Task Force Crombez appeared from the south. Sergeant Maxwell, in the second tank, saw the four tanks on the road ahead and was just about to open fire when he recognized them as friendly. The leading tanks stopped. For about a minute everyone waited, then Sergeant Maxwell dismounted and walked forward to make contact with the 23d Infantry's tanks. He asked them to withdraw and allow Task Force Crombez to get through.[35]

By this time the Chinese were in the process of abandoning their positions south of Chipyong-ni and many were attempting to escape. Enemy opposition dwindled. With enemy soldiers moving in the open, targets were plentiful for a short time and Colonel Crombez halted his force long enough to take the Chinese under fire.[36]

At 1700 Task Force Crombez entered the Chipyong-ni perimeter. It had required an hour and fifteen minutes for the tanks to break through a little more than six miles of enemy territory. Even though there were neither supply trucks nor ambulances with the column, and although the task force itself was low on ammunition, infantrymen were cheered by the sight of reinforcements.

Of 160 Company L infantrymen plus the 4 engineers who had started out riding the tank decks, only 23 remained. Of these, 13 were wounded, of whom 1 died of wounds that evening. Some members of that company already had returned to join the remainder of the 3d Battalion near the point of departure; a few wounded men lay scattered along the road between Koksu-ri and Chipyong-ni. While crossing the six miles of drab and barren country between those two villages, Company L lost about 70 men —nearly half of its strength. Twelve men were dead, 19 were missing in action, and about 40 were wounded.[37]

With only an hour of daylight remaining, Colonel Crombez had to choose between returning at once to his regiment, or spending the night at Chipyong-ni. Any enemy opposition encountered on a return trip that evening would probably delay into darkness the contact with friendly forces, and unprotected tanks operating in the darkness, he reasoned, could be ambushed easily by enemy groups.[38]

On the other hand, the 23d RCT was dangerously low on small-caliber ammunition, airdrops that day having contained only artillery shells.[39] Task Force Crombez had fired most of its ammunition during the action. Officers inside the perimeter wondered if there were enough small-arms ammunition to beat off another Chinese attack.

There was another reason for returning. Seriously wounded infantrymen within the perimeter urgently needed to be evacuated. It was also probable that men from Company L who had been wounded or stranded during the attack by Task Force Crombez were waiting near the road, according to their instructions, hoping to be picked up again as the tanks made the return trip. However, weighing the two risks, Colonel Crombez chose to stay. He arranged to station his tanks around the perimeter to strengthen the defense, but no attack came. Except for a few flares that appeared over enemy territory, the night passed quietly. Toward morning it began to snow.

At 0900, 16 February, the scheduled time for return to the regiment, Colonel Crombez informed his assembled force that the return trip would be postponed because the snow, reducing visibility at times to less than a hundred yards, prevented air cover. It was 1100 before the weather cleared and the task force was reassembled. This time Colonel Crombez stated that only volunteers from the infantrymen and the engineer mine-detecting crew would ride on the tanks. None volunteered. Instead, an artillery liaison plane hovered over the column as it moved south. The observer in the plane had instructions to adjust proximity-fuzed shells directly on the column if the enemy attempted to destroy any of the tanks. On the return trip not a single enemy was seen, nor a shot fired.[40]

Immediately upon his return Colonel Crombez ordered the assembled supply train to proceed to Chipyong-ni. Escorted by tanks, twenty-eight 2½-ton trucks and nineteen ambulances pulled out in the middle of the afternoon. For his part, Captain Barrett (the Company L commander), having returned with the task force because he wanted to find out what had happened to the rest of his company, set out in a jeep to retrace the route and search for wounded men who might still be lying along the road. He found four whom he turned over to the evacuation train at Chipyong-ni. The ambulances and seven 2½-ton trucks, all loaded with wounded men from the 23d Regimental Combat Team, left Chipyong-ni that evening. The siege was ended.[41]

★ DISCUSSION

The few details in the narrative concerning the situation before the departure of Task Force Crombez do not permit sound criticism. However, it does appear that either the enemy was underestimated or friendly capabilities for attacking were overestimated. It hardly seems likely that foot soldiers fighting a determined enemy in the rough terrain of Korea could be expected to advance fifteen miles to Chipyong-ni in one day.

Simplicity is a virtue applied to military operations. It means that units and individuals have but a limited number of clearly defined moves to make or jobs to do. It is not confined to brevity in orders; sometimes the simplest maneuver is simple only when detailed orders are issued to all participants. Simplicity of execution usually results from comprehensive and careful planning, which is frequently time-consuming and not simple. But the complexities of planning are relatively unimportant. It is for simplicity of execution that commanders must strive. The mission assigned Task Force Crombez was simple to state but difficult to execute. Task Force Crombez accomplished its mission but it paid an extremely high price. The cost can be attributed to inadequate planning and a subsequent lack of coordination.

Plans must be based on intelligence of the enemy, an evaluation of the terrain, and a knowledge of one's own capabilities. Hindsight clearly indicates that in this instance not one soldier should have ridden on top of the tanks. Friendly artillery and the tanks with their own machine guns could have provided adequate close-in protection for the armored column. No engineers were necessary to remove mines.

Coordination is neither accidental nor automatic. It comes with training, experience, and planning. When trained and experienced troops fail to coordinate their efforts, the failure must be attributed to a lack of planning. Complete lack of artillery support contributed to the difficulties of

Task Force Crombez. Coordination between the artillery commanders supporting the 5th Cavalry and the 23d Infantry could have provided artillery support over the entire distance—from the point of departure to Chipyong-ni. The absence of coordination between the tanks and their riders is outstanding. Communication failures on two different occasions further point up deficiency in planning and coordination.

★ NOTES

1. 5th Cavalry Regiment: S3 report, 15 February 1951.

2. The narrative of this action is based upon a series of interviews made and recorded in March 1951 by Capt. Martin Blumenson with officers and men of Task Force Crombez. They were submitted as part of Eighth Army: command report, section V (After Action Interviews: Task Force Crombez). In this narrative, reference to the interviews will be made by referring to separate interviews as statements by the person under interview.

3. Statement of Col. Marcel G. Crombez.

4. 5th Cavalry Regiment: command report, 14 February 1951.

5. Statement of Lt.Col. George B. Pickett.

6. Crombez, *op. cit.*

7. Statement of Major Robert A. Humphrey.

8. *Ibid.*

9. Crombez, *op. cit.*

10. *Ibid.*

11. *Ibid.*

12. Statement of Capt. John C. Barrett; statement of Major Charles J. Parziale.

13. Crombez, *op. cit.*

14. *Ibid.*

15. Barrett, *op. cit.*

16. Statement of CWO C. L. Umberger, who was unit adminitrative officer of Company L, 5th Cavalry.

17. Barrett, *op. cit.*

18. Parziale, *op. cit.*

19. Crombez, *op. cit.*

20. Statement of MSgt. Jessie O. Giddens.

21. Statement of MSgt. Lloyd L. Jones.

22. Crombez, *op. cit.*

23. Jones, *op. cit.;* statement of SFC George W. Miller.

24. Barrett, *op. cit.*

25. This estimate is based upon Barrett, *op. cit.*, which appears to be the most accurate in this instance.

26. 5th Cavalry Regiment: command report (comments by regimental commander), 15 February 1951.

27. Humphrey, *op. cit.*

28. Barrett, *op. cit.*

29. Crombez, *op. cit.*

30. Statement of SFC James Maxwell.

31. Crombez, *op. cit.*

32. *Ibid.;* statement of Lt. William R. Bierwirth.

33. Pickett, *op. cit.*

34. Crombez, *op. cit.;* statement of Cpl. Wayne O. Kemp.

35. Maxwell, *op. cit.*

36. Crombez, *op. cit.*

37. *Ibid.;* Barrett, *op. cit.* See Company L, 5th Cavalry: morning reports, 13 to 25 February 1951.

38. Crombez, *op. cit.*

39. X Corps: command report (inclosures: 23d RCT Defense, Chipyong-ni).

40. Crombez, *op. cit.*

41. Barrett, *op. cit.;* statement of Capt. Keith M. Stewart.

They say that Henri of Navarre at Ivry told his cavalry to follow the white plume on his helmet when he ordered the charge that decided the battle and the future of France. Plumes are out of fashion today, but every leader can still set before him a figurative white plume—his mission—never to be lost sight of until his objective is attained.

THE INFANTRY JOURNAL (1943)

10

Tank Support

★ Members of Company A, 89th Medium Tank Batallion, crawled out of their sleeping bags at 0330 on 7 March 1951. Breakfast was scheduled at 0345, the attack at 0615.[1]

It was snowing. The heavy wet flakes, which melted soon after they fell, made the ground wet and slippery. Through the darkness and the usual early morning fog, the drivers went off to start the engines of their tanks so that they would warm up during breakfast.

Bivouacked in the half-destroyed village of Kwirin-ni, Company A was ready to move as soon as the men finished breakfast and rolled up their sleeping bags. The company's 15 tanks and 1 tank recovery vehicle were dispersed among the buildings of the village, carefully located so that each would occupy its designated position in the column when it moved onto the road. The vehicles were already loaded with ammunition, carrying, in addition to the regular load of 71 rounds, 54 rounds that each crew had stacked on the rear deck of its tank. Fastened to the eight tanks that were to be at the head of the column were trailers, each carrying nested twelve-man assault boats.

Company A's mission for 7 March 1951 was to support the 35th Infantry (25th Infantry Division) in its assault crossing of the Han River. For the operation the tank company was attached to the infantry regiment, and further detailed to support the 3d Battalion. Orders for the crossing, originating at Eighth Army, reached the 35th Infantry on 2 March. Regimental and battalion officers had begun at once to plan for the crossing and to train troops in the use of assault boats. Commanders, flying in liaison planes above the river, had searched for possible crossing sites. The Intelligence and Reconnaissance Platoon patrolled the south bank of the river to get specific information.[2]

Since the engineers had estimated that the Han River would be 7 to 9 feet deep at the time of the crossing, division and regimental orders included no plan to get tanks across the river during the assault phase. There was a plan, however, to construct a fifty-ton-capacity floating bridge, which the engineers anticipated would be in use by early evening of the first day of the assault.[3] After delivering fire across the river in support of the infantry crossing, the tanks were to continue direct fire support of the ground movement until they could cross on the bridge.

As the planning progressed, Lt.Col. Welborn G. Dolvin (commander of the 89th Tank Battalion) considered the possibility of getting tanks across the river in time to give close and effective support while the infantrymen were expanding their bridgehead. After reconnoitering the river bank and and making several flights over the area, Colonel Dolvin suggested this possibility to the commander of Company A (Capt. Herbert A. Brannon). He did not order Captain Brannon to attempt the crossing but only suggested that he fully investigate the possibilities, and that the advantages of giving tank support when the infantrymen most needed it warranted the risk involved.

"It's worth a gamble," Dolvin said.

Captain Brannon went to the engineers for more information about the depth of the water and the condition of the river bottom. Unfortunately, there was scant information on either, since the Chinese kept the river effectively covered with machine-gun fire both day and night. Captain Brannon studied aerial photographs of the crossing site and decided to gamble one tank on the crossing.

On 4 March Brannon moved his tank company into a forward assembly area at Kwirin-ni about two miles from the proposed crossing site. That evening he called his platoon leaders to his mud hut and told them he intended to attempt to ford the river. His plan was to send one tank, towing a cable from the winch of the tank recovery vehicle, across the river. If the water proved to be too deep and the tank swamped out, the recovery vehicle on the south bank could pull it back. If the tank made it to the north bank, the others would follow the same route. The leader of the 3d Platoon (Lt. Thomas J. Allie) volunteered to take the first tank into the water.

The next morning Captain Brannon made a reconnaissance of the south bank of the Han. Hills and embankments on the right and in the central part of the regimental zone fell abruptly to the river. Only on the left, in the 3d Battalion's sector, were the banks gentle enough to permit a crossing. This area, at the point where the Pukhan River joins the Han, was of necessity the crossing site for all assault units of the 35th Infantry. About a thousand yards upstream from the confluence of the rivers, there was a small, flat island dividing the Han into two channels, the near about 250 feet wide and the far about 200.

Captain Brannon walked along the river bank until he was opposite the island or sand bar. Aerial photographs indicated he would find the most promising route at the west end of this island. After choosing a route for the tank crossing, he selected positions from which all three platoons could best support the crossing of the infantrymen.

Since all movement to the river bank on 7 March would be hidden by darkness, tank-platoon leaders, accompanied by Captain Brannon, made their own reconnaissance on 6 March, locating the routes and the positions they would occupy.

Engineers, responsible for furnishing and manning the assault boats, asked Captain Brannon to haul these craft to the river bank. There were two reasons for this: the engineers feared their trucks would get stuck in the loose sand near the river, and the regiment was anxious to have as few vehicles as possible on the roads leading to the crossing site on the morning of the assault. Each trailer carried five assault boats. Engineers were to ride on the trailers to the crossing site, unhook them, and then remain until the infantrymen arrived to put the boats into the water. After dropping the trailers, the tanks would proceed to their selected positions and prepare to fire. The schedule called for the tanks to fire a twenty-minute preparation beginning at 0555. At 0615 infantrymen of the 3d Battalion, 35th Infantry, would push the assault boats into the water and row toward the hostile north bank of the river.

Quietly, early on the morning of 7 March, Company A tankers finished breakfast, rolled up their sleeping bags, and then moved the tanks onto the road. When Captain Brannon ordered the column forward at 0430, it had stopped snowing. The tanks moved slowly; the tank commanders did not want to make unnecessary noise by racing the engines, and it was too dark at the time for the drivers to see more than the outline of the road.

Exactly as planned, the tank column proceeded to the river bank, stopped only long enough for the engineers to uncouple the trailers, then continued by platoons to firing positions. It was about 0545. From across the river came the sound of occasional shell bursts. The preparation fire was not scheduled until twenty minutes before jump-off. At 0555 four battalions of 105mm howitzers, a battalion of 155mm howitzers, and a regiment of British guns commenced firing on previously designated targets.[4] Captain Brannon's tanks opened direct fire against targets on the north bank of the Han. For this fire, the crews used the ammunition loaded on the rear decks of the tanks, keeping the regular load of ammunition for use if they could successfully ford the river.

It was still so dark that the tankers could see only the hazy outline of hills across the river. At 0615, on schedule, infantrymen pushed assault

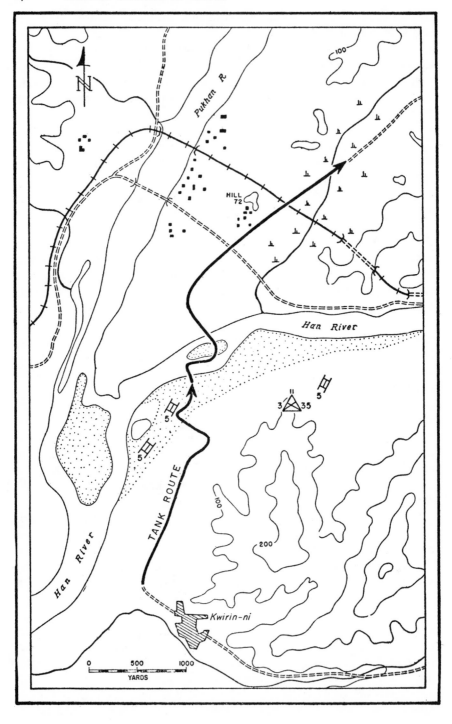

boats into the water, and the assault wave, still partly hidden from the enemy by the dim half-light of early morning, started across the river. The infantrymen crossed several hundred yards below the sand bar, following a different route than that the tankers expected to take.

The crossing progressed on schedule although enemy machine-gun fire punched small holes in several of the boats, wounding some of the occupants. Once across the river, the assault companies came under concentrated small-arms fire soon after leaving the gentle rise on the north river bank. At the same time, enemy artillery fire began falling on the south bank. Besides interfering with activities on that side of the river, the fire destroyed sections of a foot bridge then under construction.

Lt.Col. James H. Lee (infantry battalion commander) and Captain Brannon watched the river-crossing operation from the battalion's observation post. At 0740, when he received word that all assault units of his battalion were across, Colonel Lee, who was skeptical of the success of the crossing, told Captain Brannon that the north bank was secure. "You can try crossing if you wish."

Captain Brannon called Lieutenant Allie, who had offered to take the first tank into the water.

Already within two hundred yards of the river, the two vehicles moved to the edge of the water and stopped to connect the winch cable from the recovery vehicle to Lieutenant Allie's tank. About 0800 Allie's tank went into the water, heading toward the west (downstream) end of the sandy island near the middle of the river. Lieutenant Allie stood erect in the open hatch, calling out instructions to the driver over the tank intercommunication system. The water was only about three feet deep, and since the Sherman tank was designed to ford water to that depth, there was no difficulty except that the speed of the tank, limited by the speed at which the motor-driven winch on the recovery vehicle could pay out the cable, was slow. After the tank had gone two thirds of the distance to the island, the winch suddenly caught. The moving tank dragged the other vehicle for several feet, and then the cable broke, pulling apart at the coupling fastened to Lieutenant Allie's tank. Relieved to find the tank able to move freely, the tank driver (Sgt. Guillory Johnson) increased his speed. Within a few minutes after leaving the south bank, the tank reached the lower end of the sand bar.

Originally, Lieutenant Allie had planned to proceed straight across, but once on the island, he could see at its east end what appeared to be footings for an old bridge. Crossing to the up-river end of the island, Lieutenant Allie turned into the water again. The tank dipped steeply into water that momentarily covered the hatches over Sergeant Johnson and his assistant driver, wetting both men. An experienced tank driver, Johnson at once increased the speed of the tank to keep the water from closing in behind the tank and drowning out the engine. The tank climbed out of the water at each of the three old earthen bridge footings but, after a few seconds, it would plunge again into the water deep enough to come up to the turret ring. Nevertheless, after being in the water for two minutes or less, the tank reached the opposite bank.

After radioing back for the next tank in line to follow, Lieutenant Allie moved forward a short distance and then waited for the rest of his platoon. SFC Starling W. Harmon, following the same route with his tank, joined his platoon leader within five minutes. Wanting to have only one tank in the river at a time, Lieutenant Allie waited until Sergeant Harmon was on the north bank of the Han River before calling for the third tank. Because its escape hatch had jarred loose during the firing that morning, the third tank flooded out and stalled in the comparatively shallow water south of the island. Lieutenant Allie ordered his two remaining tanks, one at a time, to proceed around the stalled tank and cross.

With two tanks, Lieutenant Allie set out at 0830 to join the infantry. Having advanced a little more than a thousand yards, the infantrymen had stalled temporarily near a road that cut across the tip of land between the Pukhan and the Han. Enemy fire coming from a small hill and from a railroad embankment six hundred yards ahead had stopped them. The two tanks moved forward, directing their fire against the small hill. When fire from the hill stopped, the two tank crews turned their cannon toward the railroad embankment. There were six freight cars standing on the tracks. They had been burned and shot up, apparently during an air raid. The Chinese had placed three machine guns to fire under the cars into the area to the south. With their own machine guns and 12 or 15 rounds from their cannon, the tank crews quickly silenced the enemy guns. The infantrymen moved up even with the two tanks, a gain of six hundred yards. As the infantrymen moved beyond the railroad tracks, following the two tanks which ranged ahead, three other enemy machine guns commenced firing. Lieutenant Allie spotted one, laid on it with the 76mm gun and fired two rounds, the second of which threw parts of bodies and weapons into the air. The other two tanks of Lieutenant Allie's platoon arrived in time to take part in the firing, and a tank commanded by MSgt. Curtis D. Harrell located and silenced another machine gun. Then, all four tanks raked the enemy positions with their coaxial machine guns during a thirty-minute period while the front line advanced approximately seven hundred yards to the objective.

In the meantime, as soon as Lieutenant Allie's tanks were on the north bank, Captain Brannon started another platoon across. Within twenty minutes these five tanks were moving forward to support another infantry company and the last platoon of tanks began to cross. By 1000 all Company A's tanks except one were moving forward with the assault companies; by noon Colonel Lee's 3d Battalion had reached its objective. The remaining tank, which had flooded out earlier in the morning when its escape hatch fell out, was repaired by midafternoon and successfully crossed the river.

The river crossing was a success and, as Colonel Lee believed, the close support furnished by the tanks was a big factor in the outcome of the operation.

★ DISCUSSION

Too often there are recorded in tales of battle instances of commanders failing to remember the principle of the objective. Obstacles and fleeting attractions divert them from the accomplishment of their missions. A successful commander will always engage in a relentless pursuit of the end to be gained, but he will not be stubborn without reason. Rather, he tempers his tenacity with a spirit of adaptation to the fluid circumstances of the battlefield. Only explicit orders from a superior commander will relieve him from bending every effort of his command to the mission.

Captain Brannon and Lieutenant Allie were not content with a mere routine execution of close support. Once assigned their mission they showed courage, initiative, resourcefulness, and resolution in accomplishing it. When Scharnhorst was asked to comment on the appointment of Blücher to high command in the German Army, he wrote, "Is it not the manner in which the leaders carry out the task of command, of impressing their resolution in the hearts of others, that makes them warriors far more than all other aptitudes or faculties which theory may expect of them?"

★ NOTES

1. Unless otherwise cited, the information upon which this narrative is based was obtained from Capt. Herbert A. Brannon, Lt. Paul B. Harkness and Lt. Thomas J. Allie (all of Company A, 89th Medium Tank Battalion) in an interview by the author on 3 September 1951.

2. 25th Infantry Division, command report: 35th Infantry Regiment, March 1951 (narrative section).

3. *Ibid.*

4. *Ibid.*

II

A Rifle Company as a Covering Force

★ Toward the end of April 1951, Communist forces in North Korea launched an offensive against the peninsula-wide United Nations line. Except near Kaesong, at the west end, Eighth Army troops were ten or more miles north of the 38th parallel when the enemy attack began on the 22d day of the month. Although the attack was general in both plan and scope, North Korean units fighting on the east end of the front made only scant efforts and small advances. Chinese Communist forces concentrated on the west half of the line, aiming the heavy punch at the city of Seoul, thirty-five miles south of existing lines. The Chinese called the attack the "First Step, Fifth Phase Offensive."

This enemy activity interrupted an Eighth Army limited offensive that contemplated seizing the Chorwon–Kumhwa–Pyonggang area, an important communication and supply area commonly called "The Iron Triangle." The 3d Infantry Division was attacking north toward Chorwon and Pyonggang along the road running from Seoul through these towns and then north to the eastern port city of Wonsan. Units of the 3d were within ten miles of Chorwon and about the same distance north of the Imjin River.[1]

As usual, the Chinese waited until after dark before launching their big attack. By morning on the following day (23 April) they had penetrated United Nations' lines at widely scattered points and, under orders, units of Eighth Army began falling back. The 3d Division gave up ten miles of territory, returned to the south bank of the Imjin River, and there, by the evening of the 23d, took up previously prepared positions on an established Eighth Army fortified defense line. The 7th Infantry (3d Divi-

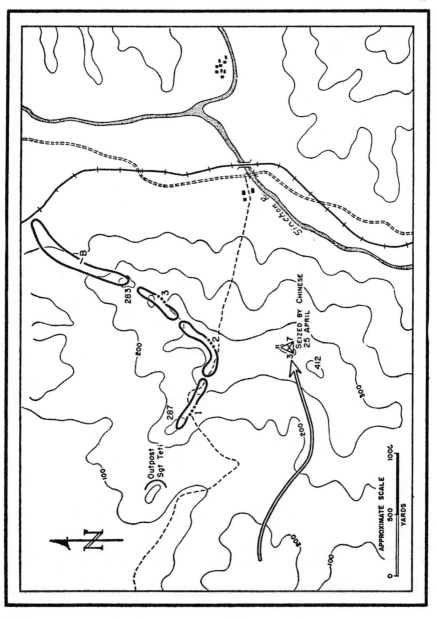

sion) was placed on a ridge overlooking the important Seoul–Chorwon–Wonsan road and the single-track railroad that parallels it. The position was especially important since it guarded the crossing site of the Imjin River. This was the same road and river crossing the North Koreans had used when they first invaded South Korean territory during the summer of 1950.

The 7th Infantry positions were not more than a thousand yards south of the 38th parallel, the former boundary between North and South Korea. The 1st Battalion occupied the east end of the regimental sector. Company B manned the bunkers and foxholes on Hill 283 and those along the ridge-line that slanted down toward the road. Company A's sector extended from Company B, southwest across a long, brush-covered saddle, then west along the top of Hill 287—a company front of 1,400 yards. Beyond Company A there was a gap of about 500 yards between its left-flank position and the right flank of the 3d Battalion, which occupied another ridgeline to the north and west.

To cover the wide Company A front, its commander (Lt. Harley F. Mooney) committed his three rifle platoons on his front line, leaving as his reserve a force of only eight men including himself, his executive officer, and his Weapons Platoon leader. Except for being thinly manned, however, Mooney's defensive positions were good. In most places the north side of the hill was too steep to permit the enemy to maneuver in front of the company.

The Weapons Platoon leader (Lt. John N. Middlemas) covered the critical areas with his weapons. He "fired-in" mortar concentrations in front of each platoon and located his mortar position near the center of the company front and only a few yards behind it so that the mortar crews would immediately be available if needed for front-line action.

Lieutenant Mooney considered his left flank the weakest section of the line since the best approach for the Chinese was at that end. In addition, the existing gap between the two battalions made that area more vulnerable. He stationed the 1st Platoon (MSgt. Joseph J. Lock) at that end. To cover the gap between the two battalions, Sergeant Lock sent his second-in-command (SFC Thomas R. Teti) with nine other men to establish an outpost on a small hill between the two battalions. Mooney then instructed Teti to make physical contact with the adjoining unit of the 3d Battalion once an hour. Company I agreed to send a patrol to contact Teti's outpost on alternate half-hour periods.

This was the position of troops when Chinese Communists renewed their attack on the morning of 24 April. Within the defensive position of the 7th Infantry, the heaviest enemy pressure was against the 3d Battalion, which was engaged throughout the day and the following night. Another enemy force struck Company B's end of the line and started a heavy fire fight that lasted from midnight until first light on 25 April. Men from Company A waited quietly and tensely between these areas of activity, watching and listening. They were not disturbed.

At 0700 on 25 April a large enemy force attacked an observation post that the 3d Battalion had established on a hill about four hundred yards south of Lieutenant Mooney's company. Since this hill was over three hundred feet higher than front-line positions of either the 1st or 3d Battalions, it afforded observation of both battalions. The enemy force, after having penetrated the lines during the night, made a sudden and strong assault against the observation-post hill, forcing the battalion commander and his group to abandon it hurriedly. In enemy hands, this hill threatened both battalions.

Sergeant Lock, in charge of the left-flank platoon, watched this enemy action and, as soon as he realized what had happened, turned his machine gun toward the Chinese to restrict their movement and help the members of the observation-post party who were escaping toward the south and the north in order to rejoin Company A. Sergeant Lock also called Mooney, who immediately had his Weapons Platoon leader (Lieutenant Middlemas) shift his 57mm recoilless rifle to the west flank from where it could be fired more effectively against the Chinese.

Meanwhile, the S3 of the 1st Battalion called Mooney to tell him the regiment had orders to move to a fortified Eighth Army line just north of Seoul.

"You and Baker Company are to cover the withdrawal of the 3d Battalion and then be prepared to move Able Company out at 1000."

The S3 designated Lieutenant Mooney's company as rear guard for the move because there was a trail from the center of Company A's position that went southwest down the hill to the road to Seoul. This was the only easily accessible route by which the three companies of the 3d Battalion and the two companies of the 1st Battalion could get down with their equipment and wounded men. The plan outlined to Mooney was for the three companies of the 3d Battalion to move through Company A in column of companies. Company B then would pass through the right flank of Company A. This action was to begin immediately. Lieutenant Mooney called his platoon leaders to tell them of the orders, then walked over to the top of Hill 283 to coordinate plans with the commander of Company B (Capt. Ray W. Blandin, Jr.). The time was about 0800.

At the opposite end of the line Sergeant Lock's platoon was still busy firing at the Chinese, who were now in full possession of the 3d Battalion's OP hill. On the north side of this hill there was a trail that the Chinese followed, and near the top the trail curved around a large rock. Sergeant Lock's machine gunner (Cpl. Pedro Colon Rodriguez) zeroed his light machine gun in on that point on the trail—a range of about three hundred yards—and fired cautiously, usually squeezing off one round at a time, throughout the morning. He did not fire at every Chinese who passed the point, but after hitting one, would allow one or several others to pass unmolested before firing again. Because he was not greedy the Chinese kept using the trail and Rodriguez hit a total of fifty-nine enemy soldiers during several hours of firing.

After returning from Company B's position, Lieutenant Mooney and his executive officer (Lt. Leonard Haley) briefed the platoon leaders on the plan for moving Company A after the other units had started down the trail. To better cover his route of withdrawal Mooney decided to peel off his line from the left. Sergeant Teti's outpost between the two battalions would follow the last element of the 3d Battalion. Sergeant Lock's platoon would follow Teti; next, the 2d Platoon would follow and move through the 3d which would hold the right flank until the rest of the company was on the trail; then it would move out.

By the time Mooney had thoroughly briefed his platoon leaders it was 0900. There were still heavy exchanges of fire between the Chinese on the OP hill and Lock's left-flank platoon. Mooney, believing that the next action would be against this platoon, went to the west end of his line where he could best observe that situation. He was also anxious to learn what was happening to the 3d Battalion, knowing that the commander had lost control at the time his group was forced to leave the observation post. Even though an hour and a half had gone by since the order to leave had been issued, none of the men from 3d Battalion had yet reached the outpost position manned by Sergeant Teti, who had orders to call Mooney as soon as the first men appeared. Teti could see only an increase of enemy activity in the zone of the 3d Battalion. At the same time, the volume of rifle and machine-gun fire from the OP hill had increased steadily.

It was about 0915 when the first of the 3d Battalion—men from Company K—came through Lieutenant Mooney's area. They were tired from the activity during the previous night and day, and walked slowly along the narrow trail. They sat down if there was any delay along the single-file column. Mooney urged them to hurry. This made little impression on the weary men, however, and the column moved haltingly. It required forty-five minutes for Company K to clear, and by the time men from the next company appeared it was after 1000. This was the hour scheduled for Company A to begin moving but Mooney, now that this was no longer possible, called his battalion headquarters again for further orders. He was told to wait until everyone else was off the ridgeline before moving his own company.

At the opposite end of the battalion front, however, Company B's commander (Captain Blandin) started his company down the trail at 1000 according to plan, unaware that the plan had broken down. Lieutenant Mooney received the information by telephone from his executive officer (Lieutenant Haley). This posed a new threat on the east flank although Mooney still believed the Chinese were most likely to strike Sergeant Lock's platoon at the west end of the line. He told Haley to send a few men to outpost the top of Hill 283, which had been Company B's left flank, and to bend the right flank of the company line south and refuse it. Haley sent a sergeant with four men to outpost Hill 283.

While these events were taking place, four planes made a strike with napalm and rockets on the OP hill causing a sudden drop in enemy fire from that area. A brief and relatively calm period followed while men from the 3d Battalion filed along the path. At 1100 the last men from Company I, still moving slowly, reached the spot where Lieutenant Mooney was waiting. Mooney urged the officers of the company to hurry, but they explained they needed litters and that the men were very tired. Mooney offered to furnish the litters, adding, "You'd better hurry or all of us will be up here and we'll be damned tired."

It had taken about two hours for two of the three companies to clear through Company A's area. In the meantime, Captain Blandin's Company B had reached the bottom of the hill where he reported to his battalion commander (Lt.Col. Fred D. Weyand). Colonel Weyand, realizing that the plans had miscarried, told him to get one platoon back on the top of the hill as quickly as possible to help Mooney hold his right flank.

Lt. Eugene C. May (a Company B officer) turned his platoon around and started back up the hill. He was near the top of the trail at 1130. When he arrived the last company of the 3d Battalion was strung out along the ridge top, and the entire company front was suddenly quiet. From the west end of the line Mooney called Lieutenant Middlemas who was now watching the east end of the line. Mooney explained that all the firing at his end of the line had stopped, and asked what was happening on the opposite flank.

"It's so quiet here," said Middlemas, "I'm just about ready to read some adventure stories for excitement."

At that instant there was the sound of scattered rifle fire from the top of Hill 283 where a sergeant and four men had been sent to outpost the right flank after Company B had vacated its sector. Hill 283 was just a large knob on the east end of the ridgeline. Between the knob and the right-flank position of Company A there was another smaller mound about forty yards beyond the last foxhole occupied by Lieutenant Mooney's men, and about seventy yards west of Hill 283.

Within a minute or two the sergeant in charge of the outpost appeared, running from the intermediate mound and yelling in a voice loud enough to be heard by the entire 3d Platoon: "They're coming! They're coming! Millions of them! They'll banzai us!"

Middlemas was near the center of the company line when he heard and saw what was happening. He took off running as hard as he could go toward the sergeant. The two men met near the right flank, and Middlemas lunged, bringing the sergeant to the ground with a football tackle. The other four members of the sergeant's outpost were following him, "just as goslings follow along after a mother goose." At the same time, three of the infantrymen at that end of the line started to abandon their holes, fearing that the right flank was crumbling.

Lieutenant Middlemas was yelling loudly and pounding several of the men on their helmets. "Get the hell back in your positions! Get up on that damned hill!"

He shoved the three men back in their holes, called to the 3d Platoon to send up one squad immediately, and then started off chasing the sergeant from the outpost and his four men back to the intermediate brush-covered knoll. They arrived there just in time to shoot one Chinese who was racing up the opposite side. There were 10 or 15 more enemy soldiers running from Hill 283 toward them. If the Chinese took this intermediate knoll they could fire down onto the top of the trail, severing the only route of withdrawal and evacuation. Lieutenant Middlemas knew he would have to hold off the Chinese for at least a half hour, or suffer heavy losses. He also knew they would probably either win or lose the battle within the next few minutes.

"Get to firing. Get to firing!" Middlemas shouted.

The action on this end of the line developed fast. There was considerable enemy fire coming from Hill 283 and a few Chinese crept within grenade range before they were killed. Within another minute or two, however, an eight-man squad from the 3d Platoon reached the knoll, making a total of fourteen men there, including Middlemas. All of them were firing rapidly.

A platoon leader of Company D in charge of the two heavy machine guns with Company A saw the critical situation as it developed and rushed the heavy machine gun from the 3d Platoon to the knoll. Then he sent for both the light caliber .30 and the heavy machine gun that were with the 2d Platoon. All of this action had taken place within five minutes after the sergeant in charge of the outpost signaled the alarm.

The platoon from Company B, meanwhile, reached the top of the trail soon after the shooting started and hurried into position. This platoon had one light machine gun. Then crews with two machine guns from the 2d Platoon arrived so that, in less than ten minutes, Lieutenant Middlemas had four machine guns firing and approximately forty-five riflemen in position. The firing swelled into a noisy roar and even the sound of the clips coming out of the rifles made considerable noise. The Chinese, who had been trying to wriggle around both sides of Hill 283 and reach Middlemas's knoll, backed away to the protection of the reverse slope.

At the opposite end of the company line, Lieutenant Mooney heard the storm of activity and realized he had allowed himself to be drawn away from the center of his company front. He was now more than a thousand yards away from the main action. He started east along the trail, but it was clogged with men from the 3d Battalion who had squatted there as soon as the fire fight flared up at the east end. Mooney hurried along the trail telling the men to keep going and looking for their officers, one of whom he found also sitting by the trail resting.

"For Christ's sake," he said, "get up and get these men moving."

Farther along the trail he met Lieutenant Haley whom he instructed to strip all ammunition from the 3d Battalion men as they turned down the trail.

Up on the knoll the sergeant who had been in charge of the outpost had recovered his composure and was now reassuring his men. "We're holding them! By God, we're holding them!"

Gradually, after the strength and fire power increased and the men realized they could hold the small hill, they overcame their fear and their anxiety changed to bravado. One of the men started yelling, "Come and get it!" and the other men took it up, either firing or screaming at the Chinese. Once, when their rate of fire dropped noticeably, there was a sudden increase in the amount of fire received from the Chinese. After that experience the Americans kept up a heavy volume of fire, and although Lieutenant Middlemas believed it was this sudden and heavy base of fire that was built up in the first ten minutes of the action that saved the flank, he was now concerned with making the ammunition last until everyone was off the hill. He went back and forth across his short line cautioning the men to fire aimed shots and hold down their rate of firing. In addition to its basic load of ammunition and that taken from the 3d Battalion, Company A had 300 bandoleers of rifle ammunition that were still intact when this action commenced. Mooney had this carried up to the knoll on the right flank. Even so, there was danger of running out.

About 1145 Mooney reached the area of activity. At that time the last of the 3d Battalion was passing through Company A's area followed by Sergeant Teti's outpost, and then the rest of Sergeant Lock's platoon. Lieutenant Mooney got in touch with his battalion commander (Colonel Weyand) to tell him of the situation and that he desperately needed some artillery support. As it happened, the artillery forward observer with Company A had been shot in the leg just before this action started, and Mooney now had no map of the area. He explained to Colonel Weyand that he wanted the artillery to fall on the hill which Company B had occupied that morning.

"Put a round out somewhere," he said, "and maybe I can hear it."

Colonel Weyand had been over this terrain and was well acquainted with it. He called the artillery, gave them the general area, and asked for one round. Mooney reported that he could neither see nor hear this round, especially through the heavy firing going on where he was standing. Weyand then asked for a shift "right 200, drop 200" and within a minute this round fell squarely on the enemy, exploding on the far side of the mound where there was apparently a concentration of Chinese troops. In any event, there were loud screams from the Chinese.

Mooney yelled over the radio, "That's beautiful! That's beautiful! Fire for effect! Throw out some more!"

The troops around him commenced yelling with renewed enthusiasm. More shells landed in battery volleys, relieving the pressure against Lieutenant Middlemas and his crew.

Meanwhile, Lieutenant Mooney revised his plan for moving his company from the hill. The 1st and 2d Platoons on the west end of his line were already moving and were not affected, but the remainder of his force —which now had become a mixture of the 3d Platoon, his headquarters group, and the platoon from Company B—could not be moved as a unit. He ordered these men to move out one at a time, Indian fashion, with the men farthest from the trail moving first so that he would be able to keep men along the trail to protect it. This plan would also release the men in the order that they became least valuable.

The two heavy machine guns, having fired twenty-six boxes of ammunition, ran out and Mooney ordered them to leave. The other ammunition was running low and Colonel Weyand kept urging Mooney to hurry since the artillery battery firing for him was almost out of shells too. Weyand arranged for an air strike and the planes soon appeared circling overhead until called in. These could not be employed until after the artillery fire stopped, and Lieutenant Mooney asked for the artillery to continue as long as the ammunition lasted.

Shortly after 1200 Colonel Weyand again called, urging Mooney to "move fast and get down from there." Except for those men still firing at the Chinese, all men from Company A had cleared the top of the trail. Mooney asked for smoke to screen the movement of these men as they broke contact. With smoke and a mixture of explosive shells to replace the machine-gun and rifle fire, men from the last group started to leave—they needed no urging. Less than five minutes elapsed from the time the first of the forty-five left their position until the last was on the trail. As the last man left, the artillery fire stopped and the planes commenced the air strike.

The entire action on the right flank had lasted from 1130 until approximately 1215. During this time two men had been killed by enemy rifle fire. When the tail of the column had gone about seventy-five yards down the trail, a single mortar round landed on the trail, killing one man and wounding four others, including Lieutenants Middlemas and Mooney, both of whom were hit in the leg by mortar fragments. By the time this happened a few Chinese were at the top of the trail and began firing down upon the withdrawing column. The last men in the column turned to fire up at the top of the trail, backing down the hill as they did so.

★ DISCUSSION

Daylight withdrawals should be avoided when contact with the enemy is imminent. Only in an emergency such as faced the 7th Infantry on 25 April, should a daylight withdrawal from enemy contact be attempted. In a daylight withdrawal the normal procedure is to pull back first the front-line platoons under the cover of the support platoon; then the front-line companies under the cover of the reserve company; and finally the front-line battalions under the cover of the reserve battalion. When a company commander has no support holding a position from which it can cover with fire the withdrawal of his front-line platoons—when he is faced with the problem that faced Lieutenant Mooney who had his company deployed along a 1,400-yard line—he must determine which platoon can best cover the withdrawal of the rest of the company, then hope to get the covering platoon out with the help of battalion and regimental fire support. Lieutenant Mooney correctly analyzed his situation and his mission. He erred only when he decided that the enemy most likely would hit his company's left flank.

The 1st Battalion, 7th Infantry, enjoyed outstanding leadership in this action. Colonel Weyand commanded the battalion but left the command of Company A to Lieutenant Mooney. Lieutenant Mooney commanded his company without usurping the duties of his platoon leaders. Lieutenant Middlemas knew his job and bent every effort to perform it. Leaders at every echelon "thought on their feet."

Colonel Weyand was quick to send a platoon from Company B back to protect Company A's right flank. He skillfully employed supporting artillery and air to help his covering force. Lieutenant Mooney saw the situation developing and urged the withdrawing troops to hurry. He thought his left flank the more vulnerable but took prompt action when Company B withdrew and exposed his right flank. Lieutenant Middlemas probably saved the day with his quick and forceful leadership and his appreciation of how to obtain and maintain fire superiority. The Company D platoon leader used initiative and did not wait for orders to employ his machine guns. The men of the 1st Battalion, 7th Infantry, responded as disciplined soldiers always will to high-caliber leadership.

★ NOTE

1. This narrative is based upon information supplied by Capt. Harley F. Mooney, Lt. John N. Middlemas, and Lt.Col. Fred C. Weyand in an interview by the author. The author also made a careful inspection of the terrain.

Regard your soldiers as your children, and they will follow you into the deepest valleys; look on them as your own beloved sons, and they will stand by you even unto death.

If, however, you are indulgent, but unable to make your authority felt; kind hearted but unable to enforce your commands; and incapable, moreover, of quelling disorder, then your soldiers must be likened to spoiled children; they are useless for any practical purpose.

SUN TZU: THE ART OF WAR

12

Artillery in Perimeter Defense

★ The U.S. IX Corps, near the center of the Korean peninsula, renewed an attack on 21 April 1951 to seize a line running generally from Kumhwa to Hwachon Reservoir. The corps included only two divisions at the time—the U.S. 1st Marine Division and a ROK division. The attack went well. Both divisions, meeting no enemy opposition, gained about three miles. They encountered only scant resistance after they jumped off again on the morning of 22 April.[1]

Front-line units advanced two more miles on the 22d. The enemy made little effort to interfere although, late in the afternoon, artillery and air observers reported an unusual amount of enemy movement north of the line.[2]

That night the Chinese struck back with their own 1951 spring offensive, a full-scale attack, which they labelled the "First Step, Fifth Phase Offensive." The Chinese limited their offensive to the western half of the front lines, the eastern prong of which pointed directly at the IX Corps' ROK division. It appeared that the Chinese had made it easy for IX Corps troops to advance so that they, in turn, could launch their own attack when friendly forces were extended and before they had a chance to dig in securely again. By 2000 enemy soldiers were several thousand yards behind friendly lines and were firing on artillery units that had displaced forward only that afternoon. Front lines crumbled within an hour or two. Infantrymen poured back on the double. Artillery units were forced to withdraw.[3]

The liaison officer from the 92d Armored Field Artillery Battalion to one of the ROK regiments (Capt. Floyd C. Hines) radioed his battalion. "Someone's pushed the panic button up here," he warned.

The battalion commander (Lt.Col. Leon F. Lavoie) received this message on his jeep radio as he was on the way to Corps Artillery headquarters where he intended to seek immediate engineer help to repair and maintain the precariously narrow supply road. From other messages it was soon evident to Colonel Lavoie that the Chinese had made a serious penetration of the lines. Stopping at the first military installation he came to, he called IX Corps Artillery to report the information he had on the front-line situation, and then, because the emphasis had suddenly shifted from repairing the supply road to defending it, he turned back to his own battalion.

The 92d Armored Field Artillery Battalion, reinforcing the fires of both divisions of the corps, had moved forward that afternoon to a point near the boundary between the ROKs and marines, a little less than half way from Chichon-ni to Sachang-ni. The road between these two villages, following a deep river gorge, was exceedingly narrow. By 2130, when Colonel Lavoie got back to his battalion, the road was jammed with vehicles and ROK infantrymen were moving back pell-mell along both sides of it. Putting his entire battalion on a man-battle-stations basis, Colonel Lavoie and his staff officers tried desperately to collect stragglers and stop the withdrawal, but the momentum was too great by the time the soldiers reached Colonel Lavoie's battalion and most of them continued determinedly on.[4]

When morning came on 23 April the Chinese, in possession of a three-mile-deep corridor west of the 1st Marine Division, turned to attack the Marine left flank. They completely overran one ROK artillery battalion and the 2d Rocket Field Artillery Battery, both of which lost all equipment.[5] The 987th Armored Field Artillery Battalion, partially overrun, lost some.[6]

Colonel Lavoie's 92d Field Artillery Battalion (a self-propelled 155mm howitzer unit) moved back battery by battery to a new position near the Pukhan River south of Chichon-ni. Batteries registered as soon as they were laid.

Battery C, in position north of a trail-size road through the new battalion position, placed its howitzers on the reverse slope of an incline that offered defilade. Battery A and Headquarters Battery were in a rice paddy south of the road with Battery A, 17th Field Artillery Battalion. Battery A of the 17th was an 8-inch howitzer outfit temporarily attached to the 92d Field Artillery Battalion to replace its own Battery B which, in turn, was attached to the 17th Field Artillery Battalion. (The lower half of the map on page 165 shows the batteries' positions in detail.)

Late in the afternoon the last howitzer was laid and ready to fire. The general military situation was tense. The artillerymen, having had little sleep during the past thirty-six hours, were tired, but immediately went to work establishing their usual perimeter for the night. Colonel Lavoie—tall, and gentle almost to the point of shyness—insisted upon always having a well-fortified perimeter. Even when smiling, as he usually was, he had a way of being obdurately firm about the condition of the battalion perimeter, as he also was about standards of performance. Convinced that his responsibility as an artillery commander was to insure continuous artillery support to the infantry, he also reasoned that the very time when the infantrymen would most urgently need supporting artillery might well coincide with an enemy attack on his own perimeter. Colonel Lavoie had therefore developed a standard defensive perimeter that, from the outside toward the gun batteries in the center, consisted of patrols covering neighboring terrain; outposts, usually centered around a halftrack, for warning and delaying; a dug-in and fully manned main battle line just beyond grenade range of the battalion's critical installations; and a highly mobile reserve in the center. This reserve force usually was made up of two or three halftracks with 8 or 10 men for each vehicle.[7]

Colonel Lavoie's acting executive officer (Major Roy A. Tucker) set up the perimeter on the afternoon of 23 April. Because of the limited time before darkness, which came about 1745, the perimeter was not as elaborately developed as usual, nor was there time to patrol nearby terrain. However, Major Tucker did establish a complete system of security outposts with trip flares ahead of the outposts, a complete telephone communication system, and a radio net as an alternate means of communication. He had laid out the main battle line but only a few positions were dug in at darkness. There was no defensive wire, demolitions were not out, nor had the men dug in and sandbagged such critical installations as the fire direction center and the communications center. These tasks had a lower priority and usually waited until the second or third day of the process of developing the battalion perimeter.[8]

Members of outpost detachments ate chow early and went to their halftracks or ground-mounted machine-gun positions before dusk in order to be familiar with their sectors of responsibility, fields of fire, and to check their communications. Thereafter, except for relief detachments, no traffic was allowed to the outposts or beyond the battalion perimeter. Colonel Lavoie wanted security guards to heed and challenge all movement or activity. Four to eight men manned each security outpost, half of them being on duty at a time. Colonel Lavoie inspected the perimeter defenses just before dark, pointing out to his men the Marine positions on the hill to the front.[9]

That night the battalion reinforced the fires of the 1st Marine Division. Corps Artillery headquarters called about 2100 with instructions for the 92d Field Artillery Battalion to prepare to remain in its present positions for several days. Colonel Lavoie promptly called the 11th Marine Regiment (an artillery unit) he was to reinforce and asked for further instructions. Wire sections laid telephone lines to the 11th Marines, completing the job

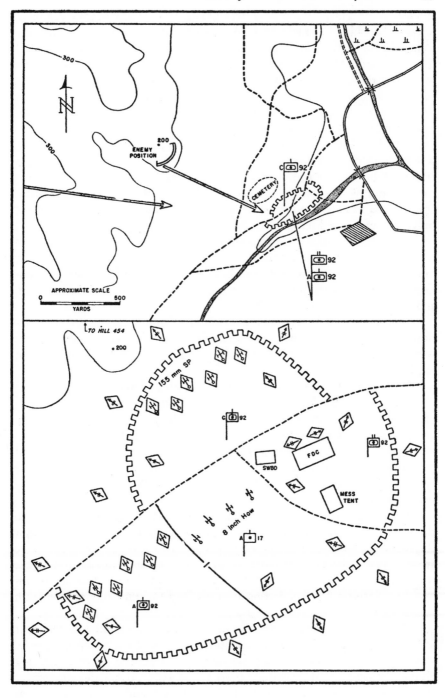

at 2300. Midnight passed and all was quiet. At 0115 the Marine regiment telephoned asking Colonel Lavoie to report immediately to its headquarters. When Lavoie arrived there, the Marine commander outlined a new plan. The 1st Marine Division, its entire left flank exposed, planned to withdraw soon after daylight on 24 April. Colonel Lavoie was to keep his howitzers in firing position until the last moment, but to be prepared to move at 0530. Battery A, 17th Field Artillery Battalion, with its heavy, towed howitzers, was to leave at 0400.

At 0230 Colonel Lavoie returned to his command post. Although he was very tired, he could not sleep and scarcely had time for it anyway. He reviewed the displacement plan, being particularly concerned about getting the 8-inch howitzers on the road at 0400. Battery commanders were called at 0315, and Colonel Lavoie gave them the complete plan and order for the move. He instructed his commanders to serve a hot breakfast.

The heavy howitzers moved out on schedule. At the same time guards were going through the battalion area waking all personnel. Within a few minutes there was the sound of trucks moving about and the usual commotion that goes with the job of getting up, packing equipment, striking tents, and loading trucks—all in the dark.

Gun sections still manned the howitzers, firing harassing and interdiction missions. The range had decreased during the night and the cannoneers were aware of increased machine-gun activity on the hill mass in front of the battalion.

Breakfast was ready at 0445. Chow lines formed in all batteries.

First sign of daylight appeared ten or fifteen minutes after 0500. Most of the men had finished breakfast. Most of the pyramidal tents, used because of cool weather, were down. In Headquarters Battery only the command post and kitchen tents were standing. In Battery A the kitchen tent was still up. The communications system was still intact but commanders had pulled in most of their outlying security installations. Equipment and personnel were just about ready for march order.

Colonel Lavoie, having eaten an early breakfast, had just returned to the mess tent where an attendant was pouring him a cup of coffee. Major Raymond F. Hotopp (battalion S3) prepared to leave on reconnaissance at 0530, placed his personal belongings in his jeep and walked over to see whether the battalion commander was ready. Capt. John F. Gerrity (commanding Battery A) was getting into his jeep to join Colonel Lavoie on reconnaissance.

An unidentified artilleryman from Battery C, with a roll of toilet paper in his hand, walked toward the cemetery in front of the howitzers. As he approached the mounds in the graveyard, he saw several Chinese crawling on their bellies toward his battery. Startled, he yelled, threw the toilet paper at an enemy soldier, turned, and ran. The Chinese soldier ducked involuntarily. At that moment, someone tripped a flare outside the perimeter. Capt.

Bernard G. Raftery (commanding Battery C) looked at his watch. It was 0520.

Machine guns opened fire. At first many thought someone had accidentally tripped a machine gun, since the marines were supposed to be in front of the artillery positions. But when the firing increased there was no more doubt. Men in the mess line scattered for cover. Major Hotopp dropped to the ground and dived under a halftrack. SFC Charles R. Linder (chief of section), warming his feet over the running "tank" motor,[10] jumped off and took cover behind the vehicle. Most of the men took cover wherever it was most quickly available.

Colonel Lavoie saw a bullet hole suddenly appear in the side of the mess tent. He ran outside. "Man battle stations!" he yelled, "Man battle stations!" and headed for his command post tent to get into communication with his battery commanders.

Captain Raftery looked at Lt. Joseph N. Hearin (Battery C executive). "This is it!" he said, scrambling to his feet. "Let's go!" He and Hearin got out of their command post tent at the same time.

SFC George T. Powell (Battery C chief of detail), anxious about some new men who had never seen combat, took off toward their section of the main battle line. When he arrived at the nearest halftracks, he found his men already manning the machine guns. Several others were setting up a machine gun on a ground mount. No longer anxious, Powell relaxed and began to enjoy the battle. Several other friendly machine guns were already in action.

SFC Willis V. Ruble, Jr. (Headquarters Battery motor sergeant), who at first thought the noise was caused by someone throwing wads of ammunition into the fire, ran for a halftrack and unzipped the canvas cover on a caliber .50 machine gun while several slugs whistled past, and he then looked about for a target. He saw four or five persons in the field in front of Battery A's positions. They were wearing dirty white civilian clothes and Ruble thought they were South Koreans until he saw one of them carrying a rifle. He fired three short bursts, knocked one of them down, spun another one around. Just then he noticed flashes on the hill in front. Figuring that the small-arms fire could take care of the enemy troops close in, Ruble turned his machine gun toward the distant flashes.

SFC James R. White (Battery A) remembered only being at a machine gun on a halftrack but did not know how he got there. By this time, a minute or two after the first shot had been fired, enemy fire was so intense that tracer bullets formed a thin red arch between the battalion's position and Hill 200, from which most of the enemy long-range fire came. The ammunition belt in White's machine gun was crossed. White was shaking so badly that he could not get it straightened, and he was afraid to expose himself above the ring mount. After a bit, he stood up, straightened the belt, and began firing.

The battalion executive officer (Major Tucker), who had started out to inspect the perimeter soon after the firing commenced, opened the rear door of White's halftrack and cautioned him and several other men in the vehicle to pick targets before firing. White then waited until he saw the location of the enemy machine guns before he fired. Visually following the tracers back toward the hill, White was able to locate an enemy emplacement. He opened fire again. He could see his own tracers hitting the hill, so he walked his fire in on the enemy position, then held it there until his belt gave out. White then reloaded his gun with a fresh belt (105 rounds) but did not fire at once. The man firing the caliber .30 machine gun on the same halftrack was playing it cool; he was firing in short bursts at enemy in a field across the road.

Within ten minutes or less the exchange of fire had become a noisy roar. Enemy bullets cut up the telephone wires that were strung overhead, forcing the battalion to rely on its radios.

Captain Raftery stood in the middle of Battery C's area trying to determine enemy intentions. The bulk of enemy fire against the battery appeared to be coming from Hill 200, where Raftery estimated there were six machine-gun emplacements, which the Chinese had reached by old communication trenches. As these entrenched troops acted as a base of fire, enemy riflemen took concealed positions in the cemetery while others, armed only with hand grenades, crawled toward the howitzers. Captain Raftery thought the Chinese were concentrating on his No. 5 howitzer—the most vulnerable because of its forward position. Enemy fire in that area was so intense that the artillerymen could not man the machine guns on the nearest halftrack. Deciding that the enemy was trying to knock out one howitzer and blow up the powder and ammunition for psychological effect, he called the chief of No. 5 howitzer section and instructed him to pull his "tank" back into defilade and on line with Nos. 4 and 6.

Behind the No. 4 howitzer, Lieutenant Hearin tried to see what the men were shooting at. Flashes on the hill were 600 to 1,000 yards away, and it seemed unusual that the enemy would attack from so far. He looked for enemy elements coming in under the base of fire. Suddenly he noticed men of the battery running from the No. 5 to the No. 6 howitzer. Several feet behind them, grenades were bursting.

Jumping on a halftrack, Hearin swung the caliber .50 machine gun around and shot a Chinese grenadier who was crawling up on the No. 5 piece. A couple of other machine-gunners swung their guns to help Hearin and, among them, they shot a half dozen enemy attempting to destroy the No. 5 howitzer.

Under cover of this fire, Sgt. Theral J. Hatley (chief of section) ran forward and backed his vehicle out of immediate reach of the enemy grenadiers, crushing one who lay concealed underneath.

After the initial scramble to their positions, Colonel Lavoie's men settled down to returning the fire with enthusiasm. Having staged so many "dry runs," the battalion commander was pleased to see the results of the practice. The firing, however, was getting out of hand and, although there was plenty of ammunition and more at Service Battery's position three miles away, Colonel Lavoie feared that they were experiencing only an initial attack calculated to pin them down while a larger force maneuvered from the west to seal the river defile and destroy the only bridge over the Pukhan. As soon as his executive officer returned from checking defensive positions, Colonel Lavoie changed places with him and set out to inspect the battle line. He wanted to see for himself the positions and the trend of the action, to be seen by the men for whatever effect that might have upon their morale, and to persuade the men to stop aimless and unnecessary firing. He sought out his three battery commanders.

"You must control and limit your fire to specific targets," Lavoie told them. "Make every bullet count."

Captain Raftery, who thought his Battery C was under the heaviest enemy fire, defended his men and their volume of fire. "Sir," he answered, "Battery C has Chinks all through its area."

"Are they dead or alive?"

"Both," said Raftery.

"Well, don't worry about the dead ones," Colonel Lavoie told him; "just take care of the live ones and make every bullet count."

Lavoie continued around the perimeter. He opened the rear doors on the halftracks and crawled up to talk with the machine gunners to ask them to cooperate in firing only at specific targets, and to tell them how successfully the battalion was holding off the Chinese.

One man told him he'd better get down. "It's dangerous up here," he explained. Others, reassured, only grinned.

On two occasions Lavoie found groups of two or three men huddled in the bed of a halftrack. He told them to get out and help: "I'm scared too. There's nothing wrong with being scared as long as you do your part." Ashamed, they promptly returned to their proper positions.

In Battery A's area, enemy fire was coming in from Hill 454 on the left-front as well as from Hill 200. Enemy snipers behind piles of rubble and rock were also firing from the field directly in front of Battery A. There was no haze and the artillerymen could clearly see enemy soldiers on the hills a thousand yards away.

Returning to his command post, Colonel Lavoie received a radio message from the Marine regimental headquarters objecting to excessive firing and ordering the artillerymen to cease fire.

"You're firing on friendly troops," the officer complained.

"Those friendly troops," Colonel Lavoie argued, "are inflicting casualties on my battalion."

While Lavoie was explaining the situation to the Marine commander,

Major Tucker made another round of the defensive position, rallying the men. The exchange of fire was still brisk, but the artillerymen appeared to be holding their own well and had recovered from their impulse to fire just to make noise.

Having persuaded the marines that his artillerymen had not been seized by panic, Colonel Lavoie called Battery A by radio and said he wanted to talk with Captain Gerrity. When the latter reached the command post tent, Colonel Lavoie instructed him to shift his battery—howitzer by howitzer —several hundred yards to the east, thereby reducing the size of the perimeter. When the battery of 8-inch howitzers had pulled out at 0400 it left a gap in the perimeter and also left Gerrity's battery vulnerable to an attack from the west, from which direction the battalion commander still thought the Chinese would probably make a larger attack designed to overrun his position. Gerrity called his battery by radio and gave it the code word for "close station and march order."

While the two officers, both of them lying on the ground near the radio and in front of the tent, were still talking, Colonel Lavoie spotted two enemy machine guns that were firing a high ratio of tracer bullets into the battalion's position. Pointing them out to Captain Gerrity, he asked him to take them under direct fire with his 155mm howitzers. Gerrity took off toward his battery position.

Bullets were still ricocheting against the "tanks" and halftracks when the close-station order reached Battery A. Captain Gerrity had given the order only to alert his men for the 300- or 400-yard shift. The artillerymen were reluctant to move and expose themselves to enemy fire while they cranked up the spades and prepared to move. Sergeant White, firing a machine gun from a halftrack, stood up, exposing himself completely, and shouted instructions at the men. Every man jumped to his job, and within a few minutes the battery was ready to move. It was about 0545—twenty-five minutes after the enemy first attacked.

Captain Gerrity, out of breath from running, returned to his battery just as the vehicles were ready to move. He shouted orders for the firing mission, the artillerymen dropped trails again and opened fire on the machine guns Colonel Lavoie had seen. The range was a thousand yards or less. After a few rounds one howitzer made a direct hit. Colonel Lavoie saw fragments of Chinese soldiers thrown twenty feet or higher in the air. Eight or ten Chinese soldiers suddenly appeared running from a trench about a hundred yards away from the last explosion. Several machine guns immediately swung toward them and killed three or four. Having destroyed the two machine guns, Battery A completed its displacement, tightening up the perimeter.

MSgt. John D. Elder appeared at the command post tent to get instructions for moving ammunition trucks from Service Battery. He wanted to know if Colonel Lavoie still planned to move.

"We were going to move," answered the Colonel, "but now we'll wait until we secure this position."

Colonel Lavoie set out to make another round of his defensive positions. His indifference to the enemy fire was a steadying influence. As he walked through the area, talking with the men and cautioning them to conserve ammunition, he noticed a great change in his troops. Over their initial scare, they now appeared to be enjoying themselves. A great deal of enemy fire continued to come into the area even though Chinese machine guns seemed subdued by this time, but the men no longer hesitated to expose themselves in order to fire their weapons effectively. Realizing that they were holding their own and winning, they had lost the fear and uneasiness Colonel Lavoie had seen on his first trip around the area. It had been replaced by a cocky sort of confidence.

A young artilleryman, usually shy, spotted a small group of Chinese crawling through weeds toward the fire direction center tent. "Look at them sons of bitches," he said. "They think they're going to make it." Standing up he aimed and fired. "I got one!" he exclaimed. Several other men began firing at the same group and soon destroyed it.[11]

Several Marine tanks rumbled down the road. No one had asked for help but the Marine commander sent them over to clean out the area in front of the battalion. Taking up positions north of the road and in front of Battery A, they blasted the hills and raked the field with machine-gun fire. Several artillerymen left their positions and set out "looking for Chinks."

Sgt. Austin E. Roberts (machine-gun sergeant) organized ten men and walked across the road toward the northwest. After they had gone only a few yards, a Chinese jumped up in front of them. One of Roberts's men fired, hitting an American Thompson submachine gun the enemy was carrying. The Chinese dropped it and held up his hand.

Roberts shouted "Don't shoot! Don't shoot!" and then sent his prisoner, guarded by two artillerymen, to battalion headquarters.

The remaining eight men, working with the tanks, went on across the field examining each hole and clearing the area for four hundred yards. They found no more enemy soldiers.

In the meantime, the Marine regiment that the 92d Field Artillery Battalion was supporting called a fire mission. Colonel Lavoie assigned it to Battery C, instructing the battery to transfer its radio to the Marine channel so it could receive the mission direct.

Captain Raftery's howitzers were engaged in delivering direct fire against nearby hills. Leaving one to continue with that mission, he relaid the other five howitzers to support the marines. This was the first "live" mission that morning, although the entire battalion had been firing harassing and interdiction missions before the enemy attack. Raftery then organized about twenty men into a skirmish line to cross the battery front. Moving through the cemetery and beyond, the force killed seven Chinese and captured one who had to be pulled out of his hole. The Marine tanks killed several others who attempted to escape back to the high ground.

Capt. Albert D. Bessler (S2), annoyed by persistent small-arms fire striking near the fire direction center tent, decided a sniper with scope must be firing from behind a pile of stones in a nearby field. He took a halftrack and investigated. Several minutes later he returned with two M1 rifles fitted with scopes. "Got two of them," he boasted.

A light aircraft overhead reported into the battalion radio net and asked if it could be of assistance. Colonel Lavoie, still apprehensive of an enemy attack from the west, requested the pilot to check the valley in that direction. The aircraft pilot reported that he saw no enemy build-up, but that two groups of 25 or 30 enemy each were in a draw near the base of the hills. Lavoie destroyed these groups with artillery fire.

By 0730 the situation permitted displacement of the batteries. The battalion suffered 4 men killed and 11 wounded during the action. It lost no equipment. Marine units later reported finding 179 enemy dead in the area around the battalion perimeter, all presumedly killed during the attack.

Colonel Lavoie was pleased with the performance of his men. The artillerymen shared a new feeling of confidence and pride. They had proved they could defend themselves.

"Artillery," the Colonel said, "if it makes up its mind, will set itself up so that it can defend itself from enemy infantry action."

★ DISCUSSION

There is no doubt that on 24 April 1951, the 92d Armored Field Artillery Battalion acquitted itself with great honor. For the military student the question is: Why? Part of the answer is found in the narrative. Good leadership is evident at all echelons—leadership based on knowledge and experience that inspired confidence and promoted cooperation. With each man accepting his share of duty the 92d Armored Field Artillery Battalion could not be made to panic. Individuals responded with the initiative of free men who know discipline without tyranny.

Although it is not mentioned in the narrative, Colonel Lavoie had, at the time of this action, commanded the battalion for about twenty months. He had trained it, and now he would fight it. Training will make or break an organization. Only by setting and maintaining high standards of performance during training can a commander expect similar standards in combat. It should be noted when estimating the state of training of the 92d Armored Field Artillery Battalion that the narrative does not once mention a weapon's jamming.

Standing operating procedures come from training. When not carried to a mechanical extreme they save time and help to minimize oversights.

Because Colonel Lavoie had insisted in training that the 92d habitually fire from a defensive perimeter, its occupation and organization of position on 23 April went smoothly. It was not a new maneuver—it was SOP.

★ NOTES

1. IX Corps: command report, April 1951 (narrative section).

2. *Ibid.*

3. 92d Armored FA Battalion: command report, April 1951 (narrative section).

4. 92d Armored FA Battalion: command report, April 1951.

5. 92d Armored FA Battalion: S3 journal, entry 2045, 22 April 1951.

6. Unless otherwise cited, this narrative is based upon "Artillery in Perimeter Defense," an account prepared in Korea by Capt. Martin Blumenson, on file in OCMH.

7. Department of Training Publications and Aids, The Artillery School: Debriefing Report 52 (Fort Sill, Oklahoma, 15 March 1952).

8. Lt.Col. Leon F. Lavoie, letter to OCMH, 12 January 1952.

9. *Ibid.*

10. Men of field artillery battalions styled their self-propelled howitzers "tanks."

11. The Artillery School, *op. cit.*

It is the part of a good general to talk of success, not of failure.

SOPHOCLES: ŒDIPUS COLONEUS. I. 1429

13

Hill 800 (Bunker Hill)

★ On the night of 16 May 1951 Chinese and North Korean Communists launched another major attack against United Nations forces. To the enemy, it was "Second Step, Fifth Phase Offensive." To soldiers of the United Nations it became known as "Second Spring Offensive," or, especially to members of U.S. X Corps, "The Battle of the Soyang River."

The First Step of the enemy's Fifth Phase Offensive had been at the west end of Eighth Army's line on 22 April. Its mission was the capture of Seoul and the encirclement of UN troops in that area. Although this offensive failed to gain its announced objective, it did force a major withdrawal at the west end of the UN line and, because of the necessity of shifting troops for the defense of Seoul, a readjustment of front lines everywhere. Near the center of the peninsula, X Corps gave up a little ground, dropping back to dominating ground just beyond, and protecting, the southwest-northeast main supply road between Hongchon and Inje.[1]

The First Step lasted eight days. By the night of 30 April, with the force of the attack exhausted, enemy troops turned north, and activity across the Korean front dropped sharply. At once the Chinese turned to preparations for the Second Step. Eighth Army, nevertheless, continued in a defensive role. In the center, X Corps proceeded to organize, occupy, and defend its new position along what it called "Noname Line." [2]

From the beginning of May Americans had reason to expect another attack, but it was several days before movement of enemy troops and supplies, reported by aerial observers, indicated the attack would be aimed at X Corps' center. Intelligence officers accumulated other substantiating evi-

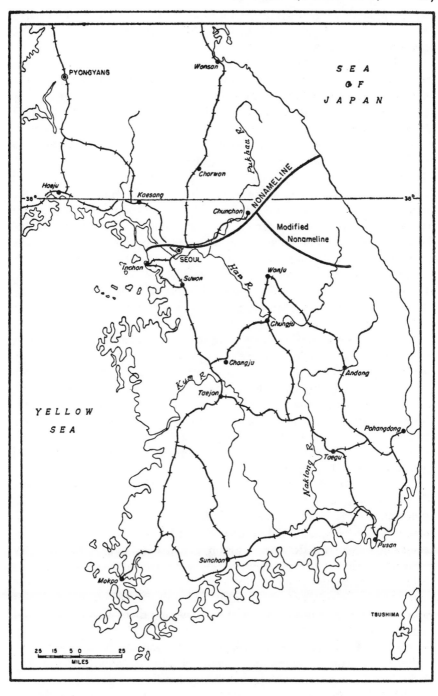

dence—including information from a captured Chinese officer who stated the next offensive would strike the U.S. 2d Infantry Division and the ROK divisions to the east.[8]

The 2d Infantry Division (Maj.Gen. Clark L. Ruffner) occupied the center position on X Corps' Noname Line, generally situated along the crest of a great, rugged hill mass separating two rivers—the Hongchon and the Soyang. The air-line distance across General Ruffner's sector was about sixteen miles. However, following barbed wire stretched from one bunker to another along the front, up and down the steep hills, and around the bends in the ridges, the distance was twice as great. Within his division, General Ruffner assigned the right half of his sector to a tank-infantry task force; the left (southwest) end, to the 38th Infantry Regiment. In turn, the commander of the 38th Infantry (Col. John C. Coughlin) stationed his 1st and 3d Battalions on Noname Line, the 3d Battalion being on the left.[4] Each of these battalions anchored its defense to a prominent hill mass: the 1st Battalion to Hill 1051 on the right of the regimental sector and, later, the 3d Battalion (on the left), to Hill 800. The initial defense sector given the 3d Battalion was about five and a half miles wide, later reduced to approximately four miles when the 9th Infantry was committed to a defense sector to the left of the 38th Infantry.

Hill 800 was typical of the terrain selected as a battle site by units of X Corps. It was ten miles or more from the main supply road and was accessible only by a single-lane dirt road that followed the curves of a small tributary of the Hongchon River. At the base of the sprawling hill mass, where the stream narrowed to a foot or two even during the spring rains, the road ended abruptly. The pointed peak of the hill was 1,600 feet above the end of the road and, for the average infantryman, more than an hour's climb away. All the tools, supplies, and equipment of war had to be carried over footpaths to the top of Hill 800.

The commander of the 3d Battalion, 38th Infantry (Lt.Col. Wallace M. Hanes) committed all three of his rifle companies to front-line defense, with Company K on the bald top of Hill 800 in the center of the battalion sector. Both horizontally and vertically, Hill 800 was the apex of the battalion's line. Having a defensive mission, Colonel Hanes gave first priority to clearing fields of fire and constructing bunkers, ordering all companies to build covered positions, one for every two or three men. Most of the men, thinking in terms of concealment and protection from heavy spring rains, dug their holes in the usual fashion, covering them with branches and ponchos, and then quit.

Colonel Hanes returned next day to inspect the positions. "*That's* concealment?" he complained to his company officers. "Dammit, I want bunkers with cover to protect you from artillery fire!"

Each day he returned and climbed the ridgelines to supervise the job of building fortifications. He made the men cut down more trees, dig more trenches, and pile more dirt on the bunkers. One company commander, when Colonel Hanes insisted on more earth over the bunkers in his area, asked for sand bags, saying he would need about five thousand.

"Five thousand!" stormed Hanes. "My God, man! You don't want *five* thousand sand bags. You want *twenty* thousand!"

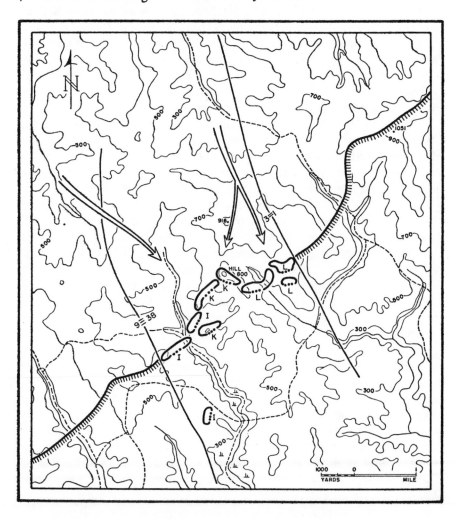

Even that number was later found to be inadequate.[5]

After a number of shifts in the battalion's sector and after laboring for a week to get the infantrymen to strengthen their positions with heavy logs and bags of earth, Colonel Hanes explained to his company commanders that if the enemy attacked in the numbers he expected, it might be necessary to fire friendly artillery on their (the Americans') own positions, using proximity fuze for air-burst effect.

"If it is necessary," he said, "I don't want you to worry about calling in the fire. I'll do that. All you have to do is fix up your bunkers so that you will have a clear field of fire to your front and to your neighbors' bunkers and won't get hit by your own shell fragments when I call down the fire."

After that, men of the 3d Battalion worked diligently. When the bunkers were completed to Hanes's satisfaction, he planned to string barbed wire and sow mines across the battalion's front. Because of the distance and the difficult terrain over which all supplies had to be carried, the infantrymen at first thought he was only joking when he talked of putting in wire. They believed him only when the Korean civilians began carrying rolls of barbed wire onto the hill and the men from the battalion's Ammunition and Pioneer Platoon arrived to supervise the work.

Seven hundred of these civilians carried supplies to the 3d Battalion. During the period of preparation, they moved 237,000 sand bags to the top of the hill; 385 rolls of barbed wire; almost 2,000 long steel pickets for installing wire aprons, and nearly 4,000 short ones; and 39 55-gallon fougasse drums. (A fougasse is a sort of dug-in, improved flamethrower made with a drum of napalm-thickened gasoline, an explosive charge of a couple of pounds of TNT or white phosphorus mortar shells, and a detonator. When detonated, the fougasse bursts into a mass of flame about 10 yards wide and 25 to 40 yards long.) This equipment was in addition to the normal supplies—rations, cans of water, and ammunition. It required eight Korean men to carry one fougasse drum up the hill; one man could carry a roll of barbed wire or a box of rations. A round trip took three or four hours. At the base of the hill were several buildings where members of the carrying parties were fed.

In addition to the laborers, the battalion used a herd of thirty-two oxen to transport a section of the heavy 4.2-inch mortars and to stockpile mortar ammunition. Because of dominant terrain features to the front of the battalion's positions, a special mountain trail was cut in the reverse slope of a mountain finger of the north-south ridgeline of which Hill 800 was a part, so as to permit the uninterrupted supply of Companies K and L and the heavy 4.2-inch mortars.

The most probable routes of enemy attack were blocked by two or more double-apron wire barriers; most of the battalion's front had at least one. As the wire situation improved, Colonel Hanes stressed other improvements—antipersonnel mine fields, trip flares, fougasse drums, buried telephone wires, and communication trenches.

On 10 May the commander of Eighth Army (Lt.Gen. James A. Van Fleet) and the commander of X Corps (Lt.Gen. E. M. Almond) landed by helicopter on Hill 800 and declared the 3d Battalion's preparations to be the most formidable in X Corps' sector.

By 12 May, when the bunkers were completed and most of the front was wired in, there were many indications that the enemy also had nearly completed preparations for his own attack.

While Colonel Hanes's battalion constructed its defenses, other units of the 2d Division sent out patrols daily to locate and engage the enemy. At the beginning of the month, patrols had made few contacts with the enemy, and none of the Chinese encountered displayed an inclination to stay and fight. Accordingly, General Ruffner ordered units to establish patrol bases several thousand yards to the front. From these bases they pushed patrols as far north as the Soyang River—a line distance of six or more miles away and parallel to the main line of resistance. Eighth Army directed that patrols be large enough to face a major attack and still fight their way back to the patrol base.[6] Within the sector of the 38th Infantry, the 2d Battalion established a patrol base in front of Hanes's 3d Battalion.

After 8 May stronger enemy patrols appeared, showing a sudden reluctance to withdraw. It became apparent that the enemy had set up a counter-reconnaissance screen and was becoming as assiduous in his attempts to locate 2d Division defensive strongpoints as were the friendly patrols in their search for enemy strength. By 10 May the enemy's build-up was in full swing.[7] Enemy vehicular traffic was heavier, patrols more numerous and more aggressive, new bridges appeared on the enemy's side, and there was a sudden flow of civilian refugees from the enemy's area.[8]

By 14 May men of Colonel Hanes's battalion had the strongest positions they had ever occupied, although they had taken a few enemy positions they considered as good. The confidence the men had in their ability to withstand an enemy attack—confidence that had increased with each log and sand bag, antipersonnel mine and roll of wire that had gone into their structure for defense—was equally strong.

General Ruffner lent his helicopter to Colonel Hanes so he could inspect the positions from the air.

"There's only one thing that worries me now, General," said Hanes when he returned. "I'm afraid those bastards won't hit us. If they've seen what I've seen today, and if they are smart, they won't even give us a nibble."

General Ruffner agreed.

If the enemy was going to attack the 3d Battalion, however, it appeared that one of his most suitable routes of approach would lead him squarely into Company K on the top of Hill 800 (by now the men who held Hill 800 had styled it Bunker Hill). Twelve hundred yards in front of Company K, and three hundred feet higher, was Hill 916. Instead of the usual steep ravine, a smooth saddle connected the two hills.

Hill 916 was a squat mass covered with patches of grass and scattered clumps of trees. There were enough trees on the south slopes to conceal the movement and assembly of enemy troops, especially at dusk. They would then be within easy range—having only to cross the connecting saddle before making the final assault on Company K's dome-shaped hill, or move down the ridge to attack Company L, which was holding the right flank of the battalion and was astride a ridge similarly connected to Hill 916.

Company K put two barbed-wire aprons across its end of the saddle. One stretched along three sides at the base of Hill 800. The other was approximately two hundred yards beyond. Members of Company K fastened trip flares and explosive charges to the wire, and planted antipersonnel mines between the aprons. This, they figured, would slow the attack when it came.

Twenty-three bunkers were located on the small but prominent top of Hill 800. Other positions of Company K were stretched along the ridgelines that slanted down to the southwest and southeast. The only apparent weakness in the defense position of Company K was its extensive front and the uncompleted prearranged close-support artillery concentrations—conditions that applied equally to the remainder of the 3d Battalion. Because of the 2d Battalion's patrol base located in front of Hanes's battalion, and because of the extensive patrolling conducted during the build-up period, firing of desired prearranged artillery concentrations was exceedingly difficult. Later, because of the numerous patrols and long-range observation posts dispatched and maintained by the 3d Battalion, artillery forward observers were unable to register all close-support fires.

The first fifteen days of May had passed without an enemy offensive. On the 16th there was a low, heavy overcast that prevented the use of observation or fighter aircraft. The Second Step of the Fifth Phase Offensive commenced that afternoon when probing patrols opened fire on United Nations positions. Stronger attacks struck both the 1st and 2d Battalions of the 38th Infantry that night. Before daylight on 17 May, the 2d Battalion was ordered to withdraw from its patrol base to positions in rear of the regimental main line of resistance. To the northeast, Chinese penetrated the lines of the 1st Battalion and seized the top of Hill 1051.[9]

Colonel Hanes's 3d Battalion, however, spent an uneventful night. The next day (17 May) men of that battalion strung more wire and prepared additional fougasses that they emplaced along probable enemy avenues of approach. They were to be set off by plunger-type detonator during the attack that everyone expected would come that night. A final adjustment was made on the left of the battalion's sector when its area was reduced by moving a unit of the 9th Infantry into line. After the long period of waiting and planning for the big attack, the suspense was over. Most of the men, confident of their positions, welcomed the attack. Morale was high. The day was hot and sultry.

Late in the afternoon, Company K's support platoon patrolled to Hill 916. It met heavy opposition where there had been no enemy before. From Hill 800 the commander of Company K (Capt. George R. Brownell) watched the progress of the patrol. He could see some Chinese troops following it back and others moving on the forward slope of Hill 916. He placed artillery and mortar fire on the enemy. The Chinese began registering their mortar and artillery fire. Enemy troops crowded against the front line across the battalion's entire sector. The battalion had numerous artillery missions fired and a number of effective air strikes were made. All patrols of the battalion were actively engaged.

With the attack imminent, Company K squared away. Captain Brownell, having previously located his command post too far to the rear, took his position at the very point of the defense in a bunker that was the battalion's observation post. His runner, an observer for the 81mm mortars, and two intelligence observers from the battalion's Headquarters Company, shared the bunker with him. Through error, his artillery forward observer was not with him. In other bunkers men rechecked their rifles and grenades —each man had twenty grenades—and waited quietly as the dusk deepened into darkness. A light fog formed and the air became damp and noticeably cold after the sultry day.

Everyone expected the attack to commence with a rapid succession of explosions from trip flares and mines. The mines would kill a lot of the enemy, they thought, and slacken the attack. But it didn't work out that way.

At about 2130 there was the sound of whistles and of a bugle or two. Nothing else happened for half an hour until the enemy troops reached the first wire barrier a hundred yards away. A flare or two appeared. Several minutes later a few of the antipersonnel mines exploded. At the same time, the Chinese opened fire. Captain Brownell's men could see none of the enemy yet, but from the steady sound of the enemy's fire, Brownell could measure the Chinese advance. Another half hour passed. The enemy's fire increased gradually. Finally the Americans could hear the Chinese soldiers talking, although they could see none of them. They wondered why more of the antipersonnel mines had not exploded.

Company K held its fire until the enemy reached the second wire barrier. Instead of moving frontally, the leading Chinese had slipped around to the west, cut the barbed wire in front of the 1st Platoon, and crawled up the steep part of the hill. At the point of first contact, the Americans opened fire with rifles and machine guns, and tossed grenades down the hill. Quickly Company K came to life, the action spreading in both directions like a grass fire.

Captain Brownell tried to get artillery fire. The artillery forward observer, however, was at a different observation post and, within a few minutes after the firing began, the telephone line went out between Captain Brownell's command post and the artillery observer's bunker. Unable to reach the observer, Brownell relayed his request to battalion headquarters, experiencing difficulties with communications in the process. In rapid succession, the lines to the 1st Platoon and to the battalion failed, apparently having been cut either by the Chinese or by their mortar and artillery fire. Company K had failed to bury all of its telephone lines.

Attached to and integrated with the defense of Company K were men from Company M manning machine guns and recoilless rifles. The lieutenant in charge was a replacement who had been recalled to active duty recently without a refresher course. He and some of his men occupied several bunkers near the point of first enemy contact. By the time the exchange of fire had increased to thunderous volume, the platoon leader left his bunker and ran a short distance to an adjoining one.

"It's getting pretty hot here," he said as he entered. After a few moments, he added, "It's getting too hot around here for me! Let's get out!"

He left and, in the darkness and through heavy enemy fire, headed toward the rear. Between 15 and 20 men followed him—those from the bunker he had just left and other men from several nearby positions.

This original break occurred near the limiting point between the two platoons on line—the 1st and the 3d. Cpl. James H. Kantner (runner from the 1st Platoon) ran to the point of the hill to tell Captain Brownell that "the line's broken." Captain Brownell gave up his attempt to adjust artillery fire and tried to get in touch with the 1st Platoon in order to determine the extent of the break. The line to the 1st Platoon was out. He sent Corporal Kantner back with instructions to tell everyone to hold where he was until Brownell had a chance to find out what happened. The runner left.

Within a minute or two, an enemy shell landed squarely on top of the command-post bunker. The explosion damaged the radio by which Captain Brownell had communicated with battalion headquarters. Thus, within fifteen minutes or less, Captain Brownell had lost communication with his platoons, his artillery forward observer, and battalion headquarters.

Leaving the battalion personnel in the bunker, Captain Brownell started toward the bunkers the men of Company M had occupied on the top of the hill. Chinese soldiers were wandering freely over the 200-yard-long point of Hill 800—the key terrain in Company K's defense. Without communication, Brownell's positions on this important part of Hill 800 crumbled quickly. Hearing the firing from the adjoining position suddenly end, the men from one bunker after another learned that the line was falling back. Chinese and Americans walked around together in the darkness.

PFC George C. Hipp, PFC Clarence E. Ricki and PFC Rodney R. Rowe occupied the northernmost bunker, guarding the approach to the hill. Not realizing the adjoining positions were abandoned, these men remained until it was too late to leave. Meanwhile, the battalion intelligence men, left in the bunker that Captain Brownell had recently occupied, moved to the bunker recently vacated by the lieutenant from Company M, and got in telephone communication with Colonel Hanes. Hanes immediately instructed his artillery liaison officer to place artillery fire in front of Company K. The first half hour of the enemy attack had created complete confusion at the very top of Hill 800.

Two men manning a 75mm recoilless-rifle position on the left side of the high point of the hill and just left of the steep ridge along which the Chinese had crawled up to Company K's position were miraculously able to make contact with the battalion's forward relay switchboard by sound-powered telephone. From their bunker they calmly reported the situation as they saw it to Colonel Hanes who, in turn, informed them of the situation known to the battalion. Hanes asked them if they could adjust artillery where they knew or suspected the enemy to be, bearing in mind that because of the confused situation and conflicting reports great care must be used so that no rounds fell on the battle positions. For a considerable time these men effectively adjusted fire as close to their bunker as was possible. Communications to this position remained effective during the entire night. With no previous experience in the adjustment of artillery, the two men helped seal off the battle position from further enemy reinforcements.

Unable to find the men of Company M at their bunkers, Captain Brownell hurried on back to the command post of the 3d Platoon. This platoon had telephone communication with battalion headquarters. He called Colonel Hanes to report the loss of the point of his hill, to request permission to use his support platoon in a counterattack (Colonel Hanes had placed restrictions on the use of this platoon), and to ask for artillery fire.

A few of the men who had abandoned their positions walked on down the trail that led south to Colonel Hanes's battalion headquarters. Most of them went back only a short distance where the leader of the 3d Platoon (Lt. Blair W. Price) stopped them and began forming a new line between the open flanks of Company K's line. Although this was soon done, Captain Brownell's defense was vulnerable since he had lost the highest and most important area of his sector, and about a third of his line was hastily formed and lacked protection of even a foxhole. Fortunately, enemy activity temporarily dropped off.

Having obtained permission to use the 2d Platoon and having moved it into position for the attack, Captain Brownell tried to precede his counterattack by placing artillery fire on his former position. A long delay followed, partly because of faulty communications, partly because Brownell was out of touch with his forward observer and was unable to adjust the desired fire properly, but primarily because Captain Brownell's situation report was in conflict with the information Hanes was receiving from the battalion's intelligence men and from the 75mm recoilless-rifle team who were adjusting artillery fire for him. Until a more accurate picture could be received, Colonel Hanes considered it advisable to seal the penetration with available artillery fire while the remainder of the 38th Field Artillery

Battalion, which was in direct support of the 3d Battalion, supported Company L, which was under tremendous pressure at the time.

Meanwhile, Lieutenants Price and Herbert E. Clark (leader of the 2d Platoon) and SFC Thomas K. Whitten lined up approximately thirty-five men who were to make the counterattack. They also arranged for 2 machine-gun crews, 2 BAR men, and 6 riflemen to fire onto the point of the hill when Clark's platoon moved forward.

At the same time, a few of the men—including the lieutenant from Company M who started the movement to abandon the position—had reached the bottom of the hill. Colonel Hanes met them.

"Get back on the hill," he told them. "We don't give up a position until we're beaten. And dammit, we're not beaten and won't be if every man does his share!"

They turned around and started the long climb up the hill. The lieutenant from Company M returned to his unit in due time although he was wounded in the side, arms, and leg before again reaching the protection of his bunker.

After waiting more than an hour for artillery fire, which could not be properly adjusted because of his faulty communications, Captain Brownell and his platoon leaders decided to launch the attack without support.

"To hell with it!" said Lieutenant Price. "We can take the damned hill ourselves."

Although he expected considerable trouble, Captain Brownell was afraid that if he delayed the attack any longer the Chinese would discover the weakly held gap in his line, break through in force, and threaten or possibly destroy the battalion's entire defensive position.

With Captain Brownell, two platoon leaders, and Sergeant Whitten guiding, the 35-man skirmish line started forward, the men firing steadily and walking erect under the supporting rifle and machine-gun fire. The enemy fired back with two machine guns—one of their own and one Company K had abandoned on the top of the hill. Both sides used American white phosphorus grenades of which there was an abundant supply on the hill. As Company K's attack progressed, the men threw one or two grenades into each bunker they passed; otherwise they and the Chinese used them for illumination. At the moment of a grenade burst the hill and the line of infantrymen stood out prominently in the eerie white light. In the alternate periods of darkness, the men could see nothing. The first white phosphorus grenade thrown by the enemy landed at one end of the skirmish line. The entire line stopped momentarily. One man fell dead with a bullet through his neck. A burning streamer from another grenade hit Cpl. Virgil J. Penwell's rifle, setting the stock on fire and burning Penwell's sleeve.

Captain Brownell's counterattack progressed steadily, moving a yard or two with each grenade-burst. As the line reached the highest part of the hill, a grenade-burst revealed three Chinese 15 or 20 feet ahead, kneeling side by side in firing position.

Sgt. Virgil E. Butler, who had thrown the grenade, yelled, "Get them where you can see them!"

Half a dozen men fired at once. At the same time, a Chinese whistle sounded and when the next grenade exploded two of the Chinese had disappeared. The third, still kneeling, was dead. A rifle left by one of his comrades leaned against his body. Enemy opposition diminished suddenly and then, except for a few rifle shots, ended.

By 0130, 18 May, Captain Brownell's counterattacking force had spread out to occupy the rest of Hill 800. Eight men had been wounded during the attack; only one had been killed. It had been easier than any of the men expected. Captain Brownell immediately reorganized the highest portion of his company's sector. The men set up machine guns again, re-allocated the supply of ammunition and grenades, and reoccupied all of the bunkers except the one farthest north. This bunker was still occupied by Hipp, Ricki and Rowe, who had remained in it throughout the enemy occupancy of the hill. They had heard enemy soldiers talking and moving nearby, but did nothing to cause a disturbance. Nor did anyone bother them. They heard the American counterattack approaching, saw the Chinese soldiers falling back, and then one of them commenced to fire a BAR to let the other men of Company K know they were still there. Men in the nearby bunkers, however, assuming that these three men were dead and taking no unnecessary chances, fired upon the bunker the rest of the night. It was not until daylight that Hipp, Ricki and Rowe were able to identify themselves.

Communications were restored, and artillery and 4.2-inch mortar fire was concentrated on the saddle leading to Hill 916. Nothing else happened on Hill 800 for the rest of the night. The men pulled blankets around themselves and sat shivering in the cold, damp bunkers while the night dragged out. About two hundred enemy had infiltrated Company K's positions through and around the battalion's right flank, and had sniped at supply and communications personnel.

While Hill 800 was secure for the rest of the night, increasing pressure was placed on the extreme left flank of Company K's front and on Company I, to its left. Preceded by heavy artillery and mortar fire, at 0415 the Chinese overran Company I's right flank and the left flank of Company K.

The reserve platoon of Company I, which had been given the mission of clearing enemy snipers from the ridge recently occupied by the reserve platoon of Company K, was immediately withdrawn in order to seal the gap between the two companies and restore the line. The reserve platoon of Company K was ordered to continue its screening mission from Hill 800 south along the ridge to Hill 754.

When morning came on 18 May, the men on Hill 800 scouted the area. They found 2 live Chinese, 28 bodies on top of the hill and in bunkers, and 40 or 50 more along the barbed wire in front of the position. Besides bodies, the enemy had left a previously captured American machine gun, fourteen burp guns, rifles, packs, and food. There were also many unexploded American grenades scattered over the hill. The Chinese had failed to pull the pins and had thrown them after only bending the handles.

Company K went to work rebuilding its defenses, replacing barbed wire the enemy had cut the night before, repairing telephone wires and—equally important—burying the wire under eight inches of earth as the men had originally been told to do. The forward observer from the 38th Field Artillery Battalion registered in artillery in a solid semicircle around the area in front of Company K.

Colonel Hanes set out to make a personal reconnaissance and inspect his defenses. He found the line intact with the exception of the one penetration between Companies K and I, and this break was larger than previously reported. He estimated that several hundred Chinese had crowded into bunkers formerly occupied by members of the two companies. With such a large break in his line, Hanes realized he would have to restore these positions before dark or his battalion would be unable to prevent a major breakthrough the next night.

Assembling the support platoons from both companies, Hanes organized a counterattacking force and quickly briefed the men on the situation. Although they were exhausted from their arduous activity during the previous night, Hanes exhorted them to make every effort to restore the line before darkness fell again. He prepared for the attack by firing more than a thousand 4.2-inch mortar shells.

As the counterattack got under way Colonel Hanes intensified the mortar fire. Under this fire—the heaviest ever observed by members of the attacking platoons—the Chinese abandoned the bunkers and broke in full retreat. Before launching his attack Colonel Hanes had instructed the mortar observers to register concentrations along the only route by which the enemy could escape. When the enemy "bugout" started, the observers yelled for more fire, shifting the concentrations to keep up with the retreating Chinese. There were two halftracks near the bottom of the hill in Company I's sector, and crews manning the quad caliber .50 machine guns on these halftracks poured enfilade fire into the Chinese as they scrambled through the double-apron wire fences through which they had crawled during the night. The mortar men fired so rapidly that they burned their tubes and bent the base plates. The attacking infantrymen, moving closely behind the well-coordinated mortar and machine-gun fire, shouted jubilantly. It was a most successful attack. Enemy losses were high and Colonel Hanes's force restored the 3d Battalion's positions without suffering any casualties.

By the end of the day, Company K had rebuilt its defenses and cor-rected the weaknesses of the previous night. Artillery observers had fired on suspected enemy movement and assembly areas throughout the day and

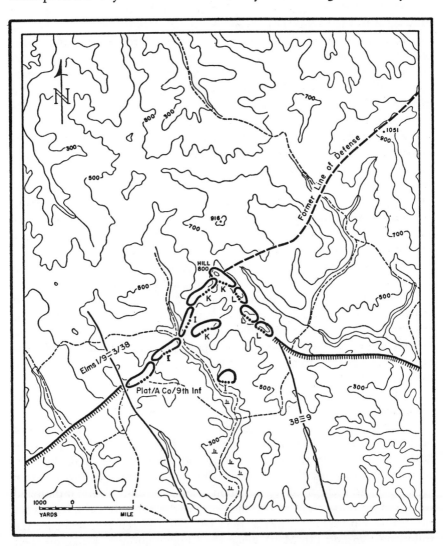

the regimental commander had given Hanes's battalion priority on air sup-port. Planes made several strikes against Hill 916. Nevertheless, toward eve-ning Chinese began moving on the southern slope of Hill 916, indicating that another attack was in the making.

East of the 3d Battalion, the enemy had dislodged two ROK divisions and parts of the U.S. 2d Infantry Division from the Noname Line. The en-tire right flank of X Corps was in process of falling back and turning its line to prevent an enemy envelopment. The new line, anchored on Company L, extended in a southeast direction to the town of Hangye on the Hongchon River.[10]

When darkness came on 18 May, Captain Brownell and his men crawled into their bunkers to wait. An hour or two passed. Beyond the barbed wire there were the sounds of whistles and horns, and the usual commotion as the enemy formed to attack. After waiting and listening for several minutes, Brownell requested artillery fire. It came promptly, interrupting the enemy attack, or at least delaying it for twenty or thirty minutes. When it was re-formed, the forward observer signalled for another concentration.

Several attacks were held off in this fashion before any enemy succeeded in reaching Company K's line. When they did, the company commander warned his platoon leaders of what he was going to do, and then asked for the artillery to drop proximity-fuzed shells squarely on top of his company. The first shell burst overhead within a minute. Two thousand 105mm shells fell during the next eight minutes.[11] It was the heaviest concentration of artillery fire any of his men had experienced. They sat in the rear of their bunkers, staying well clear of the openings.

"You think we'll ever get out of this alive?" one of the men asked his bunker companion. At the time few men thought they would.

The artillery fire ended and a sudden quiet settled over the area. It remained quiet for twenty minutes or longer before more shells—this time from the enemy—fell in preparation for the next enemy attack. Again Company K waited until the Chinese were upon its position, then asked for another concentration. In the midst of the firing, Captain Brownell reported to Colonel Hanes.

"The position is completely covered with fire," he told his battalion commander. "Nothing could live above ground in this."

Men of Company K did little fighting themselves that night. They just sat in their earth-covered bunkers and waited for the enemy. When they heard enemy activity the men would notify Captain Brownell of the location, and the forward observer would shift the artillery's air-bursts to that area. The 38th Field Artillery Battalion alone fired more than ten thousand rounds in support of the 3d Battalion during the night. It was a record for that artillery battalion.[12] Most of the shells fell between 2200 and 0400 the following morning (19 May) when the Chinese abruptly broke off their attack.

When daylight came the enemy had disappeared, this time taking all supplies and equipment from his side of the barbed wire. Emerging from their bunkers, men of Company K were in full possession of the hill. The left-wing company of the battalion (Company I) was also in its original position, but Colonel Hanes had withdrawn Company L a short distance during the night in order to refuse his right flank.

Across the Korean peninsula Hanes's battalion was the northernmost unit on the United Nations' line. Before the enemy attack, the United Nations' front lines had extended northeast from a point just north of Seoul. The east end of this line, turning on Company K's Hill 800, had fallen back during the three-day battle to a defense line that slanted southeast and became known as Modified Noname Line. Situation maps at X Corps and 2d Division headquarters, on the morning of 19 May, showed the 3d Battalion, 38th Infantry, holding the northern point of a deep bulge in the front lines.

The commanding generals of X Corps (General Almond) and the 2d Division (General Ruffner) met in mid-morning and decided it would be necessary to abandon this bulge and withdraw the 38th Infantry in order to straighten and consolidate the corps' line.[13]

When advised of this decision, Colonel Hanes protested. His defensive position, he argued, was still solid and could withstand any attack the enemy could throw against him. He preferred to stay where he was. General Ruffner ordered him to take up new positions to the south.[14]

Colonel Hanes passed the order down to his commanders who, like himself, hated to give up a position upon which they had worked hard. Hanes told his commanders to explain to all members of their companies that they were giving up their positions not because they had been beaten by the enemy, but because they had been ordered to withdraw. He ordered them to gather up all equipment and supplies in their company sectors, and march down by companies.

The regimental commander (Col. John C. Coughlin) was at the bottom of the hill when the 3d Battalion came down that afternoon. He watched the infantrymen march past. Their horseshoe packs were rolled tight, their heads were high, their shoulders were thrown back. They had proved they could beat an all-out enemy attack, and they looked proud and cocky and confident.

★ NOTES

1. X Corps: Bulletin 8, Enemy Tactics, 16 May to 1 June 1951.

2. X Corps: Operations Order No. 20, 1 May 1951.

3. X Corps: Bulletin 8, cited above.

4. 2d Infantry Division: command report, May 1951.

5. Unless otherwise noted, the narrative of this combat action is based upon after-action interviews by the author with key participants. Soon after the action the author interviewed the commander of Company K (Capt. George R. Brownell) and five members of his company (SFC Francis R. Fahey, PFC Earl Hall, PFC Samuel E. Overlease, Cpl. Roy E. Bottlow, and PFC John N. Giellis). The author also discussed the action several times with the battalion

commander (Lt.Col. Wallace M. Hanes) in Korea at the scene of the action and later after both had returned to the United States.

6. 2d Infantry Division, *op. cit.*

7. *Ibid.*

8. *Ibid.*, narrative section; X Corps: Battle of the Soyang River, May 1951.

9. X Corps, after action reports: RCT operations of the 9th, 23d and 38th Infantry Regiments during the Battle of the Soyang River, 16 May to 2 June 1951 (Annex C).

10. 2d Infantry Division, *op. cit.*, narrative section.

11. 2d Infantry Division: G3 journal, 19 May 1951, message 10.

12. Headquarters 2d Division Artillery: operations report 265, records that the 38th FA Battalion fired 11,891 rounds of 105mm between 1800 18 May and 1800 19 May.

13. X Corps: command report, May 1951 (Annex A-1); see record for 19 May.

14. Maj.Gen. Clark L. Ruffner, in an interview by the author, 13 July 1951.

An army of stags led by a lion is more to be feared than an army of lions led by a stag.

ATTRIBUTED TO CHABRIAS (*circa* 410–357 B.C.)

14

Task Force Gerhardt

★ Beginning on 16 May, the Chinese launched their second spring offensive, aiming the main effort at U.S. X Corps. They made impressive gains at first, especially on the east flank of the corps' sector, but the vigor of the attack slackened noticeably after several days. At the end of a week, the enemy units were overextended, short of supplies, and weakened by serious personnel losses. While his troops were absorbing this enemy thrust, General Almond (X Corps commander) successfully bargained with Eighth Army for an additional infantry division as well as for the 187th Airborne Regimental Combat Team. Having thus reinforced his corps, General Almond laid plans for a counteroffensive.[1]

On the evening of 22 May, realizing that his corps had contained the enemy force and that opportunity for exploitation was at hand, General Almond attached the 187th Airborne Infantry Regiment to the 2d Infantry Division. At the same time, he ordered the division commander to send the 187th on a rapid and strong thrust north along the road running from Hongchon to Inje.[2] Attacking on 23 May with two battalions, the 187th Airborne gained four miles while, across the corps front, the initiative passed to the United Nations forces as they shifted from defensive to offensive warfare.[3] Anxious to speed up his offensive operation, General Almond at 0940, 24 May, ordered the 2d Division to send a task force from the 187th Airborne to seize the bridge site on the Soyang River and, incidentally, to kill as many Chinese as possible. He ordered the task force, not yet formed, to jump off at 1200—two hours twenty minutes later.[4]

Col. William Gerhardt (executive officer of the 187th Airborne),

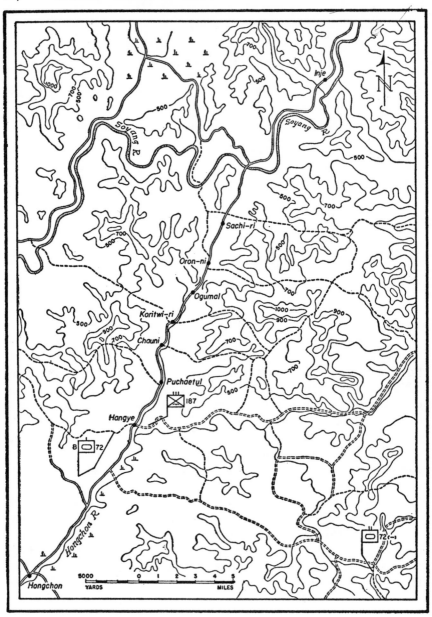

chosen to command the task force, immediately alerted those units from his own regimental combat team that would be a part of his force: an infantry battalion, a squad from the reconnaissance platoon, a company of engineers, and one battery from the airborne field artillery battalion. The 2d Division was to furnish the rest of the task force: four halftracks with quadruple caliber .50 machine guns and, according to General Almond's order, not less than two tank companies.

The 2d Division's G3 telephoned the commanding officer of the 72d Tank Battalion (Lt.Col. Elbridge Brubaker) to notify him that his battalion was to be attached to a task force from the 187th RCT, that the task force was to move out at 1200, and that he and his S3 were to report as quickly as possible to Colonel Gerhardt for complete orders. At the time of the alert, one company of tanks was serving in the sector of an adjoining corps and was not affected by the order. Company B was already supporting the 187th Airborne and occupied indirect firing positions near Hangye. The remainder of the 72d Tank Battalion was beyond a treacherous mountain pass approximately twenty miles southeast of Hangye. This distance and the condition of the road were such that the tanks would need three and a half or four hours to reach Hangye, thereby making it impossible to be on hand at the appointed hour of departure. Leaving orders for the rest of his battalion to follow as soon as possible, Colonel Brubaker and Major James H. Spann (S3) left by liaison plane for the Hangye command post.

The two officers met Colonel Gerhardt at about 1100 and from him and the 2d Division's G3 learned the composition of the task force, its mission, and preliminary plans. With this information, the two tank officers hurried to alert Company B, explaining to its commander (Capt. William E. Ross) that, since his company was the only one readily available, he would have to furnish one platoon which, together with a platoon of engineers and a squad from the 187th's Intelligence and Reconnaissance Platoon, would make up the point of Task Force Gerhardt. Captain Ross immediately reported to the task force commander and remained with him until, soon after 1200, Colonel Gerhardt instructed him to send his point platoon forward a distance of three miles to a place designated on the map as Puchaetul, selected by Gerhardt as the point of departure for the task force.

Captain Ross had chosen his 3d Platoon for the point duty. The four tanks of this platoon moved north to the initial point and there assembled in the Hongchon River bed to await the rest of the task force. The remaining three platoons from Company B followed and soon other units began to arrive. Tanks and other vehicles crowded into the sandy and rocky portions of the river bed. The day was clear and warm. Members of the task force sat in the sun, waiting.

The hour for launching Task Force Gerhardt passed, and the force was neither complete nor organized. Colonel Brubaker had hoped to put his executive officer in charge of the point of the column, but this officer was with the remainder of the 72d Tank Battalion and still two hours away. At this time Brubaker happened to meet his assistant executive officer near the 187th Airborne's command post. Major Charles A. Newman and several other men had been inspecting wreckage of tanks the Chinese had destroyed some days before. They were riding in two jeeps, one of which

Colonel Brubaker turned over to Major Spann with instructions to wait for the rest of the tank battalion and guide it forward to the starting point at Puchaetul. With Major Newman, Brubaker started forward in the other jeep to meet Captain Ross at the initial point.

"I want you to organize this point," he told Newman, "and you'll probably have to go with it."

About 1230 the two officers reached Puchaetul, where the task force was forming. Colonel Gerhardt arrived soon afterward and gave his final instructions. He already had sent the engineer platoon and the I&R squad forward to search for mines on the road, and he had obtained from the 3d Infantry Division a company of tanks that would be ready to move out with the main body of the task force. After reviewing the mission, the general situation, and advising all commanders that they could get air support simply by firing white phosphorus shells at any target, he ordered the lead tanks to get under way. It was about 1300.

The four tanks started north with the platoon leader (Lt. Douglas L. Gardiner) riding in the first tank and Major Newman in the second tank. Each of the medium tanks (M4A3E8) was armed with a 76mm cannon, a caliber .30 bow machine gun, and a caliber .50 antiaircraft machine gun. In addition to 71 rounds of ammunition for its cannon, each tank carried 49 boxes of caliber .30 ammunition and 31 boxes for its antiaircraft machine gun.

Two miles beyond the point of departure the tanks came upon the other two elements of the point—the engineer platoon and the 187th Airborne's I&R Platoon. The latter unit consisted of eleven men riding in three jeeps. Each jeep mounted a caliber .30 machine gun. The engineer platoon had two 2½-ton trucks. Major Newman re-formed his column in the following order: two tanks, a jeep, two tanks, a jeep, and then the two trucks, followed by the third jeep. In this order the column advanced another mile to a friendly advance outpost at Koritwi-ri, where it halted while engineer mine detector squads went forward to probe the road.

A helicopter descended and from it stepped General Almond (X Corps commander). He asked Major Newman the cause of the halt. Newman explained that the column had stopped temporarily to permit a check of the road by mine detectors, and to establish communications between the tanks and the squad from the Intelligence and Reconnaissance Platoon. General Almond was impatient.

"I don't care about communications!" he said, emphasizing this assertion by shaking his swagger stick at Major Newman. "You get those tanks on the road and keep going until you hit a mine. I want you to keep going at twenty miles an hour."

Newman ordered the column to move forward, instructing the tank commanders to shift to fifth gear, which would be equal to about twenty-two miles an hour.

General Almond flew back to the command post of the 187th Airborne. Standing in front of the command-post tent was Major Spann (the 72d Tank Battalion's S3) whom Colonel Brubaker had left behind to contact and guide forward the rest of the battalion. Spann reported to General Almond who, in rapid succession, asked to what outfit he belonged, why the tanks weren't moving, and the name of the commander of the 72d Tank Battalion.

"You tell Brubaker," General Almond replied when Spann had answered these questions, "to get that tank column moving whether the tanks have infantry support or not."

At this moment the 187th Airborne's S3 emerged from the tent. While General Almond was repeating his instructions to this officer, Spann left to deliver the general's message to Colonel Brubaker.

Colonel Gerhardt, in the meantime, had formed the elements of his task force in their relative positions in the column and had moved the column onto the road. Before Major Spann could relay General Almond's order through Colonel Brubaker, it had reached Colonel Gerhardt through his own staff. Gerhardt rushed up to the commander of Company B, 72d Tank Battalion, and told him to disregard the organization of Task Force Gerhardt and to get the tanks up the road to the Soyang River as fast as possible. The tank platoons, however, were intermingled with the task force column, the road was clogged with supply trucks, and it was not possible to immediately separate the tanks from the rest of the column.

After spending considerable time jockeying tanks and other vehicles around in the column, Ross succeeded in separating the tanks of the 1st Platoon which he sent along to join the leading platoon. As these tanks left the point of departure, Newman reported that he and the 3d Platoon were more than halfway to the Soyang River, having just cleared Oron-ni. He asked to have more tanks join him as quickly as possible.

When the point of the column moved out in fifth gear after encountering General Almond, the tanks reconnoitered four or five suspected enemy positions by firing at them either with the turret machine guns or the tank cannons. After advancing about a mile, the tank-platoon commander noticed two men manning a 3.5-inch bazooka near a destroyed bridge. As the tanks rolled forward, the men dropped their weapon and ran up the river bed to the northwest. Lieutenant Gardiner killed both of them with the caliber .50 machine gun. There was some enemy fire in response—from rifles and from a light machine gun which fired short bursts from about seven hundred yards away.

In the second tank in the column, the mechanic had his cap knocked off by a bullet from the machine gun. SFC Roy Goff (commander of the tank) turned his caliber .50 machine gun toward the Chinese, the other tank commanders joined him, and together they killed the enemy gunner as he attempted to change firing positions.

Since the tanks were still attracting light small-arms fire, the tankers directed the fire from all their weapons at suspected positions within a range of three hundred to five hundred yards. Eight or ten enemy soldiers then jumped out of foxholes near the bank of the Hongchon River which paralleled the road. The tankers killed 5 or 6 of them, but several escaped. The entire action lasted about five minutes.

The point of the task force column moved forward, again firing on all suspected enemy positions. (A soldier, hunting for souvenirs on the morning of 25 May, found seven dead Chinese in a cave into which the tanks had fired.) About a mile farther north, the crew of the lead tank noticed a group of 15 or 20 enemy soldiers on the road ahead. The Chinese waved their hands in a friendly manner at the tanks. Opening fire with the caliber .30 bow machine gun, the tank crew dispersed the enemy soldiers, but at the same time other groups of 4 or 5 men appeared on hills to the left of the road. These soldiers, drawing fire from all of the tanks, scampered first one way and then another as though they were uncertain about the direction in which to go.

Ahead was a mountain pass where Major Newman and the other tankers expected trouble. When Lieutenant Gardiner's lead tank reached the foot of the pass, he could see two houses at a bend commanding the road. Halting his tank, he reported this on the intertank radio. Newman told him to fire into the houses. Gardiner's fire set them ablaze, but he saw no one leave the houses.

The column continued through the pass unmolested until the last two tanks were emerging. Then two enemy machine guns, located on a fifty-foot-high knoll on the east side of the road, opened fire on the rear of the column. The machine gunner in the jeep at the end of the column returned the fire, and the last two tanks commenced firing their machine guns and cannons. Just then a liaison plane came overhead and dropped a green-smoke bomb to attract attention and then a grenade container with a message. A member of the I&R Platoon recovered the message, which said there was a large number of enemy troops on a hill east of the road, and instructed the tankers to fire several rounds of white phosphorus if they wanted an air strike placed on the enemy. Major Newman did not want to wait for an air strike. After silencing the two machine guns, the column moved forward to Oron-ni—a shabby huddle of houses at the bottom of the pass—where there was another brief exchange of fire between enemy automatic weapons and the tanks. Four Chinese surrendered. The tank crews motioned them to the rear of the column where they could ride on one of the trucks.

After reporting to Colonel Gerhardt by radio that the point of the task force column had cleared Oron-ni, Newman ordered the tanks forward again. Several small groups of Chinese appeared on a ridge west of the road, but this time the tanks did not stop although the tank commanders fired the antiaircraft machine guns at the enemy soldiers. After advancing another half mile, the lead tank crossed a culvert.

"You'd better watch the draw on the right," Gardiner radioed back to Major Newman. "There's a lot of stuff in it."

Newman had transferred from the second tank to the third in the column because the radio in the second tank had failed. Lieutenant Gardiner and Sergeant Goff (in the second tank) continued a short distance to a bridge across a four-foot-wide stream where the tanks stopped again. Gardiner had his tank crew fire the machine guns and the 76mm cannon toward the front and both flanks.

In the meantime, Newman had the tank in which he was riding (the third in the column) go just beyond the culvert so that he could see the draw about which Lieutenant Gardiner had cautioned him. He noticed several log-covered dugouts and, at about the same time, saw a platoon-sized group of Chinese run from the east side of the road into the culvert. Major Newman told the leader of the I&R squad to take his men into the draw and fire on any enemy positions there in order to stop the small-arms fire coming from that direction.

While the I&R squad deployed and moved on foot into the draw east of the road culvert, Newman and the bow gunner from his tank got out and walked back to the end of the culvert and motioned for the Chinese to come out. Enemy bullets whistled past the two men and struck the road nearby, stirring up small patches of dust. Thirty-seven Chinese soldiers came out of the culvert, hands over their heads, and surrendered. All enemy fire from the draw east of the road stopped suddenly. Newman sent the prisoners to the rear of the column, where they could ride with their four comrades in the custody of the engineers.

During all these events, the I&R squad was firing rifles, BARs, and a light machine gun at a rapid rate against what appeared to be a large enemy force at the head of the draw. The squad leader ran back to tell Major Newman that several hundred enemy soldiers were escaping at the east end of the draw. The first two tanks in the column were too far away to help, but the last two tanks fired 12 to 15 rounds of 76mm high-explosive shells into the draw. Although it was impossible to determine the results, all enemy fire ceased. The I&R squad returned to its vehicles, and the column moved off, rejoining the two tanks which were waiting at the small bridge. The fire fight lasted only about twenty minutes.

After renewing the plea for the rest of Company B's tanks, the column moved forward another mile or mile and a half to Sachi-ri, where about two hundred Chinese opened fire from both sides of the road and from hills beyond the village. The tanks stopped outside of the little village and returned the fire while the I&R squad deployed again and moved into the group of houses where thirty more enemy surrendered. At this point, Newman had to decide between mounting the prisoners on the rear decks of the tanks or leaving them on the road under guard. He chose to leave them, and placed four guards selected from the engineer platoon over all the prisoners captured thus far.

A short distance beyond Sachi-ri, the tanks came upon a group of 80 to 100 enemy foot soldiers armed with rifles and burp guns marching toward foothills on the left side of the road. They were leading about twenty pack animals. As the tanks approached them, the enemy soldiers stopped and stared as though they were in doubt as to whether the tanks were friendly or enemy. The tanks also stopped and opened fire from a range of two hundred yards with machine guns and cannons. While men from the jeeps and trucks took cover from some enemy small-arms fire, the tankers fired about twenty 76mm rounds and ten boxes of machine-gun ammunition, scattering and partly destroying the enemy group.

After ten minutes the column again moved out, this time going three quarters of a mile before meeting another group of enemy soldiers, this one about twice as large as the last one. They were marching toward the road from the northwest and were leading pack animals. After firing into this enemy column for ten or fifteen minutes and scattering it completely, the tankers believed they had killed or wounded at least half of the Chinese.

Now seven or eight miles in front of the main body, the point of Task Force Gerhardt went another mile without meeting further enemy resistance. It rounded a sharp bend in the road and approached a small hill, and minutes later, when the lead tank reached the top of the hill, Lieutenant Gardiner's men saw another enemy column marching southward toward their tank. Some of the enemy soldiers were walking in a creek bed on the west side of the road, while the others followed the road. Like the other enemy columns, this one included pack animals.

A liaison plane appeared overhead and dropped a message saying that about four thousand enemy soldiers were on the road about a mile farther north, and that two flights of jet planes were on the way to make an air strike against them. The message warned the tankers to wait until the planes had finished their napalm run before continuing forward. Gardiner, who retrieved the message, took it back to Major Newman.

"What are we going to do now?" he asked.

"We're going to attack the Chinks!" Newman answered without hesitation. "If we turn back we'll run into General Almond."

Deploying off the road in a skirmish line, the tanks opened fire on the enemy column, which was not more than five hundred yards away. After a few minutes (at about 1600) the jets arrived. They dropped napalm bombs well to the front, then circled to strafe the enemy column, flying so low that the tankers could feel the heat from the engines.

Anxious to reach the enemy column while it was still suffering from disorganization caused by the air strike, Gardiner started forward and all tanks followed. The planes were still strafing the Chinese who, scattered now and in flight, had abandoned supplies, pack animals, and some vehicles which they had previously captured from American forces. The point of the task force, now not more than a mile and a half from the Soyang River, moved into the confusion with the tanks firing all weapons. Several houses near the road were burning; along the road were dead animals and bodies of enemy soldiers killed either by the napalm strike or the advancing tanks. The tankers saw and fired at Chinese soldiers scrambling off the road trying to escape into the steep hills on both sides.

At about 1630 the tanks, still firing, reached an open area from which the members of the task force point could see the Soyang River. Besides scattered enemy soldiers south of the river, the tankers could see and fire upon enemy groups moving along a road that followed the north bank of the river.

The 1st and 2d Platoons of Company B, which Colonel Gerhardt had dispatched separately, joined Major Newman's force soon after it reached the river. The main body of Task Force Gerhardt arrived at 1830. It had also encountered some opposition on the way. That night the complete task force formed its defensive perimeter on the banks of the Soyang River.

★ DISCUSSION

Like a boxer who tries to hit his opponent when he has him off balance, the military commander times his counterpunches. When the enemy staggers, careful planning of time and space factors to insure coordination may be discarded in favor of rapid action. This narrative shows that a weak but timely jab at a faltering enemy is often effective—perhaps more so than a later, more powerful blow at a prepared opponent. "Strike while the iron is hot" refers to the blacksmith's work, but it applies equally well to the battlefield.

Strict observance of the rules of tactics in all cases is neither recommended nor advised. However, anyone who knowingly violates the rules must be ready to accept responsibility for his actions. If a deliberate violation brings about a victory, he will be a hero. If such violation results in a fiasco, he must be prepared to be the goat.

When General Almond, through the 2d Division, gave the 187th RCT a task force mission, he gave it the responsibility for carrying out a job. When he ordered the point of the task force column to move without the main body, he took upon himself the responsibility of the task force commander for the execution of his mission. Such an action is justified only when a superior commander has knowledge of the situation unknown to his task force commander and/or when time will not permit the use of regular channels—apparently true in this case. The personal intercession of General Almond is an example of positive leadership at a critical point by a senior commander.

The very existence of armored units can be justified only because of their superior cross-country mobility and their greater shock effect. When an armored unit is assigned a role that takes advantage of both these characteristics, it is being properly employed. When an armored advance guard is bold and aggressive, it is working as an advance guard should.

★ NOTES

1. X Corps: command report, May 1951 (Annex A-1); see entry at 1415 hours. Unless otherwise noted, this narrative is based upon interviews and an account of the action prepared in Korea by Capt. John Mewha. Captain Mewha interviewed the following officers and men of the 72d Tank Battalion: Major James H. Spann, S3; Capt. W. J. Richard, S2; Major Charles A. Newman, executive officer; Major William E. Ross, CO, Company B; Lt. Edwell D. Clements, Reconnaissance Platoon leader; and SFC Michael R. Huhel and SFC Glen M. Poppler. The last two were tank commanders of Company B.

2. X Corps: special report, Battle of the Soyang River, May 1951.

3. X Corps: command report, May 1951.

4. 2d Infantry Division: G3 journal and file, message J37, 0938, 24 May 1951.

Victory in war does not depend entirely upon numbers or mere courage; only skill and discipline will insure it.

VEGETIUS: MILITARY INSTITUTIONS OF THE ROMANS

15

Million Dollar Hill

★ Million Dollar Hill was one of the limited objectives of U.S. Eighth Army. It was several miles north of the northernmost line along which United Nations troops built and manned fortified positions during the summer months of 1951. Its name was an indication of the cost rather than the value of the hill. Lt.Gen. James A. Van Fleet (commander of Eighth Army) did not want to occupy and hold the hill since to do so would form a large bulge in the army's defensive line. But Million Dollar Hill was valuable terrain to the enemy, and it was chosen as the objective of one of several attempts to keep the enemy off balance, obtain information, capture prisoners, and prevent the Chinese from crowding too close against the United Nations' main line of resistance.

Accordingly, Eighth Army directed that the hill be captured. The order went to IX Corps, to the 24th Infantry Division, and then down to the 3d Battalion of the 5th Infantry. The attack was scheduled for the second day of August.

The 24th Division had made similar attacks against the same hill, had occupied it and then had abandoned it earlier that summer. From the main fortified defense line (Line Wyoming), Million Dollar Hill was prominent, not because it was higher than the ridges around it, but because artillery and air strikes had burned and blasted away all vegetation on the thousand-yard-long ridge, and it stood bare and brown among the other hills, which were green from heavy summer rains. Members of the 3d Battalion had named it Million Dollar Hill because they realized that ammunition worth at least that much had burst in flame and flash upon its crest. To the Chinese,

Million Dollar Hill afforded good observation of the 24th Division's line. In American hands, it dominated the main enemy supply route to the north.

As a terrain feature it was like other Korean ridgelines. It was so steep-sided that a grenade falling anywhere except along the trail-wide spine would probably roll on downhill. Its bare clay top, seven hundred feet above the stream at the bottom, was an hour's steady climb for an infantry-man loaded with supplies. The ridgeline was broken up into five mounds, each shaped like the hump on a camel's back. There was one large hump that was the main part of the hill and four others that became successively smaller toward the east. A few shaggy and splintered stumps remained on these humps, but the earth on the south side of the hill, where the bulk of our artillery shells had fallen, was as bare as though it had been plowed.

The attack against Million Dollar Hill commenced on the morning of 2 August and lasted for two days. Companies I and L made the assault and seized the hill. This story is the account of the defense of the hill by Company K, which relieved the attacking companies after the hill was secure.[1]

The relief of the assault companies was scheduled to begin on the evening of 3 August. It was still light when men of Company K started up the trail at 2100. Darkness during the Korean summer would not come for half an hour yet. The 2d Platoon was first in the column. Lt. Wilbur C. Schaeff-ner—a replacement officer who had joined the company three days before—was in command of the platoon.

The infantrymen moved slowly and quietly. Within a few minutes their fatigue jackets were wet with perspiration, and drops of sweat ran down their foreheads. An hour later Lieutenant Schaeffner and the thirty-one men of his platoon reached the crest of the hill and moved on out to take up positions on the east end of the ridgeline. Schaeffner split his platoon between two of the smaller mounds, leaving the smallest one—the mound at the eastern tip of the ridge—unoccupied.

The company commander (Lt. Robert H. Hight) brought up the re-mainder of the company and posted it along the two larger mounds at the west end of the ridge. This move, and the relief of the other companies, was an all-night process, and the last men were not in place until after first light the next day. As quickly as they were relieved, men from Companies I and L picked up their equipment and started down the trail and then moved back to reserve positions on the ridgeline just south of Million Dollar Hill.

Meanwhile, before dawn, the enemy was harassing Schaeffner's 2d Platoon. These men had to prepare their own positions, since neither Com-pany L nor Company I had constructed defenses on the eastern humps of the line. Because the sides of the hill were so steep, the only good approach left to the enemy was over the eastern tip of the ridge. Schaeffner put a

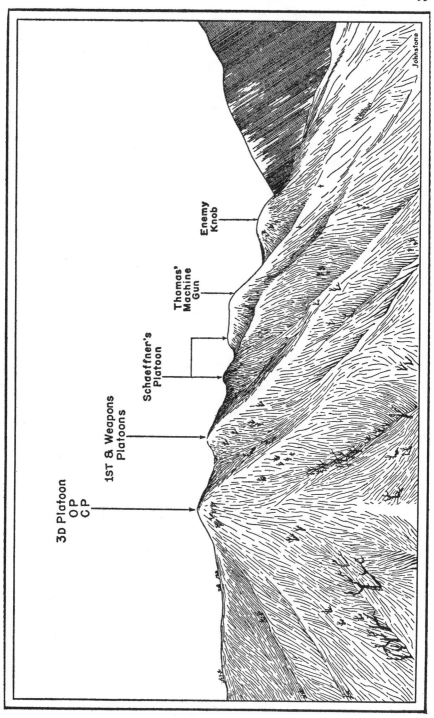

machine gun on top of his east mound and pointed it toward the saddle between this and the tip of the ridge and then placed two BAR men to protect the gun. Before the men finished digging in the gun or their own foxholes, several mortar rounds fell on the area. These tended to speed up the process of digging holes. Then one Chinese soldier walked up and threw a grenade at the machine-gun emplacement. The gunner and the two BAR men opened fire together and hit the Chinese, who dropped the gun he was carrying, fell, and rolled down the ridge side, apparently dead.

This action immediately drew fire from an enemy machine gun firing from the easternmost tip of the ridge not more than sixty yards away. The two machine guns traded short bursts for about forty minutes—enough action to worry the men since their positions were not well organized and they had only the ammunition they had carried up themselves. The carrying parties of Korean civilians had not yet reached the top of the hill with a resupply of ammunition.

When it became light again on the morning of 4 August, the commander of Company K (Lieutenant Hight) started organizing his defensive positions. After the 2d Platoon's experience during the night, Hight decided that if the Chinese were going to get that close he should have a tight perimeter rather than outposts that might become isolated and surrounded. He arranged his men around a slender perimeter that followed the thin ridgeline so that the foxholes were just a few feet below the top of the ridge, the men almost back to back. He insisted that all men dig their holes deep.

Lieutenant Hight and his artillery forward observer (Lt. Mack E. Magnum, from Battery C, 555th Field Artillery Battalion) then planned and registered their protective concentrations around their position. Altogether they could call for supporting fire from two batteries of 105mm howitzers, two batteries of 155mm howitzers, and two companies of 4.2-inch heavy mortars.

The men put out trip flares and other warning devices around their area. Throughout the day the Korean carrying parties brought up small-arms ammunition, grenades, and other supplies. In addition to forming a solid defense for the night, Lieutenant Hight made up a reserve squad of eight men, which he planned to hold at his command post near the center of the perimeter, from which point he could rush it to any spot on the line that might need help quickly during the night. Hight considered this squad an important element of his defense. It gave the men confidence to know that if any break in the line occurred, it would soon be plugged by the reserve squad.

For night illumination there were on call artillery and mortar flares that were adjusted to illuminate the northern slope of the ridge. The south side was to be illuminated by three 60-inch air-warning searchlights that were placed several miles away on the main defensive lines. One of these was pointed directly at the hill and two were aimed up so that the clouds over the area reflected the artificial moonlight.

During the afternoon and evening the men slept when they could. There were dark clouds across the sky that evening and dusk came early. Just before it got dark one of the squad leaders from the 2d Platoon (SFC Raymond M. Deckard) registered the company's 60mm mortars on the eastern tip of the ridge. The three mortars were emplaced within shouting distance of the company's command post on the highest part of the ridge so that the range was about three hundred yards.

Just as the last light left the sky it began to rain, and the searchlights came on. Lieutenant Hight set out to make the 2100 check of his positions, walking just below the rim of the ridge on the slippery clay mud. There was no enemy activity. The men were sitting quietly in the rain, waiting. Hight returned to his trench just as two flares went up in the valley between him and Companies I and L. He looked at his watch. It was 2115.

"Christ!" he said. "They're starting this thing early tonight."

The Chinese were several hundred yards away and nearer the reserve units of the 3d Battalion, which fired toward the area from which the trip flares came. Hight suspected that other groups would probe his lines soon.

Within a few minutes the machine gun at the east end of the ridge opened fire and, at about the same time, a group of Chinese came up the steep side of the ridge against the center of the company's perimeter. Hight watched the fire fights develop and decided the enemy had planned a three-pronged attack against him but that one of the groups—the one that set off the trip flares—had gone too far south and had not reached its objective at the right time.

The main action occurred at the eastern end of the perimeter in the sector of Lieutenant Schaeffner's 2d Platoon. A group of Chinese crawled up and threw about sixty grenades at Schaeffner's men. One of the grenades cut the wire on the sound-powered telephone that joined the opposite ends of the platoon. The Chinese were so close, and the ridge so narrow, that most of the grenades went over the men and exploded harmlessly farther down the side of the hill.

Since it appeared that the enemy might follow the grenade attack with an attempt to overrun the platoon positions, Sergeant Deckard and the two BAR men who were protecting the machine gun (Cpl. Philip B. Brumenshenkel and PFC Herman W. McKinney) gathered up their grenades and crawled a few feet up to the ridgeline where they knelt side by side like three crows on a limb peering at the Chinese below them. In the heavy rain it was difficult to see more than a few yards but, as one of them explained, "There were so many enemy on the hill we couldn't waste ammunition that night." The three men stayed there, their rumps prominent in silhouette, dropping grenades on the Chinese whom they could see or hear crawling through the brush below them.

At the same time, the machine-gunners and riflemen were aiming a heavy volume of fire across the tip of the ridge to keep the enemy from occupying that area. The fire fight lasted about twenty minutes before the enemy moved back. The activity gradually subsided and the close action ended, although the enemy kept up steady rifle fire and long-range supporting fire from machine guns located directly to the north. It was now close to 2200. There was loud, rumbling thunder and the noises from the fighting reverberated from the low clouds. The rain fell steadily, slanted by a hard wind.

Except for long-range firing there was a lull for half an hour or more. The second burst of activity started when one enemy soldier sneaked up to within twenty feet of the machine gun manned by Cpl. Gilbert L. Constant and PFC Robert J. Thomas. It was raining very hard at the time and the wind and rain and thunder made it difficult for the men to see or hear anything.

PFC Walter Jeter, Jr., saw the enemy first and yelled, "Look out on your left!"

Instead of a rifle or a grenade the Chinese had a signal-flare gun. From it he fired a red flare that landed on the ground directly in front of the machine-gun emplacement and bulged up in a blinding red light. Thomas —a Negro who was considered an expert infantryman by the other members of the platoon—stood up to look over the light of the flare and saw several enemy directly in front. He had unhooked the elevating and traversing mechanism so that the gun swung free on the pintle. He set off a long burst from his machine gun, then stopped long enough to shout, "Now go back and count your goddam noncoms!" Thomas killed the enemy soldier who fired the red flare, but while he was firing to the front another Chinese worked up on the left and pitched a grenade in the machine-gun pit. This seriously wounded both Thomas and Constant, who called out that they were hit. The squad leader (Sergeant Deckard) told them to come on out if they could, and sent his assistant (Cpl. John W. Diamond) to take over the gun. Just as Diamond was getting out of his hole, however, a grenade burst wounded him in the face and arm. Deckard hurried over and manned the machine gun himself since it held the critical point on the line and had to be kept in action.

At about the same time both members of one of the BAR teams with the machine gun were wounded, the BAR belonging to the other team jammed, and something went wrong with the machine gun that slowed up its rate of fire. Deckard called for the reserve squad to plug his line. By this time there were five men, a BAR, and the machine gun missing from his line —just at the time the action was beginning to reach the most furious pitch of the night.

The rain and the fighting increased in intensity at the same time. At the top of the ridge, Lieutenant Hight stood in his trench watching the action which, he thought, for wild fury exceeded anything he had experienced against the Japanese during three and a half years in the Pacific during World War II. There were four heavy machine guns on the enemy's main position 400 or 500 yards to the north which were firing into the area of the 2d Platoon. They left four red lines, only slightly arched, drawn across the narrow valley between the two ridges. Another enemy machine gun— the one on the eastern tip of the ridge—kept up a heavy and steady fire, trading tracers with the machine gun which Deckard was now operating. The lines of tracers from the two guns passed each other so closely that Hight kept expecting them to collide.

Added to the noise of this fire were about forty enemy riflemen firing at close range at the 2d Platoon, and grenade and mortar explosions which, like the other sounds, were magnified by low clouds and the rain. Searchlights against the clouds made areas of luminous white light over the ridge, and there were flares in the sky two thirds of the time during the heavy fighting. They made a hazy sort of light, like lanterns hanging out in the fog. Even in the heavy rain, which accumulated more than five inches during the night, there was light enough so that Hight could see the men slogging through the mud or occasionally standing on the ridgeline firing down at the enemy. Their helmets and wet clothing glistened in the white light. In addition to being one of the heaviest fire fights Lieutenant Hight had seen, he considered this one handled as coolly as any in which he participated. None of the men got excited, because each had confidence in the others and knew that when morning came, unless wounded, the man in the next hole would still be there.

Lieutenant Schaeffner, whose platoon was in the midst of the heavy fighting, called by telephone and asked for the special support squad, explaining that his machine gun was not working well. Lieutenant Hight dispatched the eight men at once, asked for an increase in the 4.2-inch mortar fire, and called down to his own mortar section to plaster the tip of the ridge. He also arranged to replace the machine gun with the one from the 3d Platoon. Within a short time the fire power of the 2d Platoon was restored and, as soon as the danger was past, Hight called off his supporting fire. The 2d Platoon's fire fight continued almost without abatement until half an hour past midnight. This rate of fire had used up the original basic load of ammunition and much of the reserve supply that Hight had stored by his command post near the center of the perimeter. SFC William T. Akerley was busy taking extra bandoleers from the 1st and 3d Platoons and redistributing them to the 2d. Deckard's machine gun had already fired twelve boxes of ammunition.

Lieutenant Hight called his battalion commander (Major Ernest H. Davis) to tell him that he had the situation under control but that he needed more ammunition. Davis told him to stretch the ammunition as far as he could but to hold the hill.

"Don't worry about the real estate," answered Hight. "Just get some ammunition up here."

Davis promised to have the carrying party on the way soon. Meanwhile, Hight sent out instructions for the men to conserve ammunition. They observed this to some extent, but since it was difficult to see, there were few aimed shots and the volume of fire remained high.

The enemy's second heavy assault ended before 0100. The volume of rain also slackened a little by this time but was coming down steadily. Enemy machine guns, mortars, and some small arms continued firing from a distance. But there were no assaults, although the men expected another one soon and were concerned about their lack of ammunition. They waited, but at the end of two hours they had received neither the enemy's next assault nor the ammunition.

Finally, an officer with several tanks stationed down near the road called Lieutenant Hight to tell him that the Koreans carrying the ammunition had returned to the base of the hill after having been fired upon during the trip up. This information made the ammunition scarcity a serious problem, and Hight again called his platoon leaders to say that there would be no more ammunition available until morning. One of the men explained that they were almost out as it was, and some of them had their last ammunition in their guns.

"What are we going to do when this is gone?" he wanted to know.

"Well, by God," answered Hight, "we'll just *wrestle* them when we run out of ammunition."

To save the ammunition he had on the hill, Lieutenant Hight again called for the artillery and the heavy mortars to lay down his final protective lines. The fire continued for an hour and a half—until 0430, when Hight called it off because the enemy's fire had almost ceased. During this time the 4.2-inch mortars alone fired 2,165 rounds. There had been a couple of light, probing attacks during that time, but neither had the verve or force of the first two.

The rain ended soon after it began to get light on the morning of 5 August. The enemy activity was also over except for several groups that attempted to get back—apparently to recover some of their equipment. The men counted 26 Chinese in these groups and fired upon them with machine guns and mortars, killing 7 and wounding others. They also counted 39 bodies in front of their perimeter, and believed they had killed or wounded others. Company K had suffered five men wounded from the action, but the morale and pride of the men were high.

Late that afternoon Lieutenant Hight received orders to abandon the hill at dusk that evening. The men fixed demolition charges and booby traps over it and marched off just as it began to get dark.

★ DISCUSSION

This is an example of the successful conduct of a defense. At first sight it appears to have few lessons other than the generality that a well-organized defense, adequately supported and manned by determined soldiers, is a hard nut to crack at any time. On closer examination the factors that made the defense so successful become more evident.

First of all, the defensive position selected was organized on a hilltop where the observation was excellent. To improve observation during darkness and limited visibility, arrangements were made to employ artificial lighting.

Now let us look at the organization. The platoons and squads were emplaced for mutual support. The company had a support that could be used to bolster any portion of the position which was threatened. Prior to the time of attack the supporting fires were coordinated and adjusted. The 2d Platoon's machine gun was emplaced where it could cover the most likely avenue of enemy approach, and it was protected by the fire of two BARs. Note that within the organization the integrity of the units was maintained; that communications were established within the company and with higher and supporting units; and that the company commander exercised many of the principles of good leadership by checking the positions he had ordered organized and constructed, by directing the employment of the supporting fires, by trying to maintain the ammunition supply, and finally by the use of humor to maintain morale: "We'll just *wrestle* them when we run out of ammunition."

★ NOTE

1. This narrative is based upon interviews by the author of fourteen members of Company K, including Lt. Robert H. Hight, Lt. Wilbur C. Schaeffner, SFC Raymond M. Deckard, MSgt. William L. Scholes, PFC Herman W. McKinney, and SFC Warren C. Cain, Jr. The author visited the position the morning after the attack and a week later conducted more exhaustive interviews.

*The first quality of the soldier is fortitude in en-
during fatigue and privations; valor is only the
second. Poverty, privation, and misery are the
school of the good soldier.*

NAPOLEON: MAXIM LVIII

16

Bloody Ridge

★ Bloody Ridge was so named by *Stars and Stripes*. Men of
the 9th Infantry Regiment (2d Infantry Division), fighting there, read stories of the action which, for security reasons, *Stars and Stripes* did not
clearly identify and wondered in what sector this bloody battle was raging.

Bloody Ridge consists of three hills—983, 940 and 773—and their connecting ridges. Four razor-back ridges converge on the western extremity
of Bloody Ridge to form Hill 983, a sharp and well-defined point and the
highest peak of the ridgeline. To the east, and separated from 983 by a steep
draw, the 1,100-yard-long center section of Bloody Ridge comes to a peak
at Hill 940. Another thousand yards east of this peak is Hill 773.

The maze of enemy trenches on the ridges made it appear to air observers that Bloody Ridge had been plowed. The trenches connected many
bunkers which the enemy had built strong enough to withstand artillery
fire and air strikes. The larger ones sheltered as many as sixty men. Some
protected small artillery pieces or mortars. Detection of enemy positions
from the ground was difficult because the hills were partially wooded and
enemy soldiers had been skillful with camouflage.

The planning and fighting for Bloody Ridge took place while cease-
fire negotiations droned on at the Kaesong armistice conferences. This east-
west ridgeline was considered a desirable terrain feature for purposes of
observation, but from Eighth Army's over-all point of view it had little
value. The battle for Bloody Ridge was one of several limited-objective
attacks by which Eighth Army leaned against the enemy in order to prevent
the enemy from leaning against it.

Fighting for Bloody Ridge had been going on for twelve days when the 1st Battalion, 9th Infantry, made its first attack against the hill mass. During that time an ROK division had seized the three hills, only to lose them the next day.[1] It was a bloody ridge for the South Koreans also. In ten days the ROK regiment that had made the main attack suffered more than a thousand casualties. About one fourth of these were listed as killed or missing.[2]

Supporting units were numerous during the entire Bloody Ridge battle. Included were the four artillery battalions of the 2d Division; two additional battalions of medium artillery; one additional 105mm battalion; two heavy-mortar companies; two regimental tank companies; and one company from a medium tank battalion. The fires of all these units were coordinated by 2d Division Artillery.

Beginning on the foggy morning of 17 August 1951, ROK troops launched their attack against Bloody Ridge. They secured it, finally, on 25 August. They lost it again the next day. On 27 August, the 9th Infantry, which had placed its 2d Battalion in supporting positions on Hill 940, attempted without success to seize Hill 983. The 2d Battalion withdrew that evening, going all the way back to Worun-ni. On the 28th, the 3d Battalion, attacking the long ridge from the east, failed to reach even the first objective (Hill 773). Faced with a surprise attack that night, it also fell back to Worun-ni. Thus, before the 1st Battalion made its first attack against the Bloody Ridge hill mass, UN forces had captured the long ridgeline only to lose it again, hill by hill.[3]

On 30 August, the 9th Infantry made a frontal assault, sending its 1st and 2d Battalions straight north against Hill 940. Both battalions got within a few hundred yards of the top of the ridgeline before enemy fire halted the advance. Casualties were heavy. Company A was reduced to half strength. The three aid men with the company became casualties, one platoon leader was killed, the company commander and another platoon leader were wounded. Lt. John H. Dunn took charge of the company.

When it became apparent that neither battalion would reach the objective before dark, the regimental commander ordered both to withdraw. As an artillery forward observer (Lt. Edwin C. Morrow) crawled toward a knob in Company A's area, he heard a voice behind him.

"Lieutenant, it looks like you'll have to take over."

Turning around, Morrow recognized one of the sergeants from Company A.

"Where's Lieutenant Dunn?" he asked.

"Dead."

"How many men are left?"

"Twenty-two."

"What were your last orders?"

"Withdraw and reorganize at last night's position."

While the sergeant told the men to pull back, Lieutenant Morrow arranged for fire to cover the movement.

"This is the fastest transfer of an Artillery officer to the Infantry that I've ever seen," he thought.

Seven artillery battalions fired a smoke mission as the remaining infantrymen carried the wounded men down the hill. They had to leave the dead and much equipment behind.

Not until about 0400 on 31 August did the entire 1st Battalion reassemble in the area it had occupied before the attack. Even then the men were not allowed to sleep. The battalion commander (Lt.Col. Gaylord M. Bishop) notified his company commanders that, because of an expected enemy attack, it would be necessary for all men to stay on the alert. They received rations, however—the first that many of them had eaten since the previous morning. When the expected attack had not materialized, after a two- or three-hour wait the battalion moved by trucks to an assembly area south of Worun-ni where the companies were to have two hours in which to reorganize before attacking another hill. Morale was low, the weather depressing. It was foggy and unseasonably cold.

At the assembly area the men received dry socks, hot coffee, and ammunition. There was a supply of oil, cleaning rods, and patches. There was also mail. More replacements joined the rifle companies.

Before noon on 31 August the 1st Battalion loaded on trucks again and rode two miles forward. Its mission was to attack Hill 773—this time from the east. At the detrucking point the infantrymen formed company columns and continued forward, Company C in the lead. There were dead North Korean soldiers all along the road.

At the eastern tip of the ridgeline, where Bloody Ridge ended at the road pass between Worun-ni and the Pia-ri Valley, Company C turned left and climbed toward the first knoll on the ridgeline leading toward Hill 773. The knoll was already in friendly hands, since the 38th Infantry Regiment had maintained an outpost there for several days. The main positions of the 38th were across the road on the high ground immediately east of Bloody Ridge. Since the 38th Infantry's high ground afforded the best observation of Hill 773, Colonel Bishop had established his observation post on that hill east of the road. He and his S2 (Lt. Charles W. Mallard) were already at the observation post when Company C left the road and started up the ridgeline in the attack.

Colonel Bishop watched the infantrymen, climbing slowly in single file, as they passed the outpost on the first knoll, but beyond that the attacking infantrymen were obscured by the morning fog and haze. Low clouds, as though tethered to the mountain peaks, hung over Hills 773 and 940, hiding them completely.

Beyond the outpost position Company C proceeded haltingly, the scouts setting the pace. There were frequent delays in the long column and

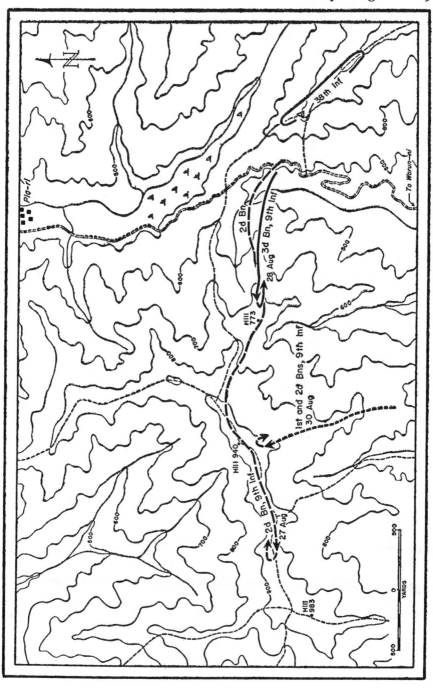

it was easy for the infantrymen, even at the rear of the column, to guess that they would soon make contact with the enemy. Those toward the rear sat down and waited quietly.

An enemy machine gun suddenly commenced firing from a knoll 100 to 200 yards beyond the front of the column, setting off a blazing, ten-minute fire fight. Striking the forward elements of Company C, the machine-gun fire wounded several men, including the company commander (Lt. Orlando Campisi) and one of the platoon leaders. Although other men returned the fire, it had little effect since the enemy gun's crew had the advantage of a substantially constructed bunker.

Because of the fog Colonel Bishop could not see the action clearly, but the radio operator with the attacking company (Cpl. John J. Truax) noti-fied him by radio that the two remaining officers of Company C were wounded and that the attack had halted. Colonel Bishop ordered Company B to attack through the stalled Company C and continue up the ridge. At the same time he sent Lieutenant Mallard to take command of Company C and provide as much supporting fire as possible for the attacking company. Fog prevented the use of artillery.

Up on the ridgeline the commander of Company B called to Lt. Joseph W. Burkett and told him to take his 1st Platoon forward. The other two companies—both with attachments from Company D—would furnish cov-ering fire for Burkett's platoon. The top of the hill was still obscured by fog, and Burkett could not see the route he was to follow. After telling his platoon sergeant (SFC Floyd Larney) to assemble the squad leaders, Bur-kett went off to question men of Company C in order to get a description of the terrain ahead and the location of enemy bunkers and automatic weap-ons. According to men of Company C, the approach to the first knoll ahead marked the trouble line.

Occasionally the fog lifted. During one of these breaks Lieutenant Burkett planned his supporting fires, then quickly briefed his squad leaders.

"Saddle up!" he called out to his men when he had completed his preparations, and started up the ridgeline.

Under the supporting fire of four machine guns, the platoon advanced without incident and against negligible enemy fire. Burkett's main concern was to maintain control over his platoon. Sixteen of his twenty-two men were replacements who had joined the company within the last two days. Although willing to do their part, they were obviously tense and had a tendency to lag or to bunch—a tendency common even among seasoned troops when attacking along a narrow ridge spine that limited maneuver-ability.

After moving about seventy-five yards, or halfway to the first knoll, Burkett stopped to check his walkie-talkie radio—his only contact with his company and his only means of shifting the supporting machine-gun fire. His radio was working.

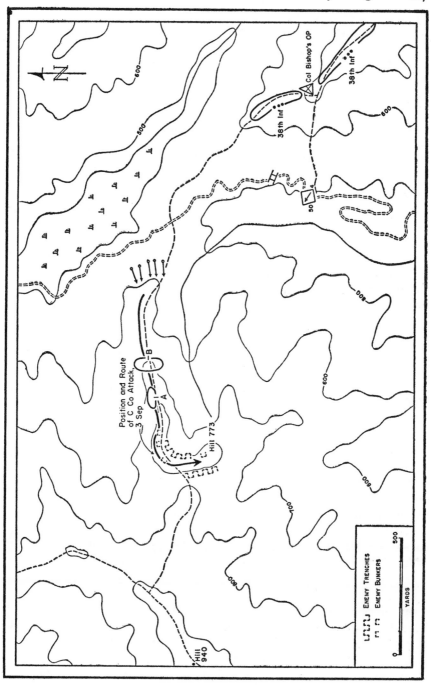

Col Bishop's OP

38th Inf

38th Inf

50

600

600

500

800

600

800

700

980

Position and Route
of C Co Attack,
3 Sep

A

B

Hill 773

Hill
940

N

⌐⌐⌐⌐ ENEMY TRENCHES
⌐⌐ ⌐⌐ ENEMY BUNKERS

0   500
YARDS

At the base of the knoll, which was actually only a small hump on the ridgeline, Burkett and his men expected enemy grenades. None came down. Enemy small-arms fire had picked up but the knoll itself protected the platoon grouped at its base, and the men could not tell whether the fire originated at the crest of the knoll or came from farther up the ridgeline. Burkett, with three men, started toward the top of the knoll, about thirty feet from the base. After asking the others to watch the top and cover him, Burkett crawled forward until he was near the crest, raised up on his knees, pulled the pin from a grenade, leaned back slightly for more leverage, and threw the grenade to the opposite side of the knoll. In so doing he leaned back so far that his helmet fell off. He watched it roll down the side of the ridge. Even before the grenade exploded, the other three men started forward, and all four went over the crest together. They found only unoccupied holes.

Fifty yards or less ahead there was another knoll. Before the platoon had gone far, Lieutenant Burkett noticed that the supporting machine guns had quit firing. He called for his platoon runner who carried the radio. At this critical time, the radio failed. Burkett tried for several minutes to get in touch with his company, but the radio was dead.

Enemy fire had increased in volume and effectiveness, and Burkett was bitterly disappointed that his only fire support had stopped. The mortars, like the artillery, had been silent all morning because of the fog. As Lieutenant Burkett later learned, the machine-gunners quit firing because the fog completely obscured the attacking platoon, which was getting too close to the line of fire as it moved higher on the ridgeline. Because he had neither visual nor radio contact, Burkett now found himself without supporting fire as well. He dropped the radio in disgust.[4]

Lieutenant Burkett tried moving his platoon forward, but as the fire increased his men strung out until not more than ten remained in a forward group with their platoon leader. About twenty yards from the crest of the second knoll Burkett and the men with him saw several grenades come over the knoll. The riflemen dropped to the ground as the grenades rolled downhill toward them. The explosions caused no damage except to blow particles of loose dirt into Burkett's bare head. More grenades followed, but the North Koreans threw them so hard they landed among the rear elements of the platoon. Burkett spotted several enemy soldiers in a well-camouflaged bunker from which the grenades were coming, and directed his men to keep the bunker under fire. Despite the fire, grenades and an occasional burst of machine-gun fire continued to come from the bunker. Although able to see each grenade as it fell, the replacements made no effort to scramble to one side and avoid them. Several men were wounded. One man was lying prone in the path of a grenade and made no apparent effort to get out of its way. The explosion picked him up and rolled him down the ridge. He was still screaming as he rolled out of sight.[5]

The commander of Company B (Capt. Edward G. Krzyzowski) sent three BAR teams from another platoon to help Lieutenant Burkett's platoon and to compensate for the loss of the machine-gun support. One of these BAR men (PFC Domingo Trujillo) walked up to Burkett, explained why he was there, and asked what he should do. He was grinning, and perfectly calm. Burkett pointed out the enemy bunker that blocked his platoon's advance. Trujillo, standing erect, fired one burst into the bunker and then lowered the gun to his waist. Behind Trujillo was another BAR man (PFC Robert L. Spain). As Trujillo lowered his weapon, Spain sighted into the opening of the same bunker just as a North Korean rose to return the fire. Spain pulled the trigger on his automatic rifle but it misfired. The burst from the enemy gun struck Trujillo in the neck and chest, killing him instantly.[6]

Several men threw grenades in the direction of the bunker, but none was close. Lieutenant Burkett told the men near him to continue firing at it while he tried to get close enough to use grenades effectively. Both the assault platoon and the bunker were on the right (north) side of the ridgeline, the bunker being just below the crest. To avoid the enemy machine-gun fire, Burkett crawled over the ridgeline to the south side, then crawled west toward the top of the knoll. He moved slowly since he could not see far in the fog and he did not want to run head-on into another bunker. When he estimated that he was about even with the bunker on the opposite side of the ridge, he crawled back to the ridgeline where he could see the top, pulled the pin and let the safety lever pop before giving the grenade a gentle toss. It exploded right on top of the covered bunker. Gaining confidence, Burkett pitched a second grenade, which exploded in the same area. He called down to a squad leader (Sgt. Charles Hartman) for more grenades in a hurry. Hartman got three and tossed them to Burkett, who pulled the pins and threw all of them. Burkett began to feel like a man who had just won a fight.[7]

About thirty seconds after the last explosion, the North Koreans opened a door at the rear of the bunker and threw five or six grenades at Lieutenant Burkett. Seeing them, Burkett slid down the ridge to get away from the explosions. He stopped by Sergeant Hartman and told him to watch out for the grenades. Just then another landed about six feet above the two men and rolled toward them. The explosion wounded both men. Lieutenant Burkett told his men to move back and establish a line beyond grenade range and hold there until he could return and get help from Captain Krzyzowski.

It was now late in the afternoon. Colonel Bishop ordered Company B to pull back and establish a perimeter for the night with the other two rifle companies. Captain Krzyzowski sent another platoon forward to help evacuate the wounded men from Lieutenant Burkett's platoon.

The fog disappeared at dawn on 1 September. The sky was clear and the morning bright. Colonel Bishop shifted Company A into the lead position for the attack and called for artillery fire to cover the ridgeline between Hills 773 and 940. Lieutenant Mallard's Company C, in supporting positions, adjusted mortar fire on Hill 773 and set up two heavy machine guns to fire at the objective.

Advancing by marching fire under this protection, the assault platoon went as far as Company B had gone the previous evening before the enemy, firing from the same bunker that had caused trouble on the 31st, again halted the advance. When the leader and several other members of the forward platoon were wounded, the company commander (Lt. Elden K. Foulk) started forward, leading another platoon to bolster the assault. Machine-gun bullets struck his leg, wounding him seriously. Several other men were wounded at about the same time. Lieutenant Foulk dragged himself back to Company C's position, explained to Lieutenant Mallard that Company A needed help, and then collapsed from shock. When information of this situation reached Colonel Bishop, he decided to commit Company B again, as he had done the day before when Company C needed help.

Captain Krzyzowski led his company through the remaining men of Company A. As two machine-gun crews and four BAR men from Company C fired on the bunker, the assault platoon of Company B worked up close enough to get grenades into it. After a five-minute grenade fight, these men seized the knoll and the bunker that had been blocking the battalion's advance. One of the platoon leaders—a replacement officer who had joined the company only fifteen minutes before it moved out—was wounded in the attack.

The action was all over by 1000. The 1st Battalion now held the three prominent knolls on the ridgeline leading to the top of the hill. The highest point on the ridge—Hill 773—was the next prominent knoll. It was about 250 yards away at the hook end of a narrow ridgeline shaped like a question mark.

At about 1400, Company B, now down to about fifty men, resumed the advance on the ridgeline. Under the control of Lieutenant Mallard, the 60mm mortar sections from the three rifle companies supported the advance by firing from positions to the rear of Company C. Mallard fired the three sections together, like artillery.

After advancing about a hundred yards along the question mark ridgeline, the lead elements of Company B came upon three enemy bunkers. Immediately, the North Koreans threw grenades which exploded and wounded five of Captain Krzyzowski's men. An enemy machine gun opened fire from a position on Hill 940.

Captain Krzyzowski ordered his company back and called Company A, asking for a bazooka and several rounds of ammunition for it. He also got in touch with Company C and adjusted the 60mm mortars so that the shells fell directly on the crest of Hill 773. This fire kept the enemy at least partly neutralized while two of Company B's new men, carrying the borrowed bazooka and ammunition, crawled forward and silenced the first bunker.

Crossing to the south side of the ridge, PFC Edward K. Jenkins crawled on his belly until he was above the second bunker, then crossed back and dropped three grenades into it. While Jenkins was knocking out this bunker, an enemy soldier in the third bunker threw a grenade into the group, wounding two men. One of the men tossed three more grenades up to Jenkins; he lobbed two of these into the third bunker and ended the interference from that enemy position.

At this point, enemy soldiers began firing at Company B from another bunker about twenty-five yards farther up the ridgeline. One of the men fired several rifle grenades at the bunker, but could not tell what damage, if any, he caused. Fire from the bunker prevented movement on the north side of the sharp ridgeline, and as men of Company B moved to the south of the question mark ridge to flank the bunker, they were exposed to machine-gun fire from Hill 773 at the top of the question mark, and from the slope of Hill 940, six hundred or seven hundred yards away.

Because of approaching darkness, Colonel Bishop ordered Captain Krzyzowski to pull his company back to the last knoll captured and, with the two other companies, establish a perimeter for the night. Only 22 men were left in Company A that evening; about 20 in Company B.[8]

Early next morning (2 September), 156 replacements, including 6 officers, joined the 1st Battalion. Companies A and B each received 2 officers and 65 men. Company C received 2 officers and 20 men. While the rifle companies distributed these replacements into their platoons, Colonel Bishop moved a tank and a quad .50 flakwagon into a position on the Worun-ni road from where they could fire at enemy positions on Hill 940.

Lieutenant Mallard, acting as the eyes and ears for the battalion commander, established an observation post on the crest of the last knoll captured and from there directed the tank fire by radio and—for the first time during the attack—made effective use of the heavy mortars. While Mallard plastered Hill 773 with massed mortar fire, an artillery forward observer covered Hill 940 and planes made strikes against the west end of Bloody Ridge.

There was no attack on 2 September. Twice during the day a platoon from Company C probed the approaches to Hill 773, but each time the enemy, armed with an abundant supply of hand grenades, made a spirited defense of his dug-up hilltop and forced the patrols back. The defensive perimeter remained unchanged.[9]

At 0900, 3 September, Lieutenant Mallard alerted one of his platoon leaders (Lt. Arnold C. Jones), a replacement officer who had joined the company the day before. Jones's platoon was to lead the next assault. But before this attack could get under way, Colonel Bishop radioed instructions to hold up until after an air strike that he had arranged for could take place. Colonel Bishop further stated that Lieutenant Mallard was to be prepared to direct the strike by radio. Since Mallard was already directing the fires of the 6omm and 81mm mortars by telephone, and tank fire by radio, he asked the commander of Company A to direct the air strike. This was Lt. Robert D. Lacaze, a battalion staff officer who had taken command of Company A after Lieutenant Foulk was wounded on the previous day.

Four fighter planes appeared over the hill at 1030. They dropped eight napalm bombs, only one of which hit the very top of the hill. But the others fell on the reverse slope and close enough to be effective. Lieutenant Lacaze directed the strike to within 150 yards of the battalion's positions—so close the men could feel the heat from the burning napalm. The infantrymen, watching the fire mushroom and turn from orange to black, cheered and shouted. A second flight followed, and this time the planes dropped eight antipersonnel bombs equipped with proximity fuze. Then the planes returned and made several strafing runs on the objective. As the planes cleared the area, Lieutenant Mallard called in the artillery and mortar fires again, some on Hill 773 and some on Hill 940.

Between 1300 and 1400, when the air strikes were over, Colonel Bishop radioed instructions for Mallard to resume the attack. Company C's strength on 3 September was about 85 men. The riflemen were divided into two platoons of experienced men and one platoon having a large proportion of replacements. Lieutenant Jones, leading one of the experienced platoons, started forward, attacking around the neck of the question mark. Although enemy bunkers blocked this route, it was still better than trying to take the direct route over the ridge in the face of machine-gun fire from Hill 940. The assault platoon reduced the first two bunkers but suffered so many casualties that the attack stalled in front of the third one. Most of the casualties were caused by grenades that came, not from the bunkers, but from enemy soldiers intrenched on the opposite side of the sharp-edged ridge, only a few yards away. Mallard committed his other experienced platoon, but by the time it had moved up even with Jones's it had lost so many men it was no longer effective. At about the same time, Jones was wounded. Although this was only his second day with the company, he had more combat experience than the other platoon leaders of Company C.[10]

Earlier that day Colonel Bishop had sent several replacements to the rear for a quick course in the use of the flame thrower. Six of these men, carrying three flame throwers, returned in the middle of the afternoon, arriving at Company C at the same time Mallard's second platoon became stalled. Lieutenant Mallard called Colonel Bishop to explain what had happened so far and to ask for permission to commit his third platoon and the three flame-thrower teams. He also wanted a platoon from Company A in order to have a reserve unit within his company. The battalion commander agreed.

The flame-thrower teams and Mallard's third platoon moved out at once. An enemy bullet pierced the pressure tank on one flame thrower, making it useless. The other two operators, however, succeeded in reaching the area controlled by the North Korean grenadiers. Crawling almost to the crest of the ridge, the two operators pointed the flame-thrower nozzles up and discharged the tanks so that the burning jelly fell on the reverse slope of the ridge, forcing the enemy out.

At the same time, the rest of Company C continued around the curve of the question mark and, after destroying two more bunkers, finally seized the very top of Hill 773. Lieutenant Mallard immediately sent the attached platoon of Company A to the hilltop with instructions to prepare to repel a possible counterattack from the direction of Hill 940. The commander of Company A (Lieutenant Lacaze) stationed his men in enemy trenches on the west side of the hill. Thus Company A held Hill 773 facing the enemy on Hill 940, a thousand yards to the west.[11]

Company C, which numbered about 85 men at noon before the action commenced, now had only about 30. Before organizing the defenses for the night, Mallard asked and received permission from the battalion commander to consolidate his company with Company A. Most of the remaining men in his own unit were experienced in combat, whereas most of the men of Company A were recent replacements. By intermingling the men, Mallard hoped to increase the effectiveness of the two companies. As he moved up to Hill 773 to accomplish the planned reorganization, a friendly artillery shell fell short, wounding him. He sent a runner forward to tell Lieutenant Lacaze to take command.

Mallard started back to the aid station. On the way he met Captain Krzyzowski, who was in the process of moving Company B into the positions vacated that afternoon by the other two companies. Krzyzowski had barely completed this move when he was killed by bullets from the machine gun on Hill 940. This left Lieutenant Lacaze and one other officer in charge of all the men who remained in the three rifle companies.

Two days later, Colonel Bishop's battalion occupied Hills 940 and 983 without opposition. The enemy had apparently moved north to strengthen positions on the next prominent terrain feature in that area—Heartbreak Ridge.

★ DISCUSSION

Until supporting weapons are much improved, they will not be able to remove a determined enemy from a well-constructed defensive position alone. On Bloody Ridge infantrymen had to go forward with flame throwers and grenades after all supporting weapons had failed to dislodge the enemy. Close infantry action is brutal, dirty, fear-inspiring work. Its reward is usually no more than the unspoken thanks of a friend or the knowledge that you have done your best. It requires stamina and individual bravery.

But individual bravery is only a contributing factor to victory in battle. Leadership, coordination, and cooperation are often as important as courage. None can deny that the men of the 1st Battalion, 9th Infantry, fought, bled, and died gallantly on Bloody Ridge. But who will testify that the battalion—its companies, its platoons, its squads—were teams when they went into action on Hill 773? Replacements cannot be fitted into a unit in two hours. Even the best leader needs time to know his men before they face the enemy together. Who wholeheartedly follows an unknown leader, or puts his life in the hands of a nearby stranger?

Cooperation among friends is the rule. Among strangers it is news!

★ NOTES

1. Capt. Martin Blumenson, "Bloody Ridge," a narrative prepared in Korea.

2. *Ibid.*

3. Unless otherwise noted, the account of the attacks on Bloody Ridge is based upon interviews made in Korea by Major Pierce W. Briscoe with the following members of the 1st Battalion, 9th Infantry: Lt. Robert D. Lacaze, Lt. Joseph W. Burkett, Capt. Charles W. Mallard, and PFC John A. Fell.

4. Lt. Joseph W. Burkett, letter to the author, 27 January 1953.

5. *Ibid.*

6. *Ibid.*

7. *Ibid.*

8. Lt. Charles W. Mallard, letter to the author, 3 January 1953.

9. *Ibid.*

10. *Ibid.*

11. *Ibid.*

Fire without movement is indecisive. Exposed movement without fire is disastrous. There must be effective fire combined with skillful movement.

INFANTRY IN BATTLE

17
Heartbreak Ridge

★ In the complex structure of enemy defensive positions protecting the seven-mile-long hill mass that became known as Heartbreak Ridge, Hill 520 was only a small, subsidiary position—a hump at the western end of a spur from the Heartbreak ridgeline.

Fighting for Hill 520 came near the end of the month-old battle for Heartbreak Ridge. On 10 October 1951, United Nations troops, holding the main north-south ridgeline, had already secured the steep part of the spur ridge that slanted down toward Hill 520. That part of the 520 ridge still in enemy hands consisted of several humps, the last and highest of which was Hill 520 at the blunt tip of the ridge. Responsibility for seizing this hump had passed from Eighth Army to X Corps, to the 2d Infantry Division, and finally to its 23d Infantry Regiment and to Company G, whose battalion commander selected it to make the attack.[1]

Fighting had been so severe on Heartbreak Ridge that at one time Company G numbered only twenty-three men. By 10 October, however, enough replacements had joined to build the strength of each of its platoons up to about twenty men. The commander of Company G had gone to Japan for the five-day rest and rehabilitation tour. Accordingly, Lt. Raymond W. Riddle, a combat-experienced executive officer, was in command for the attack. He decided to commit his 3d Platoon (under Cpl. David W. Lamb, acting platoon leader) to make the first move.

The other two rifle companies from the 2d Battalion were in positions to support the attack. Company F, located on the same ridge just behind Lieutenant Riddle's men, was prepared to pass through Company G and continue the attack, if necessary. Company E was to support the attack by firing from a parallel ridge five hundred yards to the south.

The flat top of Hill 520 was not more than two hundred yards beyond Company G's line of departure. On the ridgeline, about halfway between these two points, there was a small knoll. After considering an envelopment of the enemy position by sending Corporal Lamb's platoon into the Fluor Spar Valley—a narrow strip of flat land between his position and Company E on the next ridge to the south, and so named because of fluor spar (the mineral fluorite) mines in the valley—Riddle decided to make a direct assault along the ridgeline. There were enemy minefields in the valley. He could see some enemy movement on the objective. Hoping to draw fire so he could estimate the enemy strength there, Lieutenant Riddle ordered everyone in the company—including the mortarmen—to fire on the objective for thirty seconds. The enemy, however, did not return the fire.

When this ruse failed, Lieutenant Riddle called for supporting fires from the artillery, heavy machine guns, and Company E's 57mm recoilless rifles. At about 1300, after ten or fifteen minutes of preparation, he stopped the artillery and instructed Corporal Lamb to double-time his platoon to the intermediate knoll under cover of fire from the machine guns, the recoilless rifles, and the other riflemen in Company G. Once there, he was to set up a platoon base of fire and make the final assault on the objective.

Moving out quickly, Lamb's platoon reached the knoll without difficulty. The machine-gun crew set up its weapon and opened fire on the main objective. After deploying his platoon around the base of the knoll, Lamb reported back to Lieutenant Riddle: "No casualties yet, but receiving plenty of fire." In response to Lamb's request, Riddle instructed the support elements to intensify their fire, especially on the south side of the objective.

PFC Harry E. Schmidt, who was with Corporal Lamb's platoon, had a yellow panel wrapped around his waist. His mission was to stay with the lead assault elements so that the supporting elements would know where the platoon was. Although conspicuous himself, Schmidt made it easy for the rest of his company and for men of Company E to identify the most forward position of the attacking platoon.

While the rest of the platoon fired at bunkers on the east end of the hill, Corporal Lamb sent one squad around the left side of the objective. Brisk enemy fire drove the squad back to the platoon base, proving that both the preparatory and supporting fires had been ineffective against the enemy bunkers. Several men from the attacking squad were wounded, and enemy fire, reaching back to the intermediate knob, had caused several other casualties there. Corporal Lamb radioed to Lieutenant Riddle for reinforcements.

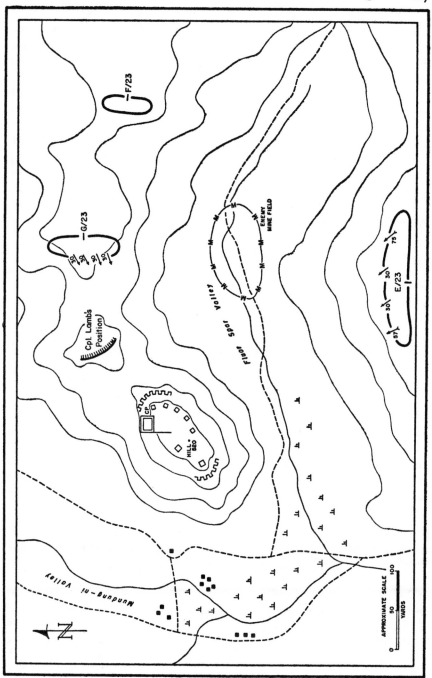

Loading the 1st Platoon with ammunition, Riddle committed it to assist in the attack. Lt. Jay M. Gano, a recent replacement, commanded the 1st Platoon. Since he was inexperienced in combat, he had instructed Pvt. Cliff R. High, who had been running the platoon, to continue to do so for the time being.

As the 1st Platoon crawled toward Lamb's position, two men were wounded not far beyond the line of departure. One of them, seriously wounded in the face and neck by a machine-gun bullet, became hysterical, and it was necessary for High to hold him down. Farther forward, Lieutenant Gano, with the lead elements of his platoon, had almost reached the intermediate knoll when he was killed on this, his first, attack. The platoon halted, pinned down by hostile fire.

Just at this time Corporal Lamb's machine gun ceased firing. "I'm out of ammo!" the gunner shouted.

Seven or eight enemy soldiers came out of their bunkers and suddenly appeared on the slope of Hill 520 descending toward Lamb's platoon. He reported that he was being counterattacked. Supporting machine-gun fire was too high to be effective. Lamb's riflemen opened fire, the ammunition bearers fired their carbines, and even the machine-gunner began firing his pistol. Part way down the slope the enemy soldiers stopped, then turned back.

A brush fire had started in the area between Lamb and the company's original position. The haze and smoke from the fire drifted north over High's immobilized platoon, making it impossible for Lieutenant Riddle to see the objective. Taking a chance, Riddle ordered his machine guns at the line of departure to fire on Hill 520. Lamb reported back that the machine-gun fire was "just right."

Under cover of the machine-gun fire and the smoke from the brush fire, High, having calmed the wounded man, sent him and another casualty to the rear and then worked his platoon forward, meeting eight or ten wounded men from Lamb's platoon who were making their way back to the company.

Corporal Lamb needed more machine-gun ammunition, and Lieutenant Riddle sent a squad from the 2d Platoon up with eight boxes. In the meantime, Lamb and High planned their assault.

Several enemy mortar shells now fell among High's platoon, wounding six more men. High sent them to the rear. He now had 11 men besides himself; Lamb had about 12. After the ammunition arrived, the two platoon leaders, leaving six men to man the machine gun and fire rifles from the intermediate knoll, called off their long-range supporting fire and then assaulted with the remaining men deployed in a skirmish line, firing as they moved forward.

Sixty yards of open ground lay between the jump-off point and enemy trenches on the slope of the objective. All went well until, halfway across, the enemy commenced firing automatic weapons. This fire was not effective, however, and did not stop the advance. When the skirmish line reached the base of the knoll, enemy soldiers stopped firing and began throwing fragmentation and concussion grenades. These caused trouble. One of the grenades wounded Lamb. Cpl. Arne Severson, seeing the skirmish line falter, picked up his machine gun and walked forward, firing as he advanced. When he reached the base of the hill an enemy grenade exploded at his feet and broke both of his legs. But he set up his gun and continued to fire until the attack stalled. Two men dragged him back.

High moved the remaining members of both platoons back to a covered position and radioed Lieutenant Riddle to bring in the machine-gun fire again and to send help, if possible. North Korean soldiers in bunkers on the objective began to taunt High and his men with phrases such as, "American, you die!"

Deciding to make a second attempt—this time a close-in envelopment of the objective—High called off the supporting fire again and led about a dozen of his men downhill toward the south, where they could move without being seen or fired upon by the enemy. They then climbed the hill, moving north to the top of Hill 520. When the men broke defilade, the enemy opened fire and began throwing grenades again. A concussion grenade knocked High down. The rest of his men, believing him dead, straggled back to the platoon base. Within a minute or two, however, High regained consciousness and returned to the platoon base where he reorganized the remaining men—about twenty in all.

In the meantime, regimental headquarters had sent three flame-thrower operators to the 2d Battalion, two of them designated for Company G and one for Company F. Lieutenant Riddle sent all three men, their flame throwers strapped to their backs, forward to help High. One operator was wounded almost immediately upon leaving the line of departure; the other two reached High as he was preparing to make another assault. He sent one flame-thrower operator and two riflemen directly to the front.

Under cover of fire, the men crawled into positions from where they could place flame on the foremost (eastern) bunker on Hill 520. As soon as this bunker was destroyed, High led the rest of his platoon around to the left and formed a skirmish line facing another enemy bunker on the south side of the hill. In position, he signalled the flame thrower to open up. As soon as the flame thrower commenced operating, High was to signal for the assault. This time the flame thrower failed to work.

By then only two enemy bunkers were interfering with the attack. A machine gun was firing from each. High decided to make the assault without the flame thrower. He sent a BAR team to knock out one bunker while he, with a rifleman and the third flame-thrower operator, walked

toward another. Firing as they walked, the men exposed themselves because High feared that if they tried to crawl they would be pinned
down. Ten yards from the bunker, the second flame thrower failed to
work. Standing exposed to enemy fire, the operator took it apart but was
unable to repair it. Finally, High told him to get out of the way because
he was too conspicuous.[2]

High stationed one of his riflemen in front of the bunker. Unable to
hit anyone in it, he nevertheless prevented the North Koreans from firing
and thus neutralized the position. Just about that time an automatic weapon
began firing from another bunker on the left, and High told Pvt. Joe
Golinda to get it. Golinda approached it from one side, High from another, while a third man covered them. Golinda threw a grenade into
the bunker, and the gun stopped firing.

With only a few men firing rifles and BARs for support, High and
four or five other men made the final assault on the top of Hill 520. Private Schmidt, still wearing the yellow panel wrapped around his waist,
stayed up with the foremost men as he had throughout the attack. The
group moved on around the hill, firing into the apertures of three other
bunkers. All were empty. Once they reached the top of the hill the men
saw eight enemy soldiers running over the hill toward the northwest, and
opened fire on them. On the north side of the hill High came upon a
bunker that had been the enemy's command post. Eight enemy soldiers,
still holding their weapons, were huddled in front of the bunker. When
High's men fired into the group the North Koreans threw up their hands
and surrendered themselves. A few minutes later, four enemy soldiers
came out of another bunker that had been bypassed and surrendered. Some
of the North Koreans were carrying United Nations safe-conduct passes
in their hands. During this final assault, other enemy soldiers were bug-
ging out off the hill.

The knoll was secure at 1600. Company G had incurred slightly over
thirty casualties, most of which were due to minor grenade wounds.
Several other casualties were sustained by the mortar men as a result of
enemy countermortar fire.

★ DISCUSSION

The attack on Hill 520 began at 1300 and ended at 1600. Company G's
advance—two hundred yards from its line of departure to its objective—
required three hours and over thirty casualties. Could Hill 520 have been
taken quicker and at a lower cost? The answer is: Yes, with one hundred
per cent effective support.

There is no doubt that fire support was planned. Private Schmidt
wore a yellow panel to indicate the position of the advance elements.
Companies E and F were in positions to aid Company G. The artillery and

mortars fired on call as requested. The assault platoons provided their own supporting fire.

But still: "The platoon halted, pinned down by hostile fire." "Supporting machine-gun fire was too high to be effective." "In the meantime regimental headquarters had sent three flame throwers to the 2d Battalion, two of them designated for Company G." "The flame thrower failed to work." "The second flame thrower failed to work."

An attack on a fortified position such as Hill 520 calls for very detailed planning. It is not enough to give machine guns a mission of firing on an objective in front of an assaulting force. A supporting machine gun should be assigned to neutralize a definite bunker embrasure. Inadequate fire-support planning and careless techniques in employment of weapons will not provide continuous fire superiority.

It was not enough to send flame-thrower operators from regiment after the attack had begun. Before Company G moved to the line of departure, the flame-thrower operators should have participated in drills and rehearsals. Forethought can, to a large extent, eliminate improvisation. Thorough training and diligent maintenance can minimize breakdowns.

It is interesting to note that immediately after Lieutenant Gano was killed his platoon halted—"pinned down by hostile fire." Probably it was not a coincidence. Although Gano had told High to continue to run the platoon, to the members of the platoon Lieutenant Gano was an officer and their platoon leader. When he stopped, the platoon stopped. Soldiers in battle look first to their appointed commanders for leadership and direction.

Lieutenant Riddle, Corporal Lamb, Private High, and the men of Company G must be commended for their courage, their determination, and their aggressive action. They accomplished their mission after they built up fire superiority with their own weapons. But they probably would have had an easier assignment had the preparations been more detailed.

★ NOTES

1. The narrative of this action on the Hill 520 ridge, written in Korea by Capt. Martin Blumenson, is based upon interviews of Lt. Raymond W. Riddle and Lt. Cliff R. High. Lieutenant High, a private at the time of the action on 10 October 1951, was awarded a battlefield commission. See also High, letter to OCMH, 3 March 1953.

2. The flame thrower, High later learned, had been improperly assembled.

18

Outpost Eerie

★ Outpost Eerie was about ten miles west of the rubble piles of Chorwon. It was a mile north of the United Nations' main line of resistance and a mile and a half south of the enemy's outpost line of resistance.[1]

In the zone of the 45th Infantry Division during March 1952, Outpost Eerie became the responsibility of Company K, 179th Infantry. Besides defending 1,400 yards of the main line, Company K kept two rifle squads, usually reinforced with a light machine gun and a light mortar, at the Eerie position. The squads had the mission of furnishing security for the main line of resistance and maintaining a base from which patrols could operate. Capt. Max Clark commanded Company K. He rotated among his rifle platoons the responsibility for manning the outpost, letting each occupy the position for a five-day period.

On the afternoon of 21 March 1952 twenty-six men of the 3d Platoon set out to take over Outpost Eerie for the next five days. These men made up two rifle squads, a light-machine-gun squad and a 60mm mortar squad. Sleet, mixed with heavy, slanting rain, began falling as the men started down toward the valley that separated the main line of resistance and the outpost line of resistance. Once across the valley floor, which was laid out in the usual pattern of rice paddies, the single-file column started up the southern tip of a two-mile-long ridge. Outpost Eerie consisted of defensive installations encircling the point peak of this ridge tip, which rose about 120 feet above the rice paddies. A rocky hill dug up by shell bursts, it had a few scrub trees and bushes and patches of thin grass.

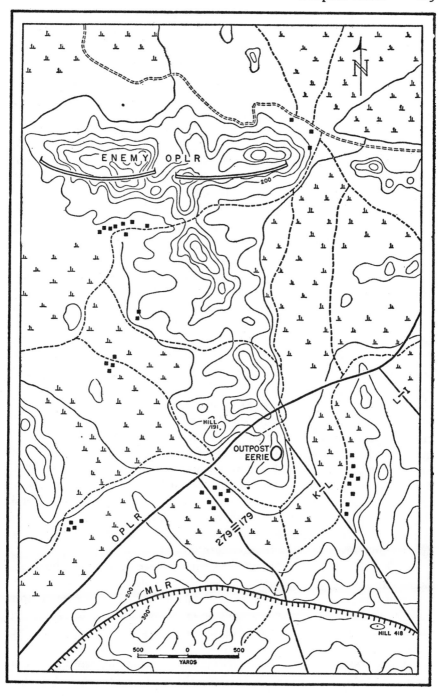

Fifty yards below the peak of the hill were three separate barbed-wire obstacles: first a coiled entanglement, then two double-apron fences —all of which circled the hilltop. Passing through the wire entanglements by a gate entrance built across the trail, the riflemen continued to the top of the hill. It was a bald hilltop, dug up from the construction of bunkers and trenches. The yellow soil uncovered during the digging was prominent in contrast to the surrounding hills.

There were nine bunkers around the top. Constructed to accommodate two or three men each, they were made with a double layer of sandbags and logs on the sides and a triple layer of logs and sandbags on top. All were but a few yards below the peak of the hill, and were for shelter only. The firing positions were in a trench that encircled the hilltop adjacent to the bunkers. The egg-shaped area circumscribed by the communication trench was about 40 by 20 yards, with the longer axis extending from southeast to northwest. The trench ran through two of the nine bunkers and just in front of, or below, the others.

At the very southern tip of a T-shaped, two-mile-long ridge, Outpost Eerie was on ground that was lower than several other high points along the same ridgeline. The crossbar of the T, upon which the enemy had established his outpost line of resistance, was higher than the shank, and dominated the entire ridgeline.

Lt. Omer Manley commanded the 3d Platoon, which effected the relief. The men who were relieved after five days on the outpost started back toward their front lines.

Most of the men in Manley's group had been on Outpost Eerie before, and each already knew to which bunker he was assigned. The most important bunkers in the Outpost Eerie defenses were three that guarded the north end of the hill. To each of these Lieutenant Manley had assigned a three-man team armed with a light machine gun and two automatic rifles. Two of these bunkers were built so that they straddled the communication, or firing, trench. The command post bunker was immediately behind the three key positions. In three of the five bunkers on the southern end of the oval there were two-man teams, three men in another, and the five-man 60mm mortar squad in the southernmost bunker.

A sound-powered telephone system connected the nine bunkers. Communication with company and battalion headquarters was by SCR-300 radio and the regular telephone; both were in the command post bunker. There were four separate telephone wires between the MLR and the outpost, thus reducing the possibility of communications failure due to cut lines.

Using Eerie as a base, the 3d Battalion maintained nightly patrols on each side of the shank of the T, covering the most likely routes by which the enemy could approach the outpost. The battalion had scheduled two such patrols on the night of 21–22 March.

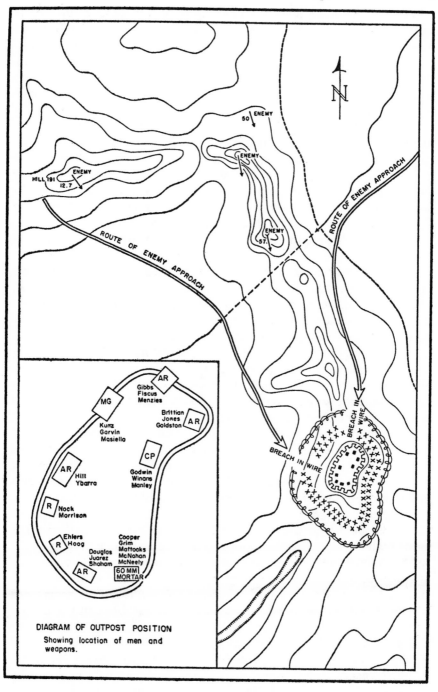

DIAGRAM OF OUTPOST POSITION
Showing location of men and
weapons.

One of these, identified as Raider Patrol, was made up of volunteers who were operating with other battalions while their own 1st Battalion was in reserve. Raider, with the mission of capturing a prisoner, left Outpost Eerie at 1900 to establish an ambush point on the east side of the long ridge, six hundred yards north of Eerie. Raider had orders to remain at its ambush site until 0130 on the morning of 22 March, and then return to Eerie at 0200.

A second patrol of nine men from Company K's 2d Platoon, and known as King Company Patrol, left Eerie at the same time to establish its ambush point in the vicinity of Hill 191—a spur ridge on the west side of the shank of the T. Hill 191 was about six hundred yards northwest of and slightly higher than Outpost Eerie. King was scheduled to man its position until 0215 the following morning and then return directly to Company K without passing through the outpost position.

Both patrols were to maintain communications by means of a sound-powered telephone tied into the outpost system.

Soon after arriving in its position, Lieutenant Manley's force test-fired all its weapons. At about 1900, Korean Service Corps personnel brought rations, water, and fuel for the small stoves in the bunkers. At dusk the men took their guard positions—one man from each bunker remaining in the trench while the others waited or slept in the bunker.

Darkness came early on the night of 21 March. It stopped raining at about 2000, soon after the two patrols had established their ambush points, but the night remained dark, misty, and cold. Since enemy patrols had probed Outpost Eerie on the two previous nights, Lieutenant Manley considered some enemy activity probable.

The infantrymen sat quietly, waiting until almost 2300 before anything unusual happened. Then King, which had set up its ambush on the western tip of the Hill 191 ridge finger, sighted and reported six enemy soldiers setting up a machine gun. The friendly patrol wanted to return to the outpost but could not because of the size and location of the enemy group.

At about the same time Raider, on the east side of the long ridge, sighted what appeared to be a platoon-sized enemy force moving south. As this column came within 150 yards of the friendly ambush point, men of Raider opened fire. The enemy group chose to ignore them, and without returning the fire continued on toward Lantern City—the name given to a small burned-out village in which the Chinese frequently used lanterns to identify themselves and to light their way among the ruins. The patrol leader called the outpost by sound-powered telephone, informed Manley of the enemy contact, and said he was withdrawing his patrol.

Lieutenant Manley immediately called the commander of Company K (Captain Clark). "The Raiders have made contact with a large group of Chinks on their front, left, and right, but did not stop them," he reported. "The patrol has broken contact and is withdrawing to the MLR. We're cocked and primed and ready for anything."

The Raider leader, however, did not inform Manley of the route by which he planned to return to the MLR. Ten or fifteen minutes later, when men in Eerie's front bunkers heard movement outside the wire below them, they passed the information on to the outpost commander.

Lieutenant Manley telephoned Captain Clark of new developments and remarked, "I'd sure like to know where the hell they [the Raiders] are!"

Manley was uncertain whether the sounds at the wire were made by the friendly patrol, or by Chinese.

The attack came at 2330. Two trip flares went off beyond the lowest barbed-wire entanglement. Seconds later, two red flares appeared. Men at the outpost interpreted the latter as a Chinese signal to notify their outpost line that they had made contact, although on that night a single red-star cluster was a United Nations sign for the return of friendly elements to the line. SFC Calvin P. Jones (platoon sergeant of the 3d Platoon) and the other men at the northern end of the outpost opened fire with automatic weapons and small arms.

Lieutenant Manley, still in doubt about the identity of the men outside the wire, rushed over from the command post bunker, yelling not to fire.

"It's the Raider Patrol returning!" he shouted.

"Like hell it is!" answered Sergeant Jones. "They're not talking English. It's the Chinese! Come on, let's get it on!"

It was then that two enemy machine guns opened fire and began sweeping the outpost position. The two weapons, emplaced about eighty yards apart on the highest ground seven hundred yards northwest of Eerie, were just a few yards above Manley's position and hence able to place grazing fire across the Eerie position. Cpl. Nick J. Masiello, manning the machine gun, alternated his bursts between these weapons and the Chinese who were attempting to breach the wire below him. The enemy gunners replied by concentrating fire on Masiello's gun. Meanwhile, the Chinese opened fire with at least one more machine gun and several 50mm grenade dischargers emplaced on the ridge to the north.

From his observation post atop Hill 418 on the MLR, Captain Clark watched the machine-gun duel. He could see tracers from Masiello's weapon apparently ricochet from the shields that protected the Chinese guns, and it appeared to him that tracers from both guns were hitting each other. When the fight broke out, he immediately signalled for prearranged supporting machine-gun and mortar concentrations. A caliber .50 machine gun, from a position on the forward slope of Hill 418 a few yards in front of Clark's observation post, fired directly over the heads of the defenders and forced one of the enemy machine guns to displace.

The mortar fire was not accurate until Lieutenant Manley made corrections by telephone to Captain Clark.

"They're giving us a hell of a battle out here, but we're OK so far," Manley reported. "Bring the mortars in closer. . . . That's too close! Move 'em out a little. . . . Now leave them right where they are."

With the first adjustment some rounds fell inside the wire, but were not close enough to the communication trench to harm the defenders.

Lieutenant Manley then headed out of the bunker to consult with Sergeant Jones, but as he started for the entrance, several machine-gun bullets ripped through the shelter half covering it. They were high and hit no one in the command post bunker, but Lieutenant Manley ducked down and crawled out into the communication trench.

Fifteen minutes after the fire fight began, a burst from one of the enemy heavy machine guns hit Corporal Masiello. PFC Theodore Garvin (Masiello's ammunition bearer) picked up the sound-powered telephone at the position and shouted, "Medic!"

Though he was manning the telephone at the command post bunker, Cpl. Herman Godwin heard the loud cry without it. Corporal Godwin was a rifleman who doubled as platoon aid man since he preferred to carry arms rather than to carry or wear any of the insignia or cards by which some medical aid men are identified as protected persons. He hurried down the communication trench to the machine-gun position, where he did what he could to stop the flow of blood and administered morphine.

PFC William F. Kunz (assistant machine gunner), markedly affected by the sight of Corporal Masiello's wounds, continuously lamented, "Poor Nick, poor Nick!"

As the machine gunner died, Corporal Godwin tried to comfort his assistant, saying, "He's not feeling anything."

Kunz went to the bunker; Godwin remained at the machine-gun position to help Garvin get the weapon in action again. The two men rapidly straightened a twisted belt, and Garvin, as gunner, resumed firing. Corporal Godwin assisted him, and at the same time kept the sound-powered telephone near him in case anyone should call for aid. When only one belt of ammunition remained, Garvin told Godwin to take over the gun while he went for more. After calling for Kunz to come back and help him, Corporal Godwin took over the machine gun.

As far as anyone in the perimeter could determine, the Chinese were trying to break through the barbed wire at only two places, the attacks coming from the north and the northeast. For another three quarters of an hour the defenders held off both attacks without further casualties. Lieutenant Manley called the company's command post and asked the artillery forward observer to fire artillery concentration No. 304, which was plotted on the Hill 191 ridge finger. Harassing artillery fire had been falling on this area throughout the evening—a few shells at intervals of about twenty minutes.

A little later, about half an hour after midnight, when Captain Clark telephoned to the outpost to ask how things were going, PFC Leroy Winans (platoon runner) replied, "Everything's OK, sir; they're not through the wire yet."

Meanwhile, both enemy assault groups steadily pressed their attempts to blow gaps in the circle of protective wire. At least one of the groups was using bangalore torpedoes.

Mortar and artillery illuminating flares contributed greatly to the defense, but whenever the illumination failed, the flash of the defenders' weapons betrayed their positions to the enemy. When the supply of mortar illumination shells was exhausted, a 155mm battery fired an illuminating mission. Most of these shells, however, burst too close to the ground to furnish effective light. Despite all efforts to adjust the height of burst, it was not corrected in time to help.

Effective illuminating fire ceased before 0100, 22 March. About this time PFC Robert L. Fiscus, an automatic rifleman in the bunker to the immediate right of the light machine gun, was wounded. Corporal Godwin, who had been assisting at the machine gun, crawled to his right through the communication trench and found Fiscus lying in the trench outside of the bunker. Carrying the wounded man inside, Godwin dressed the wound.

When Sergeant Jones learned that Fiscus was wounded, he sent Pvt. Elbert Goldston, Jr., to take the wounded man's place as automatic-rifle man. At the same time, he called over Pvt. Alphonso Gibbs, who had been Fiscus's assistant, to replace Goldston as assistant to Cpl. Carl F. Brittian, the automatic rifleman at Sergeant Jones's position—the right-hand one of the three key bunkers at the north end of the perimeter. Sergeant Jones made this shift because he considered Goldston to be the more experienced automatic-rifle man, and therefore of more value in the area closest to the threatened enemy breakthrough.

Pvt. Hugh Menzies, Jr. (a rifleman acting as Goldston's assistant) was the next man wounded. As Godwin came out of the bunker after dressing Fiscus's wound, he saw Menzies get hit by grenade fragments. Godwin pulled him into the bunker with Fiscus and administered first aid.

Officers at regimental headquarters were trying to obtain the use of a "firefly"—a plane equipped to drop illuminating flares. None was immediately available. The only aircraft in the area at that time was a B-26, which later dropped its bombs on enemy positions at the north end of the ridge-line.

By 0100 the enemy had breached the wire in two places. Lieutenant Manley encouraged his men, calling out to them, "Get up and fight or we'll be wiped out! This isn't any movie!"

Goldston was the next man wounded. As the Chinese soldiers came through the breaks in the wire and up the hill toward the outpost, he was hit in both legs by burp-gun fire, and in the arm and head by shell fragments. Of the 9 men occupying the three bunkers facing the enemy attack, 4 were now out of action, 2 were dead.

Corporal Godwin dragged Goldston through the bunker where Fiscus and Menzies lay, into the trench on the other side. After Godwin administered first aid, Sergeant Jones and Private Gibbs carried Goldston over to their bunker—the one on the right (east)—which was empty. Corporal Brittian, the BAR man who had started out the night in Jones's bunker, had previously gone over to load BAR magazines for Goldston while he was firing at the Chinese making the attack on the left. When Goldston became a casualty, Brittian took over the BAR and fired it until the ammunition was gone.

Several minutes had elapsed since the enemy broke through the barbed wire and started crawling up toward the outpost defenses. Godwin now discovered that there were no grenades left in the center bunker. He grabbed his rifle and began firing into the advancing Chinese from a position in the communication trench. The enemy troops were very near the top. Godwin fired until his ammunition was gone, threw his rifle at the nearest Chinese and saw the butt hit him in the face, knocking him back down the hill. He then ducked into the bunker to look after the two wounded men and as he did so, noticed Corporal Brittian throwing BAR magazines at the approaching Chinese. Brittian was killed very soon afterward.

At this point, ten or fifteen minutes after 0100, Kunz and Garvin remained fighting in the easternmost of the three bunkers under the heaviest enemy fire. Corporal Godwin was the only able-bodied man in the center bunker. Jones, Gibbs and Goldston, in the next bunker to the right, heard the firing suddenly stop at the center bunker when Godwin ran out of ammunition, and decided that surely they were the only ones at that end of the perimeter still living. Then they spotted enemy soldiers on top of Godwin's bunker. The three men—Jones and Gibbs helping the wounded Goldston—climbed out of the trench and rolled down the eastern slope of the hill about halfway to the wire. Taking advantage of what cover was available, they lay quiet, and remained there without further trouble during the rest of the action.

Corporal Godwin, in the center bunker with Fiscus and Menzies, also had the feeling that he must be the only able-bodied man left. Stepping out of the bunker for a look, he spotted a Chinese soldier coming along the trench toward him. He stepped back against the bunker, waited until the Chinese was within point-blank range, and shot him in the head with a caliber .45 pistol. Knowing the report would attract attention, Godwin jumped back against the side of the trench. An enemy soldier standing on the edge of the trench fired a burst from his burp gun, but then moved on without determining whether he had hit Godwin. With nothing but a dent in the lip of his helmet, Godwin went back into the bunker. Moments later an enemy soldier threw a concussion grenade through the entrance opposite the one by which Godwin had just entered, this being one of the bunkers straddling the communication trench. The explosion knocked Godwin unconscious and bent the metal cover of a small Bible which he carried in his left breast pocket.

While this action was taking place at the north end of the oval-shaped perimeter, other Chinese had moved around to the western side of the position. Sgt. Kenneth F. Ehlers (squad leader in a bunker in the left-rear sector of the perimeter) warned the platoon command post by telephone that the enemy was coming around to the west side and requested mortar fire from the outpost's one 60mm mortar. However, there was only one round left, and it was decided to save it.

Ehlers then went to the bunker south of the one where Kunz and Garvin were still operating the machine gun. There Ehlers, Lieutenant Manley (who had also come over to that position), Cpl. Robert Hill and Cpl. Joel Ybarra, fought the Chinese with their automatic rifles, M1 rifles, and grenades. As the Chinese worked up close, both Ehlers and Hill were killed. At a critical moment Lieutenant Manley ran out of ammunition for his carbine, or it jammed. He threw it at the Chinese and then started throwing grenades at them. After only a few moments, however, all action at that bunker ended; the platoon leader and Corporal Ybarra disappeared.

From the firing position of the next bunker to the south, Pvt. Elmer Nock and Pvt. Edward Morrison moved to the rear through the communication trench when the enemy began coming into the trench toward their position. Cpl. Albert W. Hoog, covering their movement from his position in the next bunker southward, shot two Chinese who were following them.

Shortly after the Chinese broke through the wire, Private Winans (the platoon runner), who by this time was the only man left at the command post bunker, called Captain Clark.

"They're coming through the wire, and it looks like a thousand!" Winans said. "It looks like we're going to have to surrender!"

"No; don't surrender!" the company commander replied. "Go get Lieutenant Manley."

This happened at about the same time the Chinese were overrunning the bunker on the opposite side of the hill where Lieutenant Manley had been.

Right after this an enemy shell—probably one from a 57mm recoilless rifle—made a direct hit on the command post bunker. It killed Winans and cut all telephone lines to Company K. There was no more communication with Outpost Eerie.

In the rearmost automatic-rifle position, manned by Cpl. Robert Shoham (BAR man), PFC David Juarez, and PFC Francis Douglas, there was not much action until the enemy had broken through the wire and was in and upon the outpost position itself. Before that time these men had fired at a few enemy troops who were on the outside of the wire near their position but had received no return fire—apparently because the Chinese below them carried grenades but not rifles. When the enemy soldiers came over the top of the outpost toward the rear positions, Shoham opened fire with his automatic rifle, Douglas with his rifle, and Juarez busied himself loading magazines for the BAR. An enemy mortar shell made a direct hit on Juarez, but it was dud. He was quick to throw the shell out of the trench. Except for a bruise and a numbed leg, he was unhurt.

With the enemy on top of Eerie, there was a lull in his supporting fire. The time was about 0120. Corporal Godwin, lying in the bunker where he had been knocked out by the concussion grenade, was beginning to regain consciousness. Hazily, he saw an enemy soldier reach into the bunker for two BARs which were standing in the corner. The barrel of the one he first touched was too hot to handle. After a few harsh Chinese words, he took the cool weapon away with him. When Godwin fully regained consciousness, he discovered his hunting knife was missing. By this time, Menzies was dead.

Back at the company's observation post, Captain Clark told his artillery liaison officer (Lt. Anthony Cotroneo) to shift his artillery fire from two concentrations being fired at the time and to place it squarely on Outpost Eerie itself. In a few minutes, 105mm proximity-fuze shells began bursting over the position. There followed the sound of a horn blown three times, and within a few minutes enemy activity stopped. The artillery shells fell, and the enemy's recall signal sounded before the Chinese troops had covered the entire outpost area. They had reached but had not searched the 60mm mortar position on the right and the bunker defended by Nock and Morrison on the left. Without further search of the area, the Chinese withdrew, assembling near the break in the wire they had made at the northwest part of the perimeter. They left two of their dead in the position.

At 0130 the regimental commander (Col. Frederick A. Daugherty) ordered Captain Clark to move the rest of Company K up to the relief of the outpost. Thirty-five minutes later, after a platoon from Company A took over its position on the main line of resistance, Company K moved out.

On the way to the outpost, members of Company K found three seriously wounded men from the outpost near the creek that flowed past the base of the outpost. The men were evacuated. Farther on, the relief men met Raider Patrol, all members of which were safe. The patrol had been caught in the open when the fighting commenced and had been unable to take an effective part in the action. Captain Clark instructed the leader to keep his patrol in its present location until further notice. Later, the patrol tapped in on a telephone line to the main line of resistance and asked to be cleared for return to the main line. Receiving it, the patrol returned and reached the front lines at 0500.

The Company K patrol returned to the main line by going southwest from the Hill 191 ridge finger. At about 0245 it arrived in front of the unit holding the main line of resistance on the left of Company K's previous position; it fired one red flare—the recognition signal. The friendly unit honored the signal, and the patrol entered the front lines at 0330. When the fight had begun at 2330, the patrol had withdrawn to the southwest, beyond the impact area of the falling mortar and artillery shells.

Company K reached Eerie at 0400, about two hours after leaving the main line. One platoon (the 2d) went around to the east side of the position, then climbed up to the peak. The 1st Platoon, followed by the headquarters group, took the direct route, using the gate through the wire at the southeastern edge. Once on top, the men searched the area for casualties, and evacuated them as they were located. After an hour's search, Captain Clark had accounted for all men except Lieutenant Manley and Corporal Ybarra, both of whom had disappeared from the same bunker.

Of the 26 men who had defended Outpost Eerie, 8 were dead, 4 wounded, and 2 were missing in action. With one exception, all men killed had suffered head and chest wounds—the parts of their bodies exposed above the firing positions in the communication trench. To the regimental commander this was significant proof of the effectiveness of the well-placed enemy machine guns. Nine of the twelve unharmed men had either manned the rear positions of the outpost, or had moved to them during the course of the action. It was Captain Clark's opinion that the artillery fire which fell on the outpost after the Chinese had entered it had prevented further casualties. He felt that the air-bursts forced the Chinese to withdraw before they were able to cover the entire outpost area in a thorough search.

The Division's artillery fired 2,614 rounds during the enemy attack. Of this number, 2,464 rounds were equipped with proximity fuzes for air-burst effect; the remaining 150 rounds were 155mm illuminating shells. Together, the regimental Mortar Company and the 3d Battalion's heavy-weapons company (M) fired 914 mortar shells, of which all were high-explosive except 10 that were white phosphorus and one a 4.2-inch illuminating—the only illuminating shell the company had ever had on hand.

Company K searched the outpost area after daylight, going as far north along the ridgeline as possible in the face of enemy fire. The men found only 2 enemy dead within the barbed wire surrounding the outpost, but found 29 other bodies to the north and northwest along the enemy's route of withdrawal. Artillery fire had been placed along the probable withdrawal routes, and it is possible this fire caused additional casualties and also influenced the Chinese to abandon bodies which they had been attempting to carry away.

Captain Clark's men also found a wounded Chinese. He had been hit in both legs—by his own supporting machine guns, he believed. This man later explained that he had been a member of the enemy force that had attacked along the west side of the long ridge—a force that apparently consisted of two platoons. On the night of 21 March, the prisoner's squad had eaten the evening meal just before dark, as usual. He and the other men of his squad had then gone to sleep. Some time between 1900 and 2000, the squad leader awakened them and told them to prepare for a patrol. After "running" for an hour or longer along the west slope of the ridge, these enemy soldiers reached the foot of the first hill north of the Eerie peak. After standing in the dark for a short while, each squad present reported its strength. There were 3 rifle squads, 2 machine-gun squads, and 1 grenade-discharger squad, having a combined total of about 60 men, according to the count.

The Chinese patrol leader then delivered a pep talk, telling his men their mission was to capture some U.S. soldiers, and that they should go out and fight gallantly. When the talk was finished, the enemy soldiers moved out to emplace their supporting weapons and prepare to attack The three rifle squads, moving in a column with one and a half yards between men, followed their leader over the Hill 191 ridge toward the outpost position. A similar enemy force was moving along the opposite side of the ridge. Thirty minutes later the fight began.

Lieutenant Manley's platoon lost some of its weapons during the fight. As the Chinese withdrew they apparently took with them a few M1 rifles and automatic rifles they had picked up as they searched the position. However, they left more American weapons than they took. A later check of these weapons proved nothing except that they did not belong to Company K.

After completing its search of the area, Captain Clark's entire company returned to the main line of resistance. And for several months, Outpost Eerie was not again permanently manned.

★ DISCUSSION

FM 7–10, *Rifle Company, Infantry Regiment*, October 1949, says: "The mission of the combat outpost is to delay, disorganize, and deceive the enemy. It aids in securing the battle position, gains timely information of the enemy, and inflicts maximum casualties on the enemy without engaging in close combat."

Note the words *without engaging in close combat.* The situation in Korea in 1952 was not clearly envisioned in 1949, when this manual was published. The Korean battle ground in March 1952 was but a strip across the peninsula between the main defensive positions of the United Nations forces and those of the Communists. While both forces had offensive capabilities, they remained in a state of static defense. Under these conditions the mission of combat outposts had to change. In order to gain timely information or to delay and disorganize an enemy attack, outposts had to be maintained. In order to have an outpost system, terrain suitable for outposting had to be denied the enemy. Had each outpost withdrawn *without engaging in close combat,* the enemy soon would have had all the advantages of a security system and the UN forces would have had none.

Too often when war breaks out situations develop that have not been foreseen by writers of military textbooks. Minor discrepancies quickly become apparent. And on all sides the cry is heard, "Throw away the book!" As the war progresses and commanders accumulate experience there soon is a reverse swing to the book and the best units are those that follow the rules—modified to fit the particular situation.

The 3d Platoon of Company K, 179th Infantry, was a good unit. It knew what it was to do, and it did the job well. With the advantage of hindsight we can see that it might have done better had it demanded a clearer message from Raider Patrol. If a message can be misunderstood, it will be. When Raider Patrol reported it was withdrawing to the main line of resistance, the message did not indicate whether or not the patrol would return through Outpost Eerie. This apparently small oversight permitted the enemy patrols to approach Outpost Eerie almost unmolested.

★ NOTE

1. The narrative of this action is based upon a thorough study, prepared in Korea by Major B. C. Mossman and Lt. Edgar Denton, of the defense of Outpost Eerie.

*A successful patrol takes time—time for planning,
time for coordination with other units, time for
thorough briefing. . . .*

THE INFANTRY JOURNAL (1949)

19

Combat Patrol

★ North of the 38th parallel and on the east side of the
Korean peninsula is a large area crowded with steep-sided hills. Most of
the valleys are wide enough for only a stream, a footpath, or a narrow road,
and a few tiny rice paddies terraced in the draws like stair steps. There is
not much land suitable for growing rice, and the houses are few, the
settlements scattered.[1]

Here, troops of the United Nations and the opposing Communist
armies stabilized their lines during the Panmunjom truce talks. Among
these wrinkled and half-barren hills, Noname Ridge was only an obscure
finger ridge. Four or five miles straight east of Heartbreak Ridge and near
the northwestern rim of a volcano-like crater called the Punchbowl, Noname Ridge was in the area between the friendly front lines and the main
defensive position of a North Korean unit. The only prominent feature
about it was a little fresh dirt left exposed by enemy soldiers who were
constructing new bunkers and trenches there. The dirt was more noticeable because of the snow which, even in early April of 1952, still covered
many of the hills, especially in the low and shaded places. Noname Ridge
was about a thousand yards from the enemy's main lines, and from positions of the U.S. 35th Infantry (25th Infantry Division). It was within
range of friendly patrols.

One of these patrols, scheduled for the night of 3 April 1952, fell to
Company A, 35th Infantry, which at the time was manning reserve positions behind the front lines. If possible, battalion commanders assigned

combat patrol missions to reserve units because they did not like to weaken their main defenses by using front-line companies for patrolling.

The regiment planned the patrol action on 28 March, naming Lt. John H. Chandler patrol leader. His mission was to conduct a combat patrol to Noname Ridge to kill or capture any enemy encountered. For the job, he was to take a force consisting of two reinforced rifle squads.

Chandler received the patrol plans on the afternoon of 2 April. He selected two squads from his 3d Platoon and several men from the other squads in order to have a total of twenty, including himself. The next afternoon (3 April) he took his nineteen men to a high point overlooking the planned route and briefed them on the patrol scheduled for that night. He pointed out the objective, one of the enemy construction sites on Noname Ridge, and explained that he hoped to surprise an enemy working party while it was digging and unarmed. If possible, the patrol would capture one or more North Koreans, or kill them if capture were impossible.

Using available maps, Lieutenant Chandler had constructed a sand model outlining the most prominent terrain features and the objective patrol. Aerial photographs were not available, and consequently, there were features of the ridges and the draws he did not include in the model. However, the model was good enough to plan the routes of advance and withdrawal and to show the known characteristics of the objective area. Just before the briefing ended, Lieutenant Chandler reminded the men of the battalion's rule concerning casualties.

"Casualties, dead or wounded," he said, "are never left by the rest of the patrol. If any man is left on the field, the entire unit will return to find him and bring him back."

When the patrol assembled after supper, Lieutenant Chandler divided the men into two sections: an assault squad of 8 men and himself, and a fire-support squad of the other 11 men.

Two men of the assault squad carried automatic rifles. For mutual assistance and for protection, Chandler paired each BAR man with another man armed with a carbine. The other members of the assault squad —Chandler, an assistant patrol leader, the two scouts (one of whom was an ROK corporal serving with the 3d Platoon), and the radio operator— also carried automatic carbines.

In the fire-support squad the leader (Cpl. David Mitchell) and the assistant squad leader (Cpl. Robert Kirschbaum) both carried M1 rifles, each with a grenade launcher and two flares. Two men carried light machine guns, two were armed with BARs, and the other five had carbines. In this squad also Chandler paired each of the automatic weapons with a carbine for mutual support.

One man in each squad carried an SCR-300 radio; a man in the support squad had a sound-powered telephone and two reels of light wire. Both wire and radio were tied in with communications at an observation post of Company C on the main line of resistance. From this observation post —manned by Company C's commander, a liaison officer from Company A, and a forward observer from the 64th Field Artillery Battalion—there was direct communication by both radio and telephone with the 1st Battalion's command post. The battalion commander (Lt.Col. Philip G. Walker) wanted to be able to direct the actions of both the patrol and the supporting artillery if it became necessary to do so.

After satisfying himself that all details of his patrol were in order, Lieutenant Chandler—a man who was both careful and thorough—waved his men forward. The patrol crossed the main line of resistance at 2100. As Chandler led his men down the finger toward the stream bed, the 105mm howitzers of the 64th Field Artillery Battalion fired their usual harassing and interdiction missions. In planning the patrol, the regimental staff had timed the departure to coincide with this evening fire, hoping it would keep the enemy under cover until the patrol was in defilade.

In spite of the difficulty of moving on the steep, snow-covered slope, the men maintained an orderly open column as they worked their way toward the draw. At 2130 Lieutenant Chandler reported to Company C's observation post that he had reached the first check point, located about halfway down the slope. After this first descent the going was easier and the patrol reported from the second check point twenty minutes later. The patrol was now about halfway to its objective. The snow, which interfered with walking part of the time, also reflected enough light to make it easier for the men to see. The moon, in its first quarter, came up at about the time the patrol left the second check point and, since the night was clear, there was good visibility thereafter.

This second check point was near the base of a draw. From this point, the fingers leading up to Noname Ridge looked quite different from the way the terrain had been shown on the map used in planning. In spite of Lieutenant Chandler's careful planning, he was still in doubt as to which of two fingers he should follow. After studying the ground for a few minutes, he chose one and decided to follow it toward Noname Ridge. If this were the correct finger ridge, he would find his objective point close to the top of it. If it were not the correct one, the added elevation would enable him to check his position against known landmarks.

When the patrol reached the crest of the finger, Chandler led his men up the slope of the ridge, through old communication trenches and close to enemy bunkers. There was no sign of the enemy—either sound or movement. The infantrymen knew the enemy had maintained an outpost line of resistance on the ridge and it seemed strange to them to be so close to enemy positions and yet to find nothing to indicate that anyone else was near. After going about ninety yards, Chandler concluded that he had chosen the wrong ridge. He turned down the steep

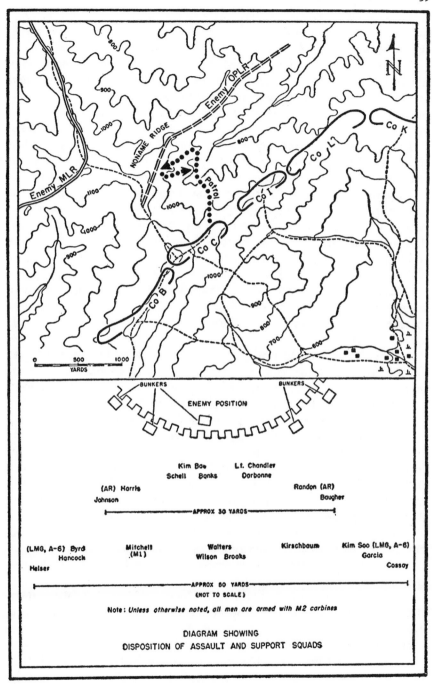

DIAGRAM SHOWING
DISPOSITION OF ASSAULT AND SUPPORT SQUADS

side of one ridge, crossed a sharp draw at the bottom and, with the rest of the men following in single file, started up the face of the next ridge, which he now realized was his original objective—Noname Ridge.

By the time the patrol reached the crest of the second finger ridge it was almost half an hour past midnight. Chandler reported his position to the observation post, using the radio because all wire for the sound-powered telephone had been used. The patrol, after travelling out of its way, had not backtracked to recover the wire. Moreover, the telephone had not worked satisfactorily after the patrol member carrying it had spliced the two reels of wire. Perhaps the splice was faulty, or perhaps the thin wire lacked sufficient insulation when the wire lay in wet snow.

By the time the patrol reached the objective, it had been out for about three and a half hours. When Chandler reported to the observation post, it had made no contact with the enemy, nor had it found any indications that there were enemy soldiers in the area. When this report reached Colonel Walker, he instructed Chandler to continue with his original mission.

"Get a prisoner if you can," the battalion commander told the patrol leader. "If you can't, shoot 'em up. Decide upon the route you are going to take to make contact, move forward a hundred yards, then report again."

When Chandler had made his decision, he called back to give it to Colonel Walker so the battalion commander could continue to plot the patrol's course. The patrol moved forward without incident. Colonel Walker told Chandler to go another hundred yards and report again.

After the second move, the patrol members saw and heard movement in the direction of the enemy's main defensive line. It appeared that enemy soldiers, still some distance away, were coming down toward Noname Ridge. Chandler called for artillery. In a few minutes, thirty-six 105mm shells fell in the area where the enemy movement had been. The movement stopped with the incoming rounds, but Lieutenant Chandler and his men could still hear voices from the vicinity of the impact area.

Though the patrol had now made some contact, it had not yet accomplished its mission of capturing a prisoner. Cautiously, Chandler led his men another hundred yards upward to a point about fifty yards from the very top of the ridge.

Here the men stopped and listened. They could hear noise above them. There were bunkers near the top of the ridge, and the men could hear North Koreans talking and laughing. There were other noises which Chandler's men identified as the sounds made by men while eating.

Lieutenant Chandler called back over the radio to Company C's observation post: "We're going on radio silence from here on, so there won't be any chance that the radio will give us away before we're ready."

Then he spent some time trying to determine the outline and construction of the enemy's position.

From the patrol's location below the crest of the ridge, the men could see a large bunker that would be a little to the left of the patrol's route of approach. On each side there were other smaller bunkers.

Lieutenant Chandler formed the patrol into two lines facing the enemy's position. The assault squad was disposed with an automatic-rifle man and another man with a carbine on each flank, and the other men quite close together in the center. Chandler and Cpl. Kim Bae were out in front; Sgt. William Schell (assistant patrol leader), Pvt. Johnnie R. Banks (scout), and Cpl. Anthony Darbonne (radio operator), were close behind them. The fire-support squad, with its weapons posted in about the same pattern, stayed about twenty yards behind the assault party.

In this formation the patrol moved stealthily ahead, the men walking upright but ready to start crawling when necessary. When the patrol had covered about twenty-five of the remaining yards to the enemy's position, PFC Van D. Randon, carrying the BAR on the right flank of the assault squad, turned to PFC Charles H. Baugher, who was walking behind him.

"There's wire right in front of you," Randon muttered. "Be careful."

Baugher stepped over the wire. There was an explosion that threw him to the ground, tipping him over on his right side. The other men of the patrol were not much later in hitting the ground. It was about 0210.

In the immediate silence that followed, Baugher, who had apparently stepped on a booby-trapped concussion grenade, felt for his foot and found it to be all right although numb. The rest of the patrol lay quietly, waiting for the enemy to come out of the bunkers to see what had tripped the grenade. Nothing happened. The sounds of laughing, talking, and eating continued.

After waiting several minutes to make certain the North Koreans had ignored the noise, Lieutenant Chandler crept forward with his assault squad. As Chandler and his South Korean interpreter (Cpl. Kim Bae) approached the large bunker in the center, they came upon a communication trench that joined at least the five bunkers the patrol members could see. Chandler and Kim Bae jumped into the trench. As they did so a North Korean came out of the big bunker a few feet away to their left. Chandler and Kim Bae climbed back out of the trench.

The North Korean muttered a few words in guttural Korean, apparently a challenge. Kim answered in Korean, but apparently the enemy was still suspicious. When he first spoke he had unslung the burp gun he carried on his shoulder; now he raised it to the ready position and fired. Several men from the assault squad opened fire at the same time. Kim Bae threw a grenade. The North Korean fell after he had fired about three rounds. No one there knew who had killed him. With the need for silence past, the men of the squad began shouting, breaking into a loud and profane argument about "who killed the son of a bitch."

Back on the main line of resistance, half a mile away, men of Company C saw the tracers scratch the night, and heard the sudden shouting. The fire fight was on.

Six North Koreans came streaming out of the big bunker. The assault squad killed the first five with carbine and automatic-rifle fire; the sixth ducked back into the bunker. One of Chandler's men threw two grenades into the big bunker and after that no one came out, but for several minutes there was the sound of yelling and screaming from inside.

There were other bunkers, however—two on each side of the large one—and North Koreans from these soon appeared in the communication trench. But the BAR men on the flanks (Private Randon and Cpl. Wilbur Harris) either killed them or drove them back into protected positions. Maintaining a heavy rate of fire, the squad managed to hold the initiative.

The North Koreans began throwing grenades. A heavy machine gun opened fire from the patrol's left, from a position above the enemy's bunkers. But the gun had to fire upward and—in clearing the ridge—put its bursts three or four feet too high. In spite of the ineffectiveness of the enemy's gun, Cpl. James A. Byrd, operating the light machine gun on the support squad's left flank, fired back until his gun jammed. Corporal Mitchell moved over to help him clear the piece, then continued firing until it jammed again. Lieutenant Chandler, still in front, watched the tracers from both guns disappear harmlessly into the darkness.

"Stop firing the machine gun!" Chandler shouted to Mitchell. "You can't hit them!"

Mitchell and Byrd then threw grenades over the crest in the direction of the enemy gun, and the firing stopped.

A couple of North Koreans from the left bunkers attempted to work their way along the communication trench. Harris, firing the BAR at that end of the line, killed them. Chandler's men tossed several grenades in the trench and toward the bunkers. After a few minutes three or four North Koreans tried to get around the patrol's right flank. As they appeared silhouetted against the skyline, Cpl. Kim Soo turned his light machine gun in that direction and saw three of them drop. He had placed his gun so that he had grazing fire.

The North Koreans relied mainly on grenades. There had been some ineffective small-arms fire at the beginning of the action, but Chandler's men silenced these weapons. The enemy preferred to remain in defilade beyond the crest of the hill or around the edge, and throw grenades into the patrol. The assault squad had some protection from these missiles by its nearness to the enemy. Men of this squad were so close to the trench—

the front of the enemy's position—that the enemy apparently hesitated to toss grenades into that area. Also, because of the short range between the assault squad and the North Koreans and because of the slope of the hill behind the squad, most of the grenades passed over it, to fall behind and below in the space between the two squads.

Nevertheless, concussion grenades wounded both radio operators and put their radios out of commission. This happened early in the action. Neither man was seriously wounded. There were two other casualties, both in the support squad. A grenade seriously wounded the assistant leader of the support squad (Corporal Kirschbaum). Besides wounding him in both legs, the explosion blew off part of his right foot. Grenade fragments also wounded the BAR man on the left flank (PFC Emmett Hancock). Of these four men, all but Kirschbaum were able to walk.

After thirty minutes of brisk firing, Lieutenant Chandler's men began to run low on ammunition. The volume of fire dropped noticeably. At about the same time, friendly artillery fire began falling on the enemy's main defensive line several hundred yards from the patrol action.

At about 0245 Chandler decided to withdraw, but when he asked the radio operators to send back the message that the patrol was breaking contact and withdrawing, he discovered the casualties and the destruction of the radios. He ordered the assault squad and the casualties to move through the support squad and start back toward the rallying point at the foot of the hill in front of friendly front lines. Several men improvised a litter in which to carry Corporal Kirschbaum.

Throughout the fire fight Chandler's men shouted and yelled. When they started to withdraw, however, this noise and the noise of firing dwindled to such an extent it was noticeable to men watching the action from Company C's observation post on the main line of resistance. Although these observers had just discovered they had no radio contact with the patrol, they could see the fire fight moving toward them and realized the patrol had begun to withdraw. They relayed this information to Colonel Walker.

The battalion commander immediately called for artillery and mortar concentrations in the vicinity of Noname Ridge. As Chandler moved back, the commander of Company C gave Colonel Walker the patrol's position, so far as he could determine it by observing the small-arms fire from the patrol toward the enemy. By the same method, he traced the location of the North Koreans as they attempted to follow the patrol. From this information battalion headquarters plotted both friendly and enemy positions on a map showing all artillery and mortar concentrations.

As the engagement moved toward the main line of resistance, Colonel Walker moved the mortar and artillery concentrations along with it. He did not call for new concentrations closer in, but rather shifted the original concentrations to keep the impact area as close as possible to the patrol.

He telephoned his decisions to the forward observer, who relayed them to the artillery and mortar units. Colonel Walker handled the supporting fires, giving the corrections himself, because he did not wish to shift to his subordinate officers the responsibility for directing the fire at night when they had no communications with the patrol they were supporting.

Just before the patrol reached the rallying point at the foot of the hill, Lieutenant Chandler sent Corporal Mitchell and Pvt. George Wilson on ahead to bring back litters and bearers from Company C. On the slippery, snowy slope of the ridge, it took the two men more than an hour to reach the main line. Once there, they learned that Company C had already alerted a relief squad and had it ready to return with them with the required items. As Mitchell and Wilson led the squad down the ridge, an enemy mortar round landed in the group, wounding four men of Company C. Mitchell and Wilson helped take these wounded men back and waited for another squad. They finally rejoined the patrol at about 0530.

Meanwhile, after forming a defensive perimeter at the rallying point, Chandler threw an illuminating grenade in the direction of the enemy as a guide for the supporting mortars. Colonel Walker shifted the mortar fire closer to the patrol and kept it well protected from North Koreans who were following with considerable determination. Besides the artillery fire, several tanks dug in on the main line fired cannon and heavy machine guns.

By this time it had become light enough for the enemy on Noname Ridge to see the patrol perimeter. Lieutenant Chandler, using the radio the relief squad had brought down from Company C, called for smoke on Noname Ridge, south of the patrol. The bursting shells obscured the enemy's observation posts, and the smoke, drifting down the draw with a light breeze, screened the patrol after the smoke had cleared the hill.

In spite of this concealment, the enemy kept the patrol pinned down until about 0630. After this the men continued on back to their base, moving slowly.

The patrol had been out more than twelve hours. Although it had no prisoner, Chandler had most successfully raided the enemy's position. He had suffered ten casualties—all from grenade fragments—during the night's action, but he and his men believed they had killed at least as many North Koreans, and had wounded others.

The effective use of more than two thousand artillery rounds on known enemy positions and on the enemy troops following the friendly patrol back toward its base prevented further casualties. Patrol members gave full credit to the artillery support for their successful return. On a small scale, infantry and artillery had teamed up to make a successful operation.

★ DISCUSSION

Lieutenant Chandler displayed a knowledge of the psychology of leadership when he repeated to his patrol the battalion's rule that no man who became a casualty would be left. The certainty of help in the event of misfortune strengthens a man's will. Thus, it is always best to assign both training and combat missions to organized units rather than to groups of individuals. For the same reason, replacements should be given a chance to become members of squads before the squads are committed to action. Lieutenant Chandler used two squads reinforced by members of his own platoon to form this patrol. He organized a *team*.

The preparation before the patrol's departure was excellent. Note should be made of the time spent. Lieutenant Chandler had more than twenty-four hours to plan and organize. He was unhurried and thorough. The only possible criticism of the preparation phase might be directed at the communications plan. With wire and radio available, Lieutenant Chandler also provided illuminating grenades. When neither wire nor radio communication was available, no use was made of the signal flares. The reader wonders why they were not used. Perhaps they had been assigned prearranged meanings that made them useless. Even the most detailed planning sometimes leaves eventualities unforeseen and uncovered.

Some credit for the success of the patrol goes to the enemy. He must be criticized for poor security measures and for not reacting to the alert provided by the detonation of his own booby trap.

Perhaps, as noted in the concluding paragraph of the narrative, major credit should be given to the supporting arms. Lieutenant Chandler's twenty-man patrol became a powerful adversary when backed by intelligently controlled fire from artillery, tanks and mortars.

★ NOTE

1. The narrative of this action is based upon a study by Lt. Edgar Denton, prepared in Korea.

L E G E N D

TOPOGRAPHIC SYMBOLS

◢, ▪▪▪, ●	TOWN OR VILLAGE
══════, ═════	ALL WEATHER ROAD, DRY WEATHER ROAD
─ ─ ─ ─ ─	TRAIL
┼┼┼┼┼┼	RAILROAD, DOUBLE GAUGE, SINGLE GAUGE
┼┼┤═══├┼┼	RAILROAD WITH TUNNEL
▄▄▄▄▄	EMBANKMENT OR CUT
⌇	CONTOUR WITH CLIFF
)(	MOUNTAIN PASS
▨▨▨▨, ∼∼∼	RIVER OR STREAM
── ··· ── ··· ──	DRY CREEK BED
⊥ ⊥ ⊥	RICE PADDY

Note: *Numbers on all contours are in meters.*

MILITARY SYMBOLS

▭	UNIT SYMBOL
⊓ (flag)	HEADQUARTERS OR COMMAND POST
△	OBSERVATION POST
▥▥▥, ━━━	FRONT LINES
➤, ●●●➤	UNITED NATIONS ROUTE OF ATTACK, PATROL ROUTE
⤧✳	ROAD BLOCK
ᴖᴖᴖᴖ, □, ⊔	TRENCHES, BUNKERS, FOXHOLES
xxxxxxx, ∼ℓℓℓℓ	WIRE FENCES
—30→	MACHINE GUN WITH CALIBER
⊜	GUN
o—→	MORTAR
o⊜	HOWITZER
⊢75→	RECOILLESS RIFLE, 75 MM
◇⊜	SELF-PROPELLED HOWITZER, (HALFTRACKED)
⊖	ANTIAIRCRAFT GUN
◇50	M16, CAL .50 (QUAD MOUNT)
⊓, ⊟, •⊓	TANK, MEDIUM TANK, TANK PLATOON
▣, ▭▭, ⟹	ENEMY SYMBOLS, UNIT, POSITION, ROUTE OF ATTACK

Index

A

Airborne infantry regiment *187th* (*RCT*), 183–192
Akerley, SFC William T, 199
Alfonso, Lt Albert F, 22, 23, 25
Allie, Lt Thomas J, 138–143
Allison, PFC Thomas S, 122
Almond, LtGen Edward M, 54–55, 61–63, 58*n*, 104, 170, 181, 183, 186–187, 191
Alston, PFC Leslie, 106
Anderson, Capt Leroy, 32–38
Anju, 39, 49
Ansong, 4–17
Antiaircraft artillery
    15th AW Battalion, 55, 69
    82d AW Battalion, 101–125
Appleman, LtCol Roy E, 18*n*, 19*n*, 52*n*, 125*n*
Armentrout, Cpl Robert Lee, 59, 68
Armored Field Artillery
    92d Battalion, 154–165
    987th Battalion, 155
Arnold, PFC Ernest R, 35
Artillery school, quoted, 31, 165*n*

B

Bailey, Lt Kincheon H Jr, 35–38
Baker, Sgt Henry E, 36
Banks, Pvt Johnnie R, 241
Barker, PFC Harold W, 34, 36
Barnes, Lieutenant, 74
Barrett, Capt John C, 128–131, 134, 135*n*

Barth, BrigGen George B, 6–17, 18*n*, 19*n*
Bauer, Capt Harold B, 71
Baugher, PFC Charles H, 241
Beauchamp, SFC Alfred, 19*n*
Bennett, Cpl Raymond, 114–115
Benoit, PFC Roy F, 105
Bessler, Capt Albert D, 164
Bierwith, Lt William R, 136*n*
Bigger, Capt Erwin B, 67, 73–74, 77, 79*n*
Bishop, LtCol Gaylord M, 204–214
Blandin, Capt Ray W Jr, 147–149
Blizzard, Cpl Billy B, 89, 98*n*
Bloody Ridge, 202–214
Blücher, Gebhard Leberecht von, 143
Blumenson, Capt Martin 58*n*, 135*n*, 165*n*, 214*n*, 221*n*
Bottlow, Cpl Roy E, 181*n*
Brannon, Capt Herbert A, 138–143
Brennen, Cpl Leo M, 23–24, 27
Briscoe, Maj Pierce W, 234*n*
British Army units
    Argyle and Sutherland Regiment, 39
    Middlesex Regiment, 39
    Royal Australian Regiment, 39–40, 43
    27 Commonwealth Brigade, 39
Brittian, Cpl Carl F, 229–230
Brownell, Capt George R, 172–181
Brubaker, LtCol Elbridge, 185–186
Brumenshenkel, Cpl Philip B, 197
Bryson, Sgt Preston L, 51
Buchanan, Sgt Alfred, 87
Bunker Hill, 166–182

Burkett, Lt Joseph W, 206–209, 214n
Butler, Sgt Virgil E, 177
Byrd, Cpl James A, 242

C

Cain, SFC Warren C Jr, 201n
Calhoun, Cpl John A, 131
Cammarano, Pvt Thomas A, 11
Camoesas, Cpl Alfonso, 73, 76–77
Campbell, Lt James G, 62–89
Campisi, Lt Orlando, 206
Castello, PFC Thomas A, 34, 36
Cavalry division
    1st, 39, 52n, 53n, 126
Cavalry regiment
    5th, 126–136
Chabrias, quoted, 183
Chandler, Lt John H, 237–245
Chichon-ni, 155
Chinju, 32
Chipyong-ni, 80, 100–125, 126, 132–133
Chonan, 13–17
Chongchon River, 39, 46
Chongju, 39–44
Chorwon, 144–146
Chosin Reservoir, 54–79
Church, MajGen John H, 20–21
Clark, Lt Herbert E, 176
Clark, Capt Max, 222–234
Cleaborn, PFC Edward O, 25–29
Clements, Lt Edwell D, 192n
Coad, Brig B A, 39, 43
Collins, SFC Roy E, 7, 18n, 21–29, 30n
Constant, Cpl Gilbert L, 198
Cook, Lt Alonzo, 41–43
Corps
    IX, 126, 154–156, 165n, 193
    X, 54–79, 80, 103, 125n, 136n, 166, 181n, 83, 192n, 215
Cotroneo, Lt Anthony, 232
Coughlin, Col John C, 168, 181
Craig, MSgt Harold M, 74–75
Crombez, Col Marcel G, 126–137
Curtis, Lt Robert, 116–123
Curtis, Maj Wesley J, 62, 67–70, 78n, 79n

D

Darbonne, Cpl Anthony, 241
Daugherty, Col Frederick A, 232
Davis, Maj Ernest H, 199
Dean, MajGen William F, 4

Deckard, SFC Raymond M, 197–199, 201n
Deland, Cpl Edward, 79n
Denchfield, Lt Raymond C, 59
Denton, Lt Edgar, 235n, 245n
DeSchweinitz, Lt Lawrence L, 131
Diamond, Cpl John W, 198
Dickson, Lt James T, 40
Division artillery
    2d, 124n
Dolvin, LtCol Welborn G, 40, 138–143
Doritsky, Sgt John, 79n
Douglas, PFC Francis, 232
Driskell, Lt Herman L, 7–9
Dunlap, PFC Bernard L, 98
Dunn, Lt John H, 203

E

Edwards, LtCol James W, 91, 99n, 101–125
Ehlers, Sgt Kenneth F, 231
Elder, MSgt John D, 162
Elledge, Capt John A, 103–112, 121–124, 125n
Engen, Maj Millard O, 84–85, 90, 99n
Euripides, quoted, 20

F

Fahey, SFC Francis R, 181n
Faith, LtCol Don C, 54–73, 77
Fell, PFC John A, 214
Field artillery
    17th Battalion, 45–53, 155–158
    37th Battalion, 101–125
    38th Battalion, 178–180, 182n
    52d Battalion, 19n
    57th Battalion, 55–79
    61st Battalion, 46
    64th Battalion, 31–38, 238–244
    503d Battalion, 101–125, 132–136
    555th Battalion, 196
Field Manual, quoted, 39, 234
Fifth Phase Offensive, 144, 154, 166
Finfrock, PFC Glenn J, 77
Fiscus, PFC Robert L, 229–230
Fluor Spar Valley, 216
Foley, SFC Regis J, 24–25
Foulk, Lt Elden K, 210, 212
Francis, Sgt Carl, 36
Freeman, Col Paul L, 90, 101–125
French battalion, 103, 107–108, 113, 114
Friesz, Maj Leonard O, 99n

G

Galard, Pvt Joseph, 131
Gano, Lt Jay M, 218, 221
Gardella, Sgt John C, 87, 98*n*
Gardiner, Lt Douglas L, 186–190
Garvin, PFC Theodore, 228–231
Gerhardt, Col William, 183–192
Gerrity, Capt John F, 158, 162
Gibbons, Cpl LeRoy, 89
Gibbs, Pvt Alphonso, 229–230
Gibson MSgt Willie C, 23–26
Giddens, MSgt Jessie O, 135*n*
Giellis, PFC John N, 181*n*
Goldston, Pvt Elbert Jr, 229–230
Godwin, Cpl Herman, 228–232
Goff, SFC Roy, 187, 189
Golinda, Pvt Joe, 219

H

Haberman, Lt Carl F, 115
Hagaru-ri, 55–78
Haley, Lt Leonard, 148–151
Hall, PFC Earl, 181*n*
Haman, 31–32
Hamhung, 54
Hammer, MSgt Frederick J, 35
Han River, 80, 82, 128, 137–143
Hancock, PFC Emmett, 243
Hanes LtCol Wallace M, 168–182
Hangye, 180, 185
Harkness, Lt Paul B, 143*n*
Harmon, SFC Starling W, 142
Harrell, MSgt Curtis D, 142
Harrell, Cpl Donald P, 131
Harrelson, LtCol Elmer H, 46–53
Harris, Cpl Wilbur, 242
Hartman, Sgt Charles, 209
Hatley, Sgt Theral J, 160
Haussler, PFC Richard G, 36
Hawkins, Sgt Harrington D, 51
Haynes, Capt Robert F, 59
Hearin, Lt Joseph N, 159–160
Heartbreak Ridge, 215–221
Heath, Lt Thomas, 103–123
Henri of Navarre, 137
Hensley, PFC Bobby G, 86–88, 97, 98*n*
Hiers, Capt Johnnie M, 128–129, 131
Higgins, Marguerite, 18*n*
High, Pvt Cliff R, 218–221

Hight, Lt Robert H, 194–201
Hill 191, 226, 229, 236
Hill 200, 160, 161
Hill 283, 146–153
Hill 287, 146
Hill 333, 83–99
Hill 397, 109–125, 131
Hill 418, 227
Hill 453, 82–99
Hill 454, 161
Hill 520, 215–221
Hill 754, 177
Hill 773, 202–214
Hill 800, 166–182
Hill 916, 171–179
Hill 940, 202–214
Hill 983, 202–214
Hill 1051, 164–172
Hill, Col John G, 20
Hill, Cpl Robert, 231
Hines, Capt Floyd C, 155
Hipp, PFC George C, 174, 177
Hite, PFC James O, 7
Hodes, BrigGen Henry I, 55–56, 66
Hoengsong, 103
Holden, LtCol Maurice C, 52*n*, 53*n*
Hongchon, 166, 183
Hongchon River, 168, 180, 185
Hoog, Cpl Albert W, 231
Hotopp, Maj Raymond F, 158–159
Hudong-ni, 66, 75, 77
Huhel, SFC Michael R, 192*n*
Humphrey, Maj Robert A, 135*n*, 136*n*
Hungnam, 55
Hwachon Reservoir, 154

I

Iho-ri, 80, 97, 104
Imjin River, 144–146
Infantry divisions
    2*d*, 31, 45–52, 80, 98*n*, 168, 181*n*, 182*n*,
        183–185, 191, 192*n*, 203, 215
    3*d*, 144, 186
    7*th*, 54–79
    24*th*, 18*n*, 29*n*, 30*n*, 52*n*, 80, 193
    25*th*, 31
    45*th*, 222, 233
Infantry in Battle, quoted, 45, 215
Infantry Journal, quoted, 137, 236

Infantry regiments (RCTs)
   5th, 193–201
   7th, 144–153
   9th, 20, 49–50, 182*n*, 202–214
   17th, 55–79
   19th, 20
   21st, 4–17, 18*n*, 19*n*, 82–97
   23d, 46, 80–97, 100–125, 126, 129,
      132–135, 182*n*, 215–221
   31st, 55, 76
   32d, 54–79
   34th, 3–17, 18*n*, 20–30
   35th, 31, 137–143, 236–245
   38th, 50, 168–182, 204
   179th, 222–235
Inje, 166, 183
Inmon, Pvt Cletis, 110, 114
Iron Triangle, 144

J

Jenkins, PFC Edward K, 211
Jensen, PFC Royce, 79*n*
Jeter, PFC Walter Jr, 198
Johnson, Sgt Guillory, 141
Jones, Lt Albert E, 195–197
Jones, Lt Arnold C, 211–212
Jones, SFC Calvin P, 227–230
Jones, MSgt Lloyd L, 130, 135*n*, 136*n*
Jones, Maj Robert E, 73–75, 79*n*
Juarez, PFC David, 232
Judd, Lt Donald, 51

K

Kaesong, 144
Kantner, Cpl James H, 174
Kelly, Sgt, Kenneth G, 114
Kim Bae, Cpl, 241
Kim Soo, Cpl, 242
King Patrol, 222–235
Kipling, Rudyard, quoted, 3
Kirschbaum, Cpl Robert, 237, 243
Kluttz, Sgt Bill C, 107–115
Knight, SFC Elvin E, 15
Koksu-ri, 126, 129–130
Konju, 14
Korean Service Corps, 226
Koritwi-ri, 186
Koto-ri, 68
Kotzur, MSgt Germanus P, 35–36
Krahel, Pvt Joseph P, 19*n*
Krizan, SFC George A, 132

Krzyzowski, Capt Edward G, 209–214
Kujang-dong, 45–46
Kum River, 14–16
Kumhwa, 144, 154
Kunu-ri, 45–53
Kunz, PFC William F, 228–231
Kwirin-ni, 137–138

L

Lacaze, Lt Robert D, 212–213, 214*n*
Lamb, Cpl David W, 215–221
Lantern City, 226
Larney, SFC Floyd, 206
Larson, Sgt Donald H, 92
Lavoie, LtCol Leon F, 155–165
Lee, Sgt Everett, 89
Lee, LtCol James H, 141–143
Lee, MSgt Jasper W, 42
Linder, SFC Charles R, 159
Line Wyoming, 193
Link, SFC Alvin W, 34–38
Livy, quoted, 80
Lock, MSgt Joseph J, 146–153

M

MacArthur, Gen Douglas, 63
MacLean, Col Allan D, 55–64, 66
Magnum, Lt Mack E, 196
Majon-dong, 66
Mallard, Lt Charles W, 204–214
Manley, Lt Omer, 224–233
Marine Corps
   1st Marine Division, 54–79, 154–165
   11th Marine Regiment, 156–165
Marshburn, Lt Herbert E Jr, 72
Martin, PFC John N, 111, 114
Martinson, SFC Odvin A, 96–97
Masan, 31–32, 37, 102
Masiello, Cpl Nick J, 227–228
Maxwell, SFC James, 131–132, 136*n*
May, Lt Eugene C, 149
May, Lt Hugh R, 73
McGee, Lt Paul J, 105–122
McKinney, PFC Herman W, 197, 201*n*
McKinney, Lt Randolph, 105, 107
McQuitty, Cpl Bobbie H, 34, 37
Meares, Cpl Cecil W, 35–36
Menzies, Pvt Hugh Jr, 229–230, 232
Mewha, Capt John, 192*n*
Middlemas, Lt John N, 146–153
Miller, Maj Crosby P, 63, 70

Miller, Lt Donald O, 125n
Miller, SFC George W, 136
Million Dollar Hill, 193–201
Mitchell, Cpl David, 237, 242, 244
Mitchell, Lt James P, 81–97, 98n, 99n
Modified Noname Line, 181
Mooney, Lt Harley F, 146–153
Moore, MajGen Bryant E, 126
Moore, Lt Henry M, 70
Moore, Lt Richard H, 60–61, 74
Moore, PFC Santford B, 34, 36
Morrison, Pvt Edward, 231–232
Morrow, Lt Edwin C, 203–204
Mortimer, PFC Thomas J, 96–97, 98n
Mortrude, Lt James O, 63, 70–73, 77
Mossman, Maj B C, 235n
Mougeat, Cpl James C, 106
Mueller, Lt Harold P, 82–97
Murphy, MSgt Edward A, 38n
Myers, Capt Allen L, 46–52

N

Naktong River, 2, 31
Napier, Lt Leonard, 95
Napoleon, quoted, 202
Navarre, Capt Vincent J, 69
Nelson, PFC Donald E, 105
Newman, Maj Charles A, 185–192
Nock, Pvt Elmer, 231–232
Noname Line, 166–182
Noname Ridge, 236–245
Nordstrom, Lt Francis G, 40–44

O

Oron-ni, 187–188
Osan, 4–17
Osburn, Capt Leroy, 5–17, 19n
Ottesen, Cpl Eugene L, 105, 109, 114
Outpost Eerie, 222–235
Overlease, PFC Samuel E, 181n

P

Pakchon, 39
Parker, MSgt William, 32–33
Parziale, Maj Charles J, 135n
Penrod, Lt William C, 82, 85–88, 98n, 99n
Penwell, Cpl Virgil J, 176
Peters, Lt Robert L, 105–108
Pia-ri Valley, 204
Pickett, LtCol George B, 135n, 136n
Pitcher, Cpl John M, 34–36

Pohang-dong, 31
Pope, Cpl William H, 106
Poppler, SFC Glen M, 192n
Powell, SFC George T, 159
Powell, Capt Wayne E, 70
Price, Lt Blair W, 175–176
Prusaitis, Maj Joseph J, 51
Puchaetul, 185–186
Pugowski, Sgt Leon, 69
Pukhan River, 138–143, 155
Punchbowl, The, 236
Pursley, Sgt Joseph R, 33
Pusan, 2, 31
Pyonggang, 144
Pyongtaek, 3–17
Pyongyang, 39, 49

R

Raftery, Capt Bernard G, 159–163
Raider Patrol, 222–235
Ramsburg, Capt John H, 116–123
Randon, PFC Van D, 241–242
Rangers, 116–123
Rawls, Sgt Herbert L Jr, 32, 34
Reed, MSgt Jimmy J, 35–36
Reidy, LtCol Richard F, 79n
Republic of Korea, units, 154
    1st Division, 53n
        Korean Service Corps, 226
Reyna, MSgt Andrew, 122
Richard, Capt W J, 292n
Ricki, PFC Clarence E, 174, 177
Riddle, Lt Raymond W, 215–221
Ridgway, LtGen Matthew B, 80, 100, 104
Ridley, Lt Robert R, 8–9
Roberts, Sgt Austin E, 163
Rochnowski, Lt Arthur, 107–111
Rocket field artillery
    2d Battery, 155
Rodriguez, Cpl Pedro Colon, 147–148
Ross, Capt William E, 185–187, 192n
Rowe, PFC Rodney R, 174, 177
Ruble, SFC Willis V Jr, 159
Ruffner, MajGen Clark L, 168, 171, 181, 182n

S

Sachang-ni, 155
Sachi-ri, 189–190
Sady, Cpl Joseph J, 25–27
Saga, 32, 36
Sanchez, Cpl Jesus A, 96–97

Sander, Cpl Boleslaw M, 108
Schaeffner, Lt Wilbur C, 194–201
Schag, Chaplain John T, 36
Scharnhorst, Gerhard Johann David von, 143
Schell, Sgt William, 241
Schiller, Lt Melvin D, 21–22, 30n
Schmidt, PFC Harry E, 216, 220
Schmitt, Sgt Donald R, 109, 115
Scholes, MSgt William L, 201n
Scullion, Capt Edward B, 59
Second Spring Offensive, 168
Seever, Capt Dale L, 59, 63, 69
Seoul, 144–147, 166
Severson, Cpl Arne, 219
Shanks, MSgt Judge, 51–52
Shea, Lt Edward L, 21–22, 29n
Shoham, Cpl Robert, 232
Simoneau, Cpl Joseph H, 23
Sinanju, 39
Sinchon, 82–83
Smalley, Lt Everett, F Jr, 61–62
Smith, LtCol Charles B, 4–17
Smith, Lt Cecil G, 58, 60, 74, 77, 78n
Sophocles, quoted, 166
Soyang River, 166–182, 183–192
Spain, PFC Robert L, 209
Spann, Maj James H, 185–187, 192n
Stai, Capt Melvin R, 82–83, 99n
Stamford, Capt Edward P, 60
Stanley, Sgt George A, 61
Stars and Stripes, 202
Stewart, Capt Keith M, 136n
Stratton, PFC William W, (*pseud*), 87, 88–90, 92
Sugua, SFC Fred, 68
Sukchon, 39
Sunchon, 48
Sun Tzu, quoted, 54, 154

T

Taejon, 16
Taenyong River, 39
Tank battalions
    6th, 126–136
    70th, 128–136
    72d, 185–192
    89th, 39–44, 137–143
Task Force Crombez, 126–136
Task Force Faith, 54–79

Task Force Gerhardt, 183–192
Task Force Hill, 20–29
Teti, SFC Thomas R, 146–153
Thomas, PFC Robert J, 198
Travis, Lt John E, 106
Treacy, LtCol Edgar J Jr, 129–130
Truax, Cpl John J, 206
Trujillo, PFC Domingo, 209
Tucker, Maj Roy A, 156, 160–162
Twin Tunnels, 80–99
Tyrrell, Capt Stanley C, 90–97, 99n

U

Umberger, CWO C L, 135n

V

Van der Leest, Lt Gerald L, 41
Van Fleet, LtGen James A, 170, 193
Vaudrevil, Capt Raymond, 68
Vegetius, quoted, 100, 193

W

Waegwan, 31
Walker, LtCol Philip G, 238–244
Ward, Pvt Jack, 105
Webb, Sgt James, 108
Weyand, LtCol Fred D, 149–153
White, SFC James R, 159–160, 162
Whitten, SFC Thomas K, 175–176
Williams, PFC Isaiah, 122
Williams, SFC Zack C, 7–17, 18n
Williamson, Maj Edward C, 52n, 124n
Wilson, Pvt George, 244
Wilson, Lt Robert D, 67–68
Winans, PFC Leroy, 229–231
Wonju, 103
Wonsan, 144–146
Woodby, PFC Gainius E, 79
Worun-ni, 203–204

Y

Yalu River, 55
Ybarra, Cpl Joel, 231–233
Yoju, 104, 126

Z

Ziebell, PFC Herbert G, 105

☆ U.S. GOVERNMENT PRINTING OFFICE : 1987 O—193-515